Talking Baseball with
Major League Stars

TALKING BASEBALL WITH MAJOR LEAGUE STARS

WAYNE STEWART

ROWMAN & LITTLEFIELD
Lanham • Boulder • New York • London

Published by Rowman & Littlefield
An imprint of The Rowman & Littlefield Publishing Group, Inc.
4501 Forbes Boulevard, Suite 200, Lanham, Maryland 20706
www.rowman.com

86-90 Paul Street, London EC2A 4NE, United Kingdom

British Library Cataloguing in Publication Information Available

Library of Congress Cataloging-in-Publication Data Available

ISBN 978-1-5381-8528-5 (cloth)
ISBN 978-1-5381-8529-2 (electronic)

♾️™ The paper used in this publication meets the minimum requirements of American National Standard for Information Sciences—Permanence of Paper for Printed Library Materials, ANSI/NISO Z39.48-1992.

To my family, who have collectively watched (and taken part in) thousands and thousands of hours of sports, including amateur soccer, track and field, basketball, football, volleyball, and swimming as well as T-ball, Little League, high school and college baseball, and on up to the majors. A great group: wife Nancy, sons Sean and Scott and their wives Rachel and Katie, and my grandson Nathan.

Also to my father, O.J. Stewart, who took me to my first big-league games and who introduced me to his old neighbor in Donora, Stan Musial. To my mother, Margaret, who always supported my writing; my maternal grandparents, Ella Mae and Louis, who introduced me to baseball on the radio and TV (KDKA in Pittsburgh); and my paternal grandmother, Julia, as well.

And to a fellow teacher, Cathy Burchell, who was part of a great bunch of colleagues she dubbed "The Wayne Train."

Contents

ACKNOWLEDGMENTS

Thanks goes out to all of the cooperative big-leaguers who shared their knowledge with me, and a special thanks to my editor, Christen Karniski, for her insights and help on this book and the others she's worked on and improved.

Introduction

I conducted my first interviews with baseball players back in 1978. Since then, I have been fortunate enough to speak with countless players, including sixty Hall of Famers and even more men who qualify as stars, along with major leaguers who may not have been in the spotlight quite as often.

That brings up the problem of defining the word "stars," as in the title of this book. A majority of the interviewees have at least one of the following accomplishments/honors on their resumes: MVP Award(s); Cy Young Award(s); Rookie of the Year; Manager of the Year; leading the league in major categories such as batting, homers, runs batted in, victories, strikeouts; and/or winning ERA crowns.

Admittedly, though, some of the people quoted in this book fall short of such lofty feats. No apologies.

First of all, some of the men a reader might contend aren't stars by any definition had very interesting insights, and many are baseball lifers. So, yes, some select interviewees may not possess glowing credentials, but all had something illuminating to say. So at worst, the book may be guilty of making the definition of "stars" a bit elastic.

Second, every single person quoted here is a star when one considers how many men devoted their young lives to the quest to become major leaguers, only to fall short.

A big-league coach was once asked a question about bench players, with the reporter referring to those men as "scrubs," an old baseball slang expression referring to players who were not on the first team and thus were inferior to the regulars. The coach chided the writer, "There are no scrubs in the major leagues."

In fact, we can learn a great deal not just from Hall of Famers, but from virtually any big-leaguer. After all, these men paid their dues on an often arduous path, working their way up from their days as a kid playing on a sandlot or on a modest T-ball field all the way to the majors. Therefore, all squabbling aside, the men interviewed here are worth listening to.

People learn things through all five of their senses, starting with newborns' reliance upon smell and taste. Then, after about a month, infants' hearing fully reaches maturation before the sense of touch comes on strong. One study says that adults process 83 percent of new information using their sense of sight and another 11 percent through hearing (leaving just 6 percent to the other three senses).[1] The pages of this book give readers the chance to see, and to figuratively "hear," so much about the game of baseball—and you'll be learning from those who know the game.

The last defense for the use of the word "stars" here is this: There are enough stars, by *anyones's* way of reckoning, in this book to form a sky chock-full of constellations.

One final note: every quote used is from the author's interviews, with the exceptions being widely quoted material and quotes that have endnotes. Stats and facts here are through the 2022 season.

CHAPTER ONE

Hitters

HITTERS' PREPARATIONS

Paul Goldschmidt not only won the MVP Award in 2022, he also finished in the top six in the voting on five other occasions. He summed up his attitude on prep work: "I can control my preparation, my mindset, my work ethic, and my focus. If I do all of that and I go out and fail—for a game, for a series or even for a career—at least I would know that I've done everything that I could, and [I] don't have regrets. . . . I'm always going to keep pushing and looking for ways to get better, and we'll see where it takes us."[1]

Gene Clines said that when he played in the 1970s, "we'd come to the park early and spend three to four hours, relaxing and playing cards. The clubhouse is your home away from home. You spend more time there than in your apartment. It's your private domain.

"Winning teams come in early. When you're winning, you can't wait to get to the clubhouse. It gives you a burst of energy. It's just like a hitter when he's hitting—he never gets tired. It's always the guys who aren't hitting who get tired."

"Ninety percent of the game is mental," Jay Buhner, an All-Star with the Seattle Mariners, agreed. "Only 10 percent is physical, so preparation is very important."

That becomes more crucial as the season wears on, especially for games down the stretch run, played under the scorching August and

September sun. "You have to step it up a bit—maybe for a salary drive and for your own personal pride [especially if your team is out of contention]. Some days when I'm not feeling as well as other days, it takes a little more time stretching and running to prepare."

Buhner also said that his prep work includes "remembering what the starting pitcher threw me the last time I faced him. I watch videos after taking BP [batting practice]—they really help. I can see the release point and the location on pitches. You can pick up tendencies."

He considers his fielding, too. "I go over defenses, how to play the hitters. Maybe have a meeting with the outfield coach. Maybe Randy Johnson's pitching for us today. We play batters a different way then."

Meanwhile, when Silver Slugger winner Adam LaRoche was with the Atlanta Braves, he said, "My pregame thing is usually by myself—taking a couple of swings off the tee either before BP or right after BP. I take a regular batting practice, but nothing extraordinary."

He, of course, did his mental homework, too: "about thirty minutes of video on that night's pitcher before the game, which is nice—you get to see what you're up against. And I usually talk with Chip [Chipper Jones] about the starting pitcher if he's faced him before, just to get a feel on how they pitch him from the left side."

Switch-hitters have to prepare to hit both ways. Omar Vizquel worked on hitting both ways daily. "You do have to keep both sides refreshed because when you switch from one hand to another, the swing is not the same, so it's hard to keep them both together. You always take extra cuts early before batting practice." He had to do that because once BP starts, all regulars get the same number of cuts—no extra swings are allowed just because a man is a switch-hitter.

All-Star switch-hitter Carlos Baerga pointed out that "it takes a lot of work to be a switch-hitter. You're going to face more righties than lefties, so you have to work really hard to maintain both sides."

Outfielder Scott Pose liked pregame peace and quiet at times. "I think even if it's just twenty minutes just to get away from everything, just so you don't even have to think about baseball; you can just read the paper. And that in itself is a way of getting mentally ready. I think it's tailor-made for every individual player.

"Myself, I just try to get by myself, think about what's going on during the game—who I'm going to face and how they might work me. It's as simple as that."

So where does a player go to find a private spot in a clubhouse often full of media, attendants, and a herd of fellow players? Pose said some players hide out in the trainer's room or other such areas that are off-limits to the media. In his case, he said modestly, "Nobody's really clamoring for me, so it's pretty easy for me to get away."

Even some of players' postgame routines can be considered preparing—getting the mind and body ready for the next grueling contest. "After the game," Buhner said, "I remove all the tape, ice my ankle down, and get a couple of carbohydrate drinks. Then I think about the day and file it away. Then it's back to the hotel."

Long ago, players sat around the clubhouse for hours after games, conducting a postmortem examination of concluded games and talking baseball in general. However, as long ago as the late 1980s (or thereabouts), Clines, then a Seattle coach, observed, "That's a thing of the past. Guys are into so many other things. Nobody sits around and talks baseball anymore. It's just the change of times—a new generation, a different breed."

Many players are rather nonchalant when it comes to BP. Former MVP and Hall of Fame manager Joe Torre noted that "too many players take BP for hitting home runs instead of hitting the way they're going to hit in the game." He felt that for practice to be effective, a player should achieve two goals. First, "you work on your timing." After that, a player should "work on his game. Pete Rose was one of the best at that. He took BP the way he played. I think that's what BP is for." Torre also praised Tony Gwynn, who often slapped at the ball and took it to the opposite field in practice. "No question. You get your timing that way."

Sparky Anderson, the first manager to win a World Series in both leagues, said players such as Hank Aaron and Ernie Banks had what many players must work on in practice: "fast hands. It all revolves around fast hands."

In the 1990s, when Torre managed the St. Louis Cardinals, he said he thought players were taking too much BP. Instead, he recommended taking fewer swings but doing so meaningfully, like Gwynn.

Next, a tale of Cecil Fielder, who led the American League in runs driven in three years running (1990–1992), and in home runs twice, with totals of 51 and 44. He and his son Prince are the only father-son duo to each have a 50-plus home run season.

One day in 1992 at Tiger Stadium, Cecil proved that hitting a ball over the fence isn't easy, even in batting practice. Teammate Mark Carreon bet Fielder that over his next five cuts he couldn't hit a homer. Fielder failed on his first four tries. "All right. Here it comes," he said, then lifted a long, lazy fly ball that fell shy of the warning track.

Perhaps he might have done better emulating Ken Griffey Jr., who once said that despite his power, "I don't think of myself as a home run hitter. I like to hit line drives. I just try to hit the ball hard."

Another example of how difficult it is to reach the fences came during the 1992 All-Star Game Home Run Derby. Players huffed and puffed, but even sluggers Barry Bonds (with just two homers), Fred McGriff (with three), and Joe Carter (with four) all struggled. The winner, Mark McGwire managed to hit twelve balls out.

Former manager Terry Collins noted, "Those guys in home run contests hit mammoth shots because they're gearing everything up, but the shorter, quicker swings that come in games, those are the balls that are hit hard.

"Because of the style of swing in BP, everything's wound up and you can get everything into the pitch. You can lengthen your swing out and do all the things you can't in a game."

J. T. Snow, a sixteen-year vet who is the son of NFL star Jack Snow, agreed. "The longest ones I've seen have been in game conditions where the pitcher is supplying part of the power."

Returning to the proper way to approach BP, Chipper Jones said he developed a strict routine. He primarily worked on hitting the ball to certain parts of the field, which he determined before seeing the pitch. Later, he liked to go with the pitch for a few cuts. Finally, he would let loose, trying to crank a few balls out of the park. However, he said he did that not to draw the inevitable "oohs" and "ahhs" from fans, who would react as if they had just witnessed a breathtaking fireworks display; instead, his purpose was simply "to get nice and loose."

Milt May was a Pittsburgh teammate of another powerful hitter, Willie Stargell. "When I played with Willie, during BP he wasn't trying to hit the ball far in most cases. He was trying to hit the ball all over, trying to sting the ball. He really wasn't up there grunting and groaning, trying to hit it out of the park. He certainly could've done that. He did it during games. He had as much power as anybody did, but that wasn't his game plan. During BP he didn't hit many balls out. He was hitting the ball the other way, trying to get loose, and working on things specifically."

Still, at times, May admitted, some BP sessions were mind-boggling sights: "There was the [1994] All-Star Game in Pittsburgh when Ken Griffey hit about six balls in the upper deck in BP. I've been here [Three Rivers Stadium] for years watching batting practice, and it's normally a routine event, and just occasionally there's one ball that'll go up there. And he takes BP and hits about six of ten up there! I've never seen that done, not close—and I've seen some pretty big guys take a lot of batting practice."

INTIMIDATING THE PITCHER

Lee Smith, who amassed 478 saves, said, "You *can't* be intimidated if you're going to be a closer. There's not one guy I fear." Easy for the confident Smith to say, but many pitchers do experience fear when facing certain hitters.

Sparky Anderson said Stargell was one of a handful of power hitters who caused pitchers to quiver. "After twenty-five years, I've seen so many sluggers. I've seen Willie McCovey, George Foster, and Stargell. Those guys hit them long and hard!"

In various roles, Hall of Famer Red Schoendienst was in the game for parts of eight decades. He rattled off his list of impressive longball hitters: "In Pittsburgh you had Stargell. Then you'd go on to the next club, especially when [talent was packed into] only eight National League teams, and there'd be more. You'd go into Brooklyn and you'd have Roy Campanella, Duke Snider, and Gil Hodges. Every team had some guys that you knew you couldn't get away with saying, 'The pitcher's gonna pitch around this guy,' because you'd have to pitch around the next one and the next one."

Other teams were similar to Brooklyn; the Braves, for example, had Eddie Mathews and Hank Aaron batting back-to-back on their way to breaking the record held by Babe Ruth and Lou Gehrig for combined homers by two teammates.

Schoendienst went on to say many intimidating hitters were not huge: "Stan Musial [175 pounds] was a great hitter who could hit the ball out of the ballpark [475 times]. A lot of guys were like that—they weren't that big in stature, but they had good bat speed—Aaron, Mays, and Mathews—that's the key."

As Anderson said, "I don't think I ever saw Henry Aaron hit the ball a long distance." And Cito Gaston, a former teammate of Aaron's who went on to manage the Toronto Blue Jays to two World Series titles, said, "Aaron was intimidating because if you threw it up there, he was going to hit you somewhere. It doesn't matter how big you are." He added, "As far as being worried about somebody going to hit a rope off you, to me the two best hitters I saw when I came into the league were Aaron along with Billy Williams, and neither one was a big person."

Lee Smith said that generally speaking, "I think size has a lot to do with it." Aside from a few exceptions, he said, "I don't think a small guy can intimidate you." However, his exceptions included Brett Butler, who could "do so many things—he might bunt or slap the ball past you. In some situations, I would much rather face a home run hitter with his big swing—guys who have a lot of holes you can pitch to—than to face some of the smaller guys who hit the ball where it's pitched and put the bat on the ball." Even so, he said, "there hasn't been a .400 hitter in a long time, and even then, he made six outs out of every ten."

Gregg Jefferies said that the "little guys aren't real intimidating, but they can get respect by hitting with men in scoring position. Like Keith Hernandez—they'd rather pitch to Darryl Strawberry, who is very intimidating."

Mike Hargrove began by saying, "I don't think you can intimidate a pitcher with long homers. It's more amazing than anything. The old saying goes, 'No matter how far you hit it, you still only get one run.'" Then, thinking of Albert Belle, he reconsidered: "Though where he hits it, you ought to get more than one run."

Still, sheer size is one thing that can cause pitchers' hearts to palpitate. Hall of Fame pitcher Bert Blyleven said, "Stargell hit a shot off Wayne Twitchell like a golf shot. It went out so quick. It almost put the whole stadium into complete silence for ten to fifteen seconds." That not only silenced a crowd, but it planted the idea in pitchers' heads that this was a man to be feared.

Nolan Ryan recalled another sky-high shot: "I saw Stargell hit two over the right field roof at Forbes Field." In all, just eighteen baseballs flew over that target, which loomed eighty-six feet above the field. Stargell launched two balls that cleared the roof during a six-day span, and seven in all. The first to hit it out of the park in that vicinity was Babe Ruth, who managed this during a three-home-run barrage for the final homers of his career.

Chuck Tanner, who managed Stargell, is widely quoted as saying, "He doesn't just hit pitchers. He takes away their dignity."

Stargell was a pretty big man, but he was five inches shorter than the 6-foot-7 Frank Howard, who outweighed Stargell 255 pounds to 188. Over a period of six games in 1968, Howard annihilated pitchers by racking up a record ten home runs in twenty at-bats. Pitcher Dick Bosman, a teammate of Howard's on the Washington Senators, said, "When he hit those ten home runs, the last two were off Mickey Lolich. The last one, Lolich tried to sneak a fastball past him. Frank top-handed that bat. It had topspin on it and was kinda hooking—you've hit it hard when it does that. It hit the roof and, bonk, gone."

Howard, though very mild mannered, could even intimidate nonpitchers. A widely told story has it that a group of obnoxious fans pushed him too far. Howard challenged them all, saying, "The big guys can come one at a time, and the little guys, you can come all at once."

That tale is reminiscent of another oft-told story of what another intimidator, the 6-foot-6 Dick Radatz, did. When a fight broke out between his Montreal Expos and the Pittsburgh Pirates, Radatz came across Freddie Patek, Pittsburgh's 5-foot-6 shortstop, and bellowed, "I'll take you and a player to be named later."[2]

Like Howard, the 6-foot-6 Dave Winfield played college basketball. All-Star pitcher Charles Nagy called Winfield an "awesome presence in the box with his size. He's impressive with the way he carries himself."

Hall of Famer Andre Dawson said Mike Schmidt was another batter to be wary of: "He just had that 'awe' about him, especially when you fell behind on him. The ball would jump off his bat and carry real well. And he was a good cripple hitter, a good mistake hitter. He was one guy who you'd really hate to face, especially with men on base."

Blyleven added Dave Kingman, who hit 442 homers, to his list of scary hitters: "In Minnesota, he hit one that went up in a hole in the roof for a ground rule double. He hit one that left Olympic Stadium completely. They had to paint a foul line on the roof due to that homer." Actually, with no foul line markings at the time, the umpires called the shot a foul ball. Kingman also hit a towering 550-foot blow at Wrigley Field that they say left the park and didn't land until it went *over* Waveland Avenue.

HITTING STANCES, STYLES, AND THEORIES

Baseball has produced men with diverse looks and thoughts on hitting. Chipper Jones said it all boils down to a matter of "to each his own. I mean, every guy's different. The fundamentals of each guy's swing [are] different." Further, it's obvious that any style *can* work for talented individuals.

Nevertheless, there are some basic theories on hitting that everyone should heed. Willie Upshaw, the first Blue Jay to drive in more than one hundred runs (and a cousin of NFL Hall of Fame guard Gene Upshaw), said that is especially true for aspiring big-leaguers: "Learn how to get behind the ball and stay closed. From there it's learning how to use your hands. Don't open up too soon, don't push the ball—throw the bat at the ball, and hit the ball consistently where it's pitched."

After all that, it's a matter of a young hitter "[catching] up to the speed of the game" since there is no doubt that the game played at the big-league level is vastly different from what he has experienced before. "That's tough for young hitters," he emphasized. Upshaw mentioned another thing that young players may not want to hear: "Most guys who can hit have always been able to hit." Many agree that the ability to play pro ball is, for the most part, God-given. You either have it or you don't.

And if you have it, you succeed even employing unorthodox methods. Terry Francona, who managed the Boston Red Sox to a world championship in 2004, pointed out that Matty Alou won a batting title in 1966 while hitting .342, and managed to hit that high while sometimes shifting his feet.

In any event, there can be no question that some hitters' approaches to their craft and their stances appear to be quite odd. Some players have such unique batting stances that even if their faces were obscured, fans would still recognize them.

Arguably, nobody looked more out of the ordinary at the plate than batting champ Stan Musial. He led his league in hitting seven times despite a stance which made him appear, according to pitcher Ted Lyons, like "a kid peeking round the corner to see if the cops were coming."

In a 1995 interview, Joe Carter remarked on Jeff Bagwell's strange stance, with his legs spread very far apart: "He hits down in a crouch, but I mean, he hits the ball. He's got tremendous hang time—he hits the ball not only far, but up high. He's looking for over the roof, over the moon. He's got a lot of power because if he can hit them as high as he does and they still go out of the ballpark, just think if you straighten it out a little bit and hit it on a line."

Dawson commented, "You throw it in his swing and he gets all of it, he's going to hit a long one. He's not that big in stature, he's compact—very strong. He's got an uppercut type of swing, and he gets the bat head through the strike zone real quick."

Many big-leaguers take a relatively short stride when hitting, maybe six to twelve inches or so. Bagwell's stride was more like six to twelve millimeters, if that. At least one broadcaster contended that Bagwell's front foot did not stride toward the pitcher—he raised his foot, but placed it back down in the same (or nearly the same) spot where it had originally rested. Some batters simply don't fit into the bell-shaped curve of human endeavor.

Take those hitters who have been known to shift their feet even as the pitch is on its homeward flight. "It's those little, young scatbacks," observed Jones. "They're constantly moving their feet, trying to fake out the third baseman—is he going to bunt, is he not going to bunt. A lot of times they've showed bunt and tried to slap it past me."

When asked if two-time batting champ Ichiro, a .311 lifetime hitter, fits that description at least in part, Jones elaborated, "Well, Japanese players are completely different. They're leaving the boxes, but they're making contact anyway, or 90 percent of them. Ichiro doesn't bunt that often; he's more of just a slash guy."

Francona said that while Ichiro moved his feet around quite a bit, he "kept his hands back. He may have jumped around, but his hands were always where they were supposed to be."

Some players change their stance; others stay consistent. Cal Ripken Jr. was known to experiment quite a bit. One example: when Ripken was thirty-eight, his manager, Ray Miller, said the stance he was using allowed him to "use his hands instead of his body so much. When you get older, I think you experiment a little bit and start trying to generate power with your body."

Upshaw said some hitters change their stance a bit depending upon the pitcher they're facing, especially if they are "having trouble getting around on the ball, so they change to help their timing mechanism again."

HITTING TECHNIQUES

From 1987 through 2004, Ellis Burks drilled 352 home runs, but he learned not to be pull crazy. When Burks was with Boston, veterans Dwight Evans and Jim Rice taught him to quit being strictly a pull hitter. Burks remembered, "They told me, 'There's a lot of money to make over in right field.' Meaning, hit the ball to right field if the ball is pitched outside—go with it instead of trying to pull everything.

"I respected everything that they said, and, of course, it's true, you can go up there and try to pull everything, and you're going to get yourself out. Try to go to right field sometimes, it works out for you.

"Instead of thinking about [going the opposite way], all you have to do is let the pitch travel a little bit further in the zone. If you try to pull the ball, you catch it out front. If you want to hit the ball to right field, let it travel a little further."

There are those stars whose technique is so simple it's boiled down to the old line that Hall of Fame fireballing reliever Lee Smith paraphrased concerning Andre Dawson: "He wasn't a technical hitter; he just saw the ball and hit it. And he hit it hard. I faced him a few times when he swung and missed—man, I didn't even know if he hit the ball or not because he swung so hard you could hear the bat swing when he came through. He worked hard and he went out there every day wanting to play."

In some way, Griffey Jr. also simply relied upon his skills. As Goose Gossage once put it, the Kid didn't complicate things, he just "goes about his business like you did when you were eight years old. He reminds you of a Little Leaguer. He plays the game for fun."

Tony Gwynn exemplified the axiom, "If it ain't broke, don't fix it." His way of hitting was never busted, so there was never a need for repairs. He hit .300 or better in each of his final nineteen seasons, feasting on pitches middle of the plate and out by driving them to the opposite field. That talent, which began in childhood, helped him win eight batting titles and hit .338 lifetime, #11 on the all-time list of men who played their entire career from 1900 on. Simply put, he was a force, and one as constant as gravity.

While Gwynn confessed that when he was a very young player he used to simply get in the box and whack at the ball, that was before he had begun to study his craft, especially as a pioneer in the use of video. He had been like Jonas Salk before getting his first microscope in that his love of the science and his raw ability existed but was undeveloped.

As late as his eleventh season in the majors, he still insisted that aside from some minor tinkering, "I use a basic approach to hitting. Keep it simple. *Never* change. I stand in the same spot, use the same bat. I don't move up in the box. I don't move back in the box. My trigger [mechanism] is when the pitcher comes with the pitch, my weight is balanced. Then, like every good hitter, the weight transfer must be crisp. I want to hit the ball to left field, but if they come inside, I have to pull it. The majority of balls I hit do go to left."

When he said, "Never change," that is not to say that he didn't factor in how he was being pitched in a given game and by specific pitchers. For instance, during a 1992 interview he said, "Of course, I'm gonna be hitting the ball in different areas. For example, last night right-hander Bob Walk threw me mostly fastballs. I looked for the ball away and adjusted if it's in. Today, with [lefty] Danny Jackson, the angles I'm gonna see and the locations will be different. I'll adjust my swing.

"A lot of guys will see the defense and try to do something different. Over the course of a season this will hurt you more times than not. I'm gonna stick with my strength." If some highly unusual set of circumstances in, say, a crucial playoff situation made him decide to change his way of thinking at the plate, he conceded, "I might, but only until I got two strikes. Then I'd go back to my normal approach."

That approach to hitting early in his career featured him slapping solid line drives for a bundle of singles and doubles. From his rookie season in 1982 through 1992, he reached double figures in home runs just once, averaging roughly six homers per season.

During the 1992 season, Gwynn had his first tête-à-tête with the doctor of hitting, Ted Williams. The two spoke hitting at length again on a 1995 Bob Costas television program. Williams was able to convince his pupil that he should really stress turning on inside pitches, pulling them hard for occasional extra base hits to right. Using the entire field with a command of both inside and outside pitches would keep pitchers honest.

"I'm just the opposite of most guys," Gwynn declared, in an obvious understatement. "My strength is outside; if they come inside, I turn on it. I know I can, so I look for the ball outside, but if it's inside, I *will* turn on it."

From 1994 through 1997, Gwynn methodically claimed four consecutive batting crowns. After his 1992 meeting with Williams, Gwynn upped his home run output to about 10 per season, including a career high of 17 when he was thirty-five years old. Two years later, he produced his career high for runs batted in (RBI) with 119, 47 more than during his best pre-Williams advice days.

Johnny Damon, a veteran of two World Series, critiqued another batting champ: "Ichiro is definitely in that Japanese 'game'—it's very easy to come over to America and see guys are hitting home runs, but he's staying with his same game plan. He's keeping the ball on the ground; that gives him a much better chance for a hit. He keeps his hands back because he 'travels.' A lot of times when a guy 'travels,' their hands travel with them, but he's able to keep his hands back and force the bat through the zone. I think that's what makes him successful." Damon said that unlike most hitters who have "hands that drift," Ichiro not only gets away with it, but thrives.

As Damon noted of the star who racked up 450 hits in his first two seasons in the majors, "He's moving sometimes out of the box [as he swings], but because his hands are back, he's able to react."

Yet another great hitter is Rickey Henderson. Among his astonishing feats is his record of leading off eighty-one games, the equivalent of a half season, with home runs. He had at least one leadoff homer in each of his twenty-five seasons, including his final one when he was forty-four. What's more, his leadoff home run total is way ahead of the #2 man on the list, Alfonso Soriano with fifty-four.

While debates rage concerning who is the greatest slugger of all time, Henderson is the indisputable greatest leadoff man in baseball history. When he was thirty-nine, he swiped 66 bases to become the oldest man ever to win a stolen bases title. Putting runs on the board is, of course, the way to win games, and Henderson crossed home plate a record 2,295 times, an average of 121 runs for every 162 games he played. Many a time he'd reach base to open a game, pilfer one of his 1,406 bases, and score to put his team on top early.

Henderson explained his leadoff power success by quoting one of baseball's oldest adages: "First pitch, fastball." Knowing pitchers generally like to get ahead in the count early on, he would focus on the fastball, salivate, then tee off. However, he also said that wasn't his overall modus operandi: "Nowadays, everybody's trying to get 'big' and hit home runs. I'm not a master of the home run, I master little things. I analyze everything." He felt the fundamentals of the game should apply rather than merely relying upon gargantuan swinging for the fences, and that's why he accumulated 3,055 hits, including 297 homers.

Meanwhile, Lee Smith praised Schmidt: "He had some of the quickest and strongest hands as I've ever seen on a hitter. He was unbelievable. You could make good pitches and he'd just golf balls right off the ground. I think his key is he just waited until the last minute to see if the ball was going to break and then read the spin on the ball."

Finally, 1995 AL MVP Mo Vaughn spoke of what is, to most observers, a hidden technique of hitting. Usually, fans think in terms of the pitcher being in control, setting a hitter up for a pitch that will retire him, but it can work the other way around. In the battle between pitcher and hitter, Vaughn knew of batters who were effective at tricking pitchers—"working the pitcher"—into throwing them a pitch they wanted to see. "The offensive game is definitely a cat-and-mouse game. Barry Bonds is one of the best at this. Albert Belle and Manny Ramirez are good at it, too."

According to Vaughn, it works like this: A batter might take a pitch early in a game "when you know you can drive it" so that later in the game, in a more important situation, the pitcher will be lulled into serving up that juicy pitch again. This time a skilled hitter will pound it. An aging Hank Aaron once faced a hard throwing reliever and looked lost, flailing at a pitch. In that same at-bat, he sat on that pitch and crushed it.

SWINGING FOR THE FENCES

Jay Buhner hit 320 homers, most coming when he wore a Mariners uniform. By the early 1990s, he was following solid advice about not swinging for the fences. "I have to learn to control the swing and not try to hit homers, just try to hit line drives, put the ball in play. If power hitters hit a hard line drive and get it up in the air, it'll go. Ken Griffey Jr. has about as much power as anyone in the game, and he's still learning that, the same as I am."

Still, putting up crooked numbers on the scoreboard later became a trend as team home run records tumbled like dominoes set up by ancient, palsied hands. The power surge reached a crescendo in 2019 when the Minnesota Twins set the all-time record with 307 homers, just one more than the New York Yankees hit in that slugfest of a season. The two next-highest home run totals also came in 2019: the Houston Astros with 288 and the Los Angeles Dodgers with 279. As a matter of fact, through 2022, 110 of the most productive seasons for total homers came after 1993.

By way of a comparison, which admittedly is not entirely an apples-to-apples comparison, in 1961, the Yankees set the record for team home runs with 240, led by Roger Maris and his then-record 61 shots. In 2019, the *average* home run output for each and every team was just under 226.

One player from the 1960s, Carl Warwick, noted that in his day, "I never saw anybody with their little finger or two fingers on the end of the knob of the bat. In those days, you get two strikes, even Stan Musial, and you might choke up the bat an inch or so. Then it was, 'Make contact. Make contact.' Today it's, 'Hit it out of here.' That's the difference."

"Hit it out" is truly the motto of recent years—in 2019 and 2020, the Cincinnati Reds' (at 23.1 percent over that two-year span), Dodgers' (20.5 percent), and Yankees' (20.3 percent) home run totals represented 20 percent or more of all their hits.

According to many stars, certain pitches are a lot more tantalizing than others for smashing. Tom Henke, who piled up 301 saves, said, "I think the pitch that goes the furthest *is* your fastball. The harder you throw it, the faster it's going to go out when you meet it solidly. That goes hand in hand with game conditions. In BP conditions a guy's just laying it in there, but you get a guy who connects against a good 90-plus-mile-per-hour fastball, and connects solidly, that ball's going to go a long way."

Many hitters disagree. Chris Chambliss—who gained fame, among other things, for his walk-off home run in Game Five of the 1976 American League Championship Series, lifting his Yankees to the AL pennant—was one.

He said that when it came to a pitch he could drive for distance, he always preferred sliders. He said the speed of a slider is a key, since the batter "doesn't have to supply all the power." He knew of sluggers who often got hold of pitches around 85-plus miles per hour and deposited them in distant places: "Frank Howard, Dave Kingman, Frank Thomas—those guys are going to hit long, towering balls. I saw

Kingman hit a high changeup, up and in, off Catfish Hunter that was a bomb. Major league bat speed is something special. When those big hitters catch it, it'll go!"

He stressed that the type of pitch is crucial, but hitting tape measure shots is a "combination of both the speed of the pitch and the hitters with their quick bats. Batters want something fairly fast. Obviously they don't want a Nolan Ryan fastball because he throws *really* hard, but I would actually say even a changeup that's thrown high and a little too hard becomes a batting practice type fastball. That can go the farthest, too."

He said the reason a hitter can drive a pitch with some speed on it is obvious: "When you throw really slow," he said, "the batter has to supply all the power himself. So, again, you *do* want the pitch to be fairly fast."

Chambliss said that when he was young, though, he was the kind of batter who hit the changeup very well. "If you threw me a changeup, I'd hit it a mile, but a fastball, I'd fight it off.

"So I didn't have as quick a bat as, say, Joe Carter, who has a real quick bat. He can time anything, even 95-plus miles per hour."

For his part, Carter said that contrary to what some people think, "the hanging curveball goes farther than a fastball or a knuckleball. Anything off speed is going to go a little bit farther than a regular fastball. A curveball is especially going to go the farthest. Those are the ones that you hit high up in the air, and they tend to go far because the wind kind of catches them a little more." For Carter, the majestic home runs often come off hanging curves.

Jesse Barfield ticked off reasons why such curves get blasted: "Number one, you're looking for the fastball, so by the pitch being a little slower, you've got a chance to get the bat head out. When you get that full extension, the ball really travels.

"And because of the height of the ball, it's already up there, you can drive it." A high pitch seems ideal for the many sluggers who loft the ball with a big uppercut. "Oh, do you ever have a chance to get under them," continued Barfield with a grin and the gleaming eyes of a power hitter.

He did disagree with Carter a bit, preferring a slider that stays up too high, but said that in general, "the hanging balls you can get under. The longest ball I ever hit was in Yankee Stadium. It was measured at 485 feet in 1991. It went over the flagpole on a hanging slider from a lefty. I'm looking for a fastball in, so I got the head out. He left it out over the plate a little bit, and I hit the ball and it just kept carrying."

Barfield noted what goes through a slugger's mind when a delectable pitch comes his way: "You look at the location of the pitch and you can see the spin on it, and if it's up there in your eyes, you're trained to swing at it. If you miss it, so what, but I'm not going to let it go by. Your eyes light up, no question about that."

He concluded by saying that hanging pitches "give you the chance to get that good backspin. You want to have that big backspin like Frank Thomas or Fred McGriff when he really extends on one.

"Now Ted Williams was one in a million. Some of his homers had topspin." Balls hit like that usually result in grounders, not balls that fly out of parks.

As to what is the ideal pitch to drive, Chambliss reached the conclusion that ultimately it varies from hitter to hitter "because their bat speed is different. There are a lot of hitters with 'slider-speed bats'; they're pretty good off-speed hitters. There are some hitters who really hit the changeup. Then there was Graig Nettles, who I played with, who could hit the fastest fastball out."

Two-Strike Hitting

Geoff Zaun earned a World Series championship ring with the 1997 Florida Marlins. As a catcher with sixteen seasons of experience, he studied a lot of hitters. He said that when it comes to two-strike hitting, "you can't hit .300 for a lengthy period of time in this game and not be able to hit with two outs or two strikes, so I would say the guys who year in and year out pile up the numbers are hitting in all different situations. You going to have to learn how to hit in all situations, and when you're hitting .300 every year, you know how."

Still, some men seem to excel at hitting in the clutch. Rico Carty was, from a pitcher's perspective, infamous for hurting them even when hitting in the hole—having a two-strike count didn't faze him. The cliché "You could wake him up in the middle of the winter and he'd get a base hit" applied to Carty.

Vinny Castilla hit more home runs—320—than any other Mexican-born big-leaguer. He observed, "When you've got two strikes, it's hard to hit, especially at this level. The pitchers know what to throw, but you have to stay focused and try to swing at a good pitch. It's hard—you check all the numbers of a lot of players with two strikes [and very few have a] big average.

"When you've got two strikes, you have to stay a little shorter with your swing and try to get a good pitch to hit hard somewhere. It's easy to say, but it's hard to do."

In 2005, David Eckstein of the division-winning Cardinals got a lot of ink for his ability to make contact. Wire reports noted that "hitting with two strikes is white-knuckle time for most batters. Not David Eckstein." He finished second among NL hitters for his .279 batting average with two strikes. In fact, a disproportionate six of his eight homers and 37 of his 61 ribbies came with two strikes.

The 5-foot-7 shortstop said he remained calm in such situations, confident that, if nothing else, he could battle and foul off pitch after pitch to avoid whiffing. As a leadoff hitter, he said, his function was to make the pitcher work hard, so he delighted in fouling off their good and even borderline pitches.

Jason Bay, a Silver Slugger winner, said the speedy Juan Pierre was great at hitting with two strikes because "that guy never strikes out and he's a leadoff guy, so he's taking a ton of pitches. He's the type of guy that his swing is a little bit easier, just to kind of get the ball in play. And if he hits it on the left side, nine times out of ten he's going to [be] safe at first base, so that helps."

In spring training of 2005, Bay said he detested hitting with an 0–2 count. "Definitely. Nobody likes to be 0–2. You're on the defense right away. Some people just deal with it or are better off [than others]—usually the guys who have been around for a few years and kind of know the league, the pitchers, and know *themselves*—I'm still getting to that point."

Being down 0–2 isn't exactly frightening, "but it's not ideal," he continued. "When you get 2–0, 3–1, you're kind of like, 'Okay, now relax a little bit.' With 0–2, you have a tendency sometimes to tense up."

Kyle Davies was a promising youngster in the Braves organization in 2005. From his pitcher's point of view, he said, "There are some guys who get really defensive and foul off pitches—pesky, pesky, pesky.

"The sluggers, when they get a pitch, they're going to hit it right then, and it's going to be hit hard, or they'll swing and miss it. Whereas the little guys, if they don't get their pitch, they'll still try and foul it off and get something that they can hit hard." They, of course, tend to have shorter cuts, "but you got to be careful—those guys will get you, too, if you leave something in."

Two-Out Hitting and Hitting with Men in Scoring Position

Managers love it when one of their players has the ability to come through with, say, a two-out hit to score a run or more. In fact, they love *any* time a guy comes through with men in scoring position.

Most hitters say they find it difficult to hit in such situations. Bay said, "Edgar Renteria [2010 World Series MVP] was pretty good—I mean, at *all* times hitting, but he was also a guy where, all of a sudden you get the first two guys out, he gets on, and a stolen base or a double [follows], and before you know it, from two outs and nobody on, all of a sudden they got a run."

Castilla said the key to his RBI success, and to hitting with runners in scoring position, is "to be more selective in those situations because the pitcher is going to be more careful than when there's nobody on, especially when a guy is known for getting a lot of RBI."

Sometimes that means letting some pitches go by, but "you still got to be aggressive because sometimes he will throw it down the middle and you have to be able to take advantage of that. But most of the time they have to try to work the count, because the pitchers don't want to just lay it in there for you, so you do have to be more selective."

Varying game situations also alter batters' strategy. For instance, if the bases are loaded, the advantage swings sharply to the hitter, and he can really look for a fat pitch because "they have to come to you."

In a crucial two-out, bases-loaded situation, Castilla said, "you still have to stay focused, still aggressive, too, but selective at the same time.

It doesn't mean that because you're aggressive you want to swing at everything. You're aggressive, but you swing at strikes and lay off of the bad pitches. Get a good pitch and hit it hard."

HITTERS' CONFIDENCE

Baseball legend Stan Musial brimmed over with confidence, possessing the calmness of a safecracker, knowing he'd come through even under duress. Hank Aaron recalled the 1955 All-Star Game, when that attitude was vividly on display. The game labored on until the twelfth inning, when Musial led off. American League catcher Yogi Berra grumbled to Musial that his feet were killing him, prompting Musial to tell him not to worry, the game would soon be over. It was, on a first-pitch homer to deep right field.

In a 2009 interview, Aaron said that just before strolling to the plate Musial told him, "'They don't pay us to play overtime.' I know a lot say Babe Ruth pointed, but I know Stan called his. I heard that myself."

Julio Rodriguez has no lack of self-confidence, either. The 2022 Rookie of the Year wound up earning more MVP votes that season than Mike Trout, thanks in part to his 28 home runs in just 132 contests. He told *Baseball Digest*, "I don't worry about expectations. No matter how high the expectations go, they'll never be higher than my own."[3]

Kevin Maas lasted only five seasons in the majors, but in his rookie season of 1990, he hit 21 homers in just 254 at-bats, good for an impressive average of 8.26 homers per 100 at-bats. In fact, he set a since-broken record for the fewest at-bats needed—72—to reach double digits in homers. He began to feel like, "If I turn on the ball and get a piece of it, you don't always have to get all of it to hit it out, [especially] down the line." He was smart enough to realize that he was "a better hitter to gaps," doing well when he didn't "try to hit 'em out." Plus, he said, "when I'm hitting well, no park can hold me.

"I've struggled in the past, going through some tough streaks, but I never lost faith in my ability. They pitch more careful with me; they know I can put it over the fence with one pitch."

It may shock most fans, but according to "Sudden" Sam McDowell, who led the AL in strikeouts per nine innings six times, many players do not exude confidence. "Most have low self-esteem," he said. "They've been taught since they were seven years old that he's important *if* he's winning. He gets this from his parents, from Little League, from high school coaches."

Interestingly, McDowell said that some big-leaguers suffering from low self-esteem will seek professional guidance or counseling, but this is less often seen in the minor leagues. He explained, "In the minors, they still view a request for help as a sign of weakness."

FACING AN UNFAMILIAR PITCHER

Stepping into the batter's box to face a pitcher one has never seen before is no easy task. Josh Barfield, son of Jesse Barfield, concurred. "Especially the first time you see them, because you don't know what the ball's doing; you don't know the release point. It's one thing to watch on TV, but it's another thing to get in there and see it in the box. So after you had a couple at-bats against them, you feel a lot more comfortable."

Casey Blake, who belted 28 home runs in 2004, pretty much agreed: "Maybe just see a pitch or two, and just kind of pick up where it's coming from, and just try to see the ball the best you can."

Paul Molitor faced a whole lot of pitchers over his twenty-one-year career, during which he ripped 3,319 hits against pitchers old and new. His strategy against a pitcher he wasn't familiar with was pretty basic: "I tried to let the ball get as deep as I could and go up the middle with the ball."

Any odd style of pitching can be disconcerting to a batter—again, especially if the hitter hasn't faced the pitcher before—but not overwhelming to some. Prior to Shane Victorino's first start against Paul Byrd, who used an exaggerated windup, the Philadelphia Phillies outfielder said, "I saw him in spring last year [2006], but, no, it's just something different. In the end, you ultimately find out where his release point is no matter what he does before he pitches. He's got to get to where his release point is, and that's what you look for."

HITTERS AND THEIR COACHES

Listening to the advice of veterans and a good hitting coach helps batters. In 1996, Ellis Burks reached career highs with 40 homers, 128 RBI, and a lusty .344 batting average under Ken Griffey Sr.

"He had a great influence on me when I had the best year of my career," Burks said of Griffey. "He reminded me not to do too much with a pitch, telling me, 'You don't have to go up there trying to swing for the fences every time. All you have to do is put the bat on the ball. You don't have to swing hard, just put it there and let the pitchers generate the power.' You need those reminders. You're a big-leaguer, you've been around for years, but it's the little things that take you back. And you go, 'Hmm, he's right.'"

Burks also came to realize that some hitters who seem to be easy outs can become late bloomers, men who "become more patient" with age. And that's a lesson even a good hitter will apply to himself. "The older you get," he went on, "you become more patient. You think more instead of just using your talent all the time—you use your brain a little more. The older you get, you use every little advantage you have." Those advantages come from coaches like Griffey and from within.

Chipper Jones, one of the rare modern big-leaguers who played his entire career with one club (Atlanta, for nineteen seasons), agreed that there is always something to learn or be reminded of: "It's pretty universal. Good hitting coaches are able to pick stuff up real fast. You know, the fundamentals of hitting are pretty simple to describe, but they're not very easy to imitate. 'Keep your head still. Keep your feet slow. Keep your hands quick.' That's pretty much it, and it *is* that simple.

"This game is all about making adjustments and keeping the fundamentals as basic as possible. I think whenever you keep things simple at the plate, don't think too much, things are going to work out good for you. When it's done right, man, it sure is fun."

Sometimes even big-leaguers slip into basic habits such as pulling one's head off the ball. Jones confided, "I do it all the time. I get quick with my feet, lunge a little bit, my head moves forward. As long as you keep your head still you've got a chance."

Most of the times, he said, a player is too close to the situation, so a coach is more apt to spot such flaws quicker. "Most of the time you can't feel it; you don't know why you're rolling over balls or why you're jumping out there. It's just something that a coach has to be able to recognize quickly, and good hitting coaches will be able to tell you when a hitter gets a little out of whack."

Griffey Jr. said he benefited from his very own and *very* personal hitting coach: his father. "He knows my swing better than I do."

FAILURE

The Pittsburgh Pirates franchise dates back to 1882, when they were known as the Alleghenys. The organization is famous for producing great hitters. From 1900 through 2006, eleven Pirates won twenty-five batting titles. However, they have had only one Rookie of the Year: Jason Bay in 2004.

Bay said that the toughest part of the hitting game for him is "going up there knowing that the best players fail seven out of ten times. It's dealing with that failure. You're up there four or five times a day, every day, and you're bearing down trying to get a hit every single time, and obviously you can't do that. It's tough offensively to deal with not being able to produce every single time.

"When you're going well, you're like, 'Hitting is easy.' Then all of a sudden, the next day, you're like, 'I got no idea what I'm doing.' That's what makes it tough—how it changes from day to day, but it's the same game."

So, is he a perfectionist? "I think everyone tries to be, yeah. You're out there and some days it feels so easy, but as soon as you get complacent, it turns on you."

Another Rookie of the Year winner, Ryan Howard, often faced failure. Going into the 2023 season, only eighteen men had ever struck out as many times as Howard. Based on an imaginary scenario in which he played every one of his team's 162 games each season, he would have averaged 190 strikeouts a year. Another way of looking at it: over his thirteen-year career, he averaged 1.7 strikeouts per game.

Unabashed, he addressed his fatal flaw. He remembered how, during his days in the minors, "that's all everybody ever talked about. Even when I started putting up numbers that were always close to the top [of the league leaders] . . . I guess everybody was always looking at 'if he doesn't strike out as much, how would his numbers look.'

"To me, I got to the point where I'm not going to worry about strikeouts because strikeouts are part of the game. If I can go out there and do what I do and put up the numbers I put up, and have my number of strikeouts, what's the problem? That was my mind-set."

He said he tries "to forget bad at-bats real quick, come back, and do the best I can," realizing, of course, that the strikeouts are part of the package that comes with so many sluggers, something Jim Thome used to say all the time. "If you can still go out and put up numbers or just have good at-bats, you can't control the outcome of whatever's going to happen. You know sometimes umpires are going to make calls, and sometimes you're going to chase bad pitches," Howard concluded.

There no longer is the stigma there once was attached to strikeouts. Rich Hofman, the highly successful high school coach who sent such stars as Alex Rodriguez and Doug Mientkiewicz to the major leagues, said, "A lot of the great hitters strike out a lot, and it's not important to people anymore.

"I read an article in our paper about strikeouts. Years ago, somebody like Lou Brock had 99 strikeouts, and he sat out the last game so he wouldn't have 100 strikeouts in a season. I think that mentality has changed."

STRUGGLES

In 2005, Ryan Howard played in just eighty-eight games as a rookie. The next season, at the age of twenty-six, he won the MVP Award while leading his league in homers (58) and RBI (149). In 2008, he again led the NL in those categories. However, in between those years he experienced some serious struggles for the first time in the majors.

In 2007, he hit only .268, a plunge of 45 points, and he struck out a humbling 199 times. What made matters worse was a galling, frustrating visit to the disabled list. He coped by saying, "Adversity definitely made me stronger. The worst part was probably just being on the DL [disabled list], not able to play, because you want to be out there playing. Just sitting and watching is probably the toughest thing."

Being pestered daily by the media about how he felt was frustrating. He said, "You know what bugged me was just having to answer the same thing every day—everybody struggles, everybody has slumps and they struggle here and there."

Through it all, Howard seemed to have control of the situation, from coping with slumps to handling the huge expectations of fans and the media. "After winning Rookie of the Year and taking over at first base for Jim Thome, I already knew people were always talking about filling his shoes and all the expectations."

Again, he dealt with the obstacle of expectations. His attitude was that he wasn't there to wear Thome's spikes; "I could only do what I could do. If you go out and try to fulfill everybody's expectations, that's when you're in trouble."

As for rebounding from injury, he said he simply was shooting for "getting as consistent as possible: get good [at-bats] and see better pitches." Howard comes across as one who, when doing well, can be pleased with his swing but never satisfied and certainly never complacent. His attitude paid off with some sterling numbers offsetting his low batting average and high strikeout rate. In 2007, he finished second for homers (47) and runs driven in (136) despite missing eighteen games.

Another type of struggle is that for recognition and appreciation. Al Oliver made seven All-Star teams but felt he was overshadowed by fellow Pirates such as Roberto Clemente and underappreciated by the media.

"I think it's quite obvious," said Oliver in 1981. "The people who are responsible for giving a player his just due have not done their job." Lack of media coverage meant that many fans never realized he ended his career in the 3,000-hit vicinity (2,743) and hit .303.

The media seemed to favor another Pirate who came along around the same time as Oliver, in the late 1960s: Bob Robertson. "We were compared, but should not have been. First of all, he was a power hitter and I was a line drive hitter, but it was a mistake the Pirates made, but I'm happy—I'm still around."

Oliver lasted through 1985 and put up a 43.6 career wins above replacement (WAR); Robertson had a 9.4 WAR when he left the game after the 1979 season. In the long run, Oliver even out-homered Robertson, 219 to 115. No wonder Oliver felt slighted.

SLUMPS

Joe Cunningham, a two-time All-Star, said the dreaded topic of slumps is a puzzler. "It's hard to explain—every good ballplayer has troubles at times. No one's ever figured out a slump. They figured out everything else—they figured out how to get to the moon, and this and that, but no one's ever figured out the solution to a slump."

Former hitting coach Rudy Jaramillo said that hitters know when things aren't right. They also realize that even when things are off *just a wee bit*, they can swoon into a full-fledged slump. He empathized, "You get lost in that rhythm, the timing with the pitcher. It's something real small all the time that gets you off, and that's, as a coach, what you have to figure out so these guys don't stay in a prolonged slump. You got to try to cut it off when you see it, not let it go three, four days and say, 'Well, let's see if he's going to adjust,' because you're losing at-bats."

Jaramillo said the theory of letting a hitter work his way out of a slump is nonsensical. "You can't do that. You got to start building that confidence back in him through drills and early work and whatever it takes."

Johnny Damon, who led the AL in steals and runs scored in 2000, lamented, "When I go into slumps, I hit a lot of lazy fly balls. Lazy fly balls aren't going to fall in too much, but if you keep the ball on the ground, make the defense work, you also have a chance to get the ball through the infield."

By way of contrast, he said a rare player like Ichiro can usually avoid slumps. "He's what every team wants, a guy who can keep it in play. He's just a great handler of the bat."

As a rule, power hitter Ryan Klesko believes, it's easier for a veteran to shake out of a slump than an inexperienced player. "You accept it. You know you're going to go through your slumps. You also have your ways of getting out of it—you know yourself and your swing as a veteran."

STREAKS

Joe DiMaggio's record 56-game hitting streak is well chronicled, but how about a player's torrid stretch that lasted for a season? Take Joe Torre's superlative 1971 season as an example. "I hit the ball hard pretty much all year," he said of his .363 season. "I hit between .360 and .370 all year long. I was very locked in mentally. That was the big thing focus-wise. I don't think I ever went two games without a hit, and I don't think that happened after July. It was just one of those freak years and I made the most of it.

"I was confident. I knew I was going to hit the slider off this guy, or he's going to give me a fastball to hit. And I just tried to think, 'Go up the middle' all the time."

He was doing so well, he became tentative off the field. "I started holding on getting in and out of the shower because I didn't want to twist or break anything." A streak is a precious, fragile commodity, one requiring overprotectiveness.

MAKING ADJUSTMENTS

Good hitters often make day-to-day and even at-bat-to-at-bat adjustments. Rob Picciolo was a San Diego Padres coach who marveled at Tony Gwynn and "his ability to make an adjustment after one pitch. Throwing Tony batting practice for all those years, the one thing Tony did better than anybody I've ever seen is he tracked the ball longer and let it get deep in the strike zone before he made his decision whether to swing or not, and he could hit a ball on the plate, deep in the strike zone better than anyone.

"There were many times when I threw batting practice to Tony and I thought he was going to take the pitch, but his bat would come out of nowhere. Great hand-eye coordination, as good as I've ever seen. That's something that is very difficult to teach."

Those men who can't adjust in the big leagues become baseball's version of a one-hit wonder. This happens, said Jeff Bagwell, "when the league makes adjustments to you. So you have to make adjustments to the league. The people who can't do it, they don't continue to be at that same level."

The Bat

When Gwynn was a minor leaguer, he used a thin, light fungo bat, playing soft toss and taking full cuts. He said he was taken aback by the bat speed he was generating. That led to his employing a small bat in games. He began using a 32-inch, 31-ounce bat in the minors before going to a 33-inch, 30 1/2-ounce stick, saying that short bats also helped his bat control. His highest number of strikeouts in a season was a mere 40, and he averaged only 29 K's per 162 games played. With his falcon-like vision, a Gwynn strikeout was as rare as a Haley's Comet sighting.

In the days before Gwynn, the topic of bats could be a touchy one. Ron Blomberg was with the Yankees from 1969 through 1976. "Players have a hundred different bats that they use now—they got the maple, the ash, the this, and the that," he said. "We had, like, three, four bats. If we broke them, we'd go to the traveling secretary. 'Well, you used two dozen bats already. We can't order you more for another month.' You'd have to use someone else's bat.

"I had a Louisville Slugger and an Adirondack, the only two bats I had. And they'd order about a dozen bats for us for a month, even for guys like Reggie Jackson, and half of the bats were no good. When I came up to the majors, I used to ask Mickey Mantle about this. They used to give Mickey a dozen bats—that's all they'd give him.

"You'd pick out the bat you want to use for the games, but when you break them, you don't have any bats that you can use. I remember I used to go to Bobby Bonds and have to get bats from him to use. And I remember Thurman Munson used to use my bats sometimes.

"A lot of times you'd keep your bats in your locker so people wouldn't use them for batting practice. Unfortunately, when we'd go on road trips with all [our] bats, the pitchers didn't have bats, so they used to use ours when they took batting practice.

"You go out there looking for your bat. You can't find it. Then you find it laying down on the ground—the pitchers used it. They used anything they wanted to. Remember how the pitchers used to play pepper against the screen, behind home plate? Then you'd come in the clubhouse and your bat's broken. You had no idea who did it. That's why I always took my bat with me and kept it in my locker so they wouldn't take it."

HITTERS DISCUSS STAR PITCHERS

Chipper Jones deeply respected the skill of former teammate Greg Maddux. He said one of the most special players he ever saw was "Maddux, as far as a pitcher goes—just an artist, truly a pleasure to play behind."

Jones said that the first time they faced each other after Maddux left the Braves was contrary to what many might expect: "It was no big deal; I faced him a ton in spring training. I knew what to expect, and he knew what I was looking for. It was a fun confrontation."

Most hitters did not find facing Maddux to be much fun. His personal catcher, Eddie Perez, revealed why: "He throws his fastball over the top, and his ball moves a lot. He throws sinkers and cutters to both sides of the plate, that's what makes him so tough to hit."

In 2005, the Los Angeles Dodgers' Todd Hollandsworth won the NL Rookie of the Year Award. He mentioned three relievers whom he found to be real challenges. "Brad Lidge has one of the best sliders in the game. He's got a lot of movement and good velocity on it. Best cut fastball's probably Mariano Rivera; it's a grenade. I know people say he's made a living off only one pitch, but he knows how to pitch, there's no doubt about it. His cutter is definitely the best in the business. For pure velocity, I'd go with Billy Wagner."

Norman Lumpkin, who played in the Negro Leagues, said he vividly remembered Satchel Paige. "Early in his career, he'd spot his fastball as his only pitch—but he'd hit spots. He threw the curve late in his career," he claimed.

"When he was in a good mood he'd put on a show. He'd put down a handkerchief and the catcher put out a target, and he'd hit it. He was a drawing card."

Another veteran of the Negro League, Robert Williams, recalled a classic matchup between Paige and Roy Campanella. "Campy" was touring with a group of major league All-Stars and faced Paige, then in the Negro League. "The game was in Columbus, South Carolina," said Williams, "around 1948. Campy got a single and ran down the line jumping and doing crow hops. He was so happy to get a hit off Satch." Paige was so talented, just about anyone would have been elated to hit safely against him.

PLAYERS DISCUSS TOP BATTERS

Let's begin here with baseball's largest legend: Babe Ruth. No need to list the Bambino's stats, but when Don Mattingly was growing up, he had heard so many Herculean tales of the man, he became incredulous. He thought Ruth must be a mythical figure, like the hulking Paul Bunyan. "I always thought Babe Ruth was like a cartoon character, I didn't relate him to a real player."

Jim Palmer paid the ultimate tribute to Ruth, saying if he had had to pitch to him, red warning flags would have been wildly fluttering high over the park. One of Palmer's catchers, Elrod Hendricks, simply said, "I'd find a way to walk him four times."

Skipping ahead to more modern players, Jeff Francoeur said one of his favorite players to watch was Gary Sheffield. No wonder—Sheffield, the nephew of Dwight Gooden, is a member of the 500-home-run club who hit .292 and drove in 1,676 runs.

"I never got a chance to play with him," said Francoeur, "but I was in camp when he was with Atlanta. I loved to watch him hit because he was always aggressive. He's always on the front foot; he's got an unorthodox swing, but at the same time he gets the job done. And he used to always tell me that 'you get paid to drive the ball and to drive in runs. If you can do that and do it successfully for 162 games, then you'll be pretty darn good.'"

Andre Dawson liked David Justice's tools: "He has that real nice and easy stroke, and the ball just seems to jump off his bat, too. He's one of the bigger guys, and with that stroke he generates a lot of bat speed."

Bo Jackson was a talented athlete in two sports: he won the Heisman Trophy in 1985, drove in 105 runs and was named MLB All-Star MVP in 1989, and was named to the NFL Pro Bowl in 1990. Powerful Mickey Tettleton appreciated Jackson, saying, "Bo is extremely strong. He can put a kiss on the ball."

Jackson surely did, hitting a high of 32 home runs in 1989. Teammate Damion Easley said Jackson's leviathan homers were so awe inspiring, opponents would stop whatever they were doing to watch him take batting practice.

Alan Trammell was impressed with former Detroit Tigers teammate Kirk Gibson's longball prowess. "He hit probably the longest one I ever saw. It went just to the right of the transformer that Reggie Jackson hit in the 1971 All-Star Game. They estimated the ball went 525 feet and hit a lumberyard across the street." That was one of 255 home runs he drilled in his career.

Joe Carter had glowing words for 2023 Hall of Fame inductee Fred McGriff, the author of 493 home runs (top thirty all-time): "He's the only guy I know who can hit the ball out of all parts of the field and sit at home plate and watch it go out.

"Freddie has got that huge backswing where he gets a lift, and he hits the ball to the opposite field, and he can just sit there with that big follow-through. I mean he's tremendous. He's got a lot of raw talent. He's probably one of the strongest guys in baseball as far as hitting the ball out of the ballpark."

Tettleton said McGriff "hits 'em where most guys need a [golf] driver or three wood to get to." And Dawson said, "He amazes me because he doesn't even seem to swing very hard and the ball jumps off his bat. Most of his home runs are tape measure shots. He's a joy to watch."

Muscular Detroit catcher Lance Parrish, once the bodyguard for singer Tina Turner, pointed out that some good hitters don't need bulk. "It doesn't necessarily take a big man to hit a ball a long way. I remember seeing Lou Whitaker hit one over the roof at Tiger Stadium. It's wrist, it's bat speed. It's everything put together." The Whitaker package of attributes led to his becoming a five-time All-Star after being named the 1977 AL Rookie of the Year.

UMPIRES FROM THE HITTER'S VIEWPOINT

Matt Lawton, who hit a personal high of .305 in 2000, said hitters are always aware of which umps are working the plate and other factors influencing the men in blue. For instance, he knew that a pitcher such as Pedro Martínez was going to have a "little bigger strike zone—or if you're playing the Yankees and you're in Yankee Stadium, you know you better be swinging the bat because their pitchers are going to get a wider strike zone."

Lawton said that such situations are "like an unwritten rule. You know what it's going to be like before the day starts, so you better go up there ready to swing, because if you take [pitches] that day, you're going to be walking back to the dugout a lot. When you see certain guys back there, you know you need to [get in the] batter's box ready to swing."

Hitters even consider what day a game takes place: "especially day games when umpires have flights to catch—all those things factor in. You just know how the game's going to be played that day."

CHAPTER TWO

Pitchers

MOUND INTIMIDATION

Many pitchers over the years have almost arrogantly held to the position that home plate belongs to them. It's seen less often nowadays, but there was a time when a batter crowding the plate did so at his own peril, because the next pitch would either brush him back, knock him down, or drill him in his ribs or back. Many intimidating pitchers would even throw at, or at least near, the head.

One such pitcher was Early Wynn, who recorded 300 victories. Stories of his aggressiveness are legendary. He once said a pitcher could never be successful until he came to the point where he hated hitters. Another time he snarled, "I've got a right to knock down anybody holding a bat." One widespread, though apocryphal, story had it that Wynn said he would knock down anyone, including his own mother.

Wynn perpetuated the legend: "I'm tired of hearing all those stories that I'd throw at my mother." He paused for effect, then added, "Unless she had a bat in her hand." Jerry Walker, a former roommate of Wynn, commented, "He didn't like to lose—*ever.*" And former Cleveland Indians teammate Bob Feller said Wynn clearly was "a very tough competitor," but that the line about brushing back his own mother was actually never uttered by Wynn. Instead, said Feller, it was part of the Wynn legend—a legend that nonetheless was well earned.

Lee Smith had a much less prickly personality than Wynn, and he said that sometimes hitting a batter isn't very wise. The 6-foot-5 Smith confided that as part of his job he wouldn't hesitate to brush people off the plate when needed. "Yes, I did, but it was tough for a guy being a closer to do that. You hit a guy, and then you got the tying run on base. I think for retaliation it was easier for starting pitchers, but if the situation comes, I don't really think that you had to hit a guy to get your point over. If you throw that ball in tight and get a guy off the plate, then you get respect. There are some times when you got to hit guys, but you don't want to end anybody's career."

Of course, when considering the speed of a pitch and the damage it can do, one man always comes to mind: Nolan Ryan. Among pitchers who plied their trade exclusively from 1900 on, four especially hard-throwing pitchers stand out among the lifetime leaders in hit batsmen: Walter Johnson (#1 with 205), Randy Johnson (#2 at 190), Roger Clemens (#8 with 159), and Ryan (#9 at 158).[1]

Does it pay to strike fear and make batters quiver in their spikes? Well, almost every pitcher named here is a Hall of Famer.

With Ryan there was constantly a fear factor. As Ken Griffey Jr. observed, "He's the only one that I felt was different [to face] because of stories my dad and Andre Dawson and Shawon Dunston told me . . . that he was mean and nasty."

Jeff Torborg had the privilege of catching a no-hitter thrown by Ryan and a Sandy Koufax perfect game. In fact, he has caught more no-hit games—three—than all but two catchers. "When you talk velocity, Nolan threw the hardest," he asserted. "Nolan threw it down the strike zone harder than any human being I ever saw. In 1973, against the Boston Red Sox, Nolan threw a pitch a little up and over my left shoulder. I reached up for it and his pitch tore a hole in the webbing of my glove and hit the backstop at Fenway Park."

Ryan, the all-time leader in walks with 2,795, led his league in walks eight times and in wild pitches six times, a category in which he ranks #2 all-time. He was wild enough to make hitters realize they had better stay loose in the batter's box.

Dizzy Dean was another pitcher who always wanted batters he faced to feel uncomfortable. Dean was colorful and often clowned around, even during games, but when he was on the mound, opposing batters usually found him to be as serious and as frightening as a biopsy. Once, when a brash rookie was laboriously digging in on him in the batter's box, Dean glared at him, waited for the batter to finally settle in, then bellowed, "You all done? You comfortable? Well, send for a groundskeeper and get a shovel cause that's where they're going to bury you."

All-Star Mark Grace related to that tale, saying, "Intimidation works for pitchers—that's what 'chin music' is all about. If a Nolan Ryan or Dwight Gooden throws tight, it sends a message—don't dig in."

Pitching tight to hitters is a strategy that dates back forever. Feller, aka "Rapid Robert," debuted at the age of seventeen, just days after reporting to the Indians straight from the halls of his Iowa high school. His fastball was frightening, and he used it to pitch inside from his very first game. He recalled, "The first strikeout I ever got was in July of 1936, in Washington in my first inning in relief of Johnny Allen. My first strikeout was of Buddy Lewis. I had thrown too close to the first man I faced, and then came Lewis, and he was nowhere *near* the plate. He *couldn't* possibly have hit the ball—yes, he struck out."

It was a combination of the speed of his pitches, his unfettered wildness, and the merciless appearance of another Hall of Famer, Rich "Goose" Gossage, that made batters tremble. Gossage sported a menacing Fu Manchu, but insisted he never consciously took to the mound trying to be intimidating—regardless, the net result was the same.

He was a great reliever in part due to his pitching style. He once said, "I mean, when you throw 95 or better, and I'm all arms, legs, and I'm not looking at the hitter—I never got a good look at the plate—my delivery was very intimidating. They couldn't pick the ball up. I'd hide it very well. It was a combination of those three things, I think, that really made me successful.

"It was never an act for me. My demeanor on the mound was always natural. I felt like a Jekyll and Hyde. When I went between the lines, something snapped in me. The hitter was the enemy."

Gossage confessed that he had "hit a few guys in the head, but never intentionally." Of course, that's not much consolation for those victims. They would probably moan, "Who cares if it was an accidental beanball? It still hurt like hell."

Gossage also said that it took a lot of energy and effort to stay intimidating over the years. In 1994, still active at the age of forty-three, he said that he somehow managed to "get pumped up, but I don't know that I'm as intense or as intimidating as I used to be." Hitters, no doubt, felt he was just as petrifying as ever.

Jay Buhner said, "When I first came up, Roger Clemens was very intimidating. Some pitchers, just by the way they carry themselves, guys like Ryan and Gossage, were very intimidating people. I think more of your intimidating pitchers were your big guys who threw harder, and the ones who gave you 'the look.' And the way they carried themselves, and maybe it's the facial hair—the goatee or mustache. The way they pull the hat down over their eyes like Goose. I mean, it's a lot of things—the way they throw their first pitch, or like Ryan who used to come up and stare you down. Everybody's got their own little style."

Griffey Jr. said he was intimidated by Gossage even when "Junior" was a young kid. The reason? "That mustache. The way he pulled his hat down over his eyes. He never smiled." Gossage downplayed his Fu Manchu as a weapon. "I had success before I had my mustache. It was never an act for intimidation." He said he first grew his mustache simply to irritate and to break the rules imposed by George Steinbrenner, the meddling owner of the Yankees when Gossage was with them.

Nevertheless, Gossage certainly had his own style and demeanor, even if he didn't consciously try to develop it. "Nothing I did out there was premeditated; that's just the way I am out there. I never consciously thought about intimidation." He once said that his own wife wouldn't know him when he was pitching. He calmly said, "Hate is an ugly word, but I hate hitters."

While Gossage also said that he "never faced a hitter that intimidated me, that I was afraid of—never," early on there was one fleeting moment of fear. "One day I threw one up and in on Willie Horton, and it just got away from me when I was a young kid back with the White

Sox. He stood there and I got the ball back from the catcher and I walked around the mound. Then I felt something staring right through me; I looked back at home plate and his eyes were as big as saucers. I turned around and went, 'Woah! This guy can scare you.'

"Then I turned toward Horton and said, 'F— him, I'm not gonna let him intimidate me,' and I threw another one up and in. It was stupidity, really." Ultimately it was far from being stupid. He had sent a message: If there's anybody around here doing any intimidating, it's going to be me.

"Gossage was an idol of mine," Lee Smith freely admitted. "I used to admire him in the bullpen. I'd get in there and I'd throw the ball as hard as I could to the plate and turn my back on home plate like he did."

Smith also critiqued Pedro Martínez, a former teammate of his on the Expos. He said of the 5-foot-11, 180-pound Martínez, "I think Pedro actually thinks he's about 6-foot-9 and about 240. He pitches like he does because he's aggressive and he uses both sides of the plate. He doesn't let the hitter get comfortable up there. He moves the ball in and he makes good pitches.

"He's a hard worker also, but I think he got bent out of shape a little bit early in his career when everybody was labeling him as being too little—'Oh, he's not big enough, he can't do this, and he can't do that.' The reason the Dodgers got rid of him was they said he was too small. He showed them that he could do it. That's one thing I like about him. Proving somebody wrong with the stuff that he has is unbelievable. It's amazing how hard that man can throw a ball, and with good movement."

Smith said it's quite possible Martínez began throwing tight as another way of proving himself to others. Then Smith added, with a knowing laugh, "That and the fact that he didn't have to hit; that helped a little bit."

However, it should be noted that even in his young days pitching in the NL, which at the time didn't allow designated hitters, Martínez insisted that he made his living throwing tight to hitters. He said no matter the repercussions, he wasn't about to change.

Paul Shuey was a reliever for eleven seasons, and he had a somewhat different take on Martínez's methods: one of respect, mixed with some scorn. "Hitters know Pedro's been very consistent about smoking people with regularity, and usually smoking them right around the face. That's happened to us [the Indians], and that's why we've gotten in brawls with him in the past. Then he usually runs and hides in the dugout—and that's not a good deal there.

"He's maybe the best pitcher in the game, and pitching like that may be a way to keep guys off edge, and you can do it, but it's certainly not going to make you any friends on the other teams.

"A guy can gain some respect by showing that he does throw inside occasionally, but it's a different thing when you're throwing at heads. You can get the same effect by throwing at somebody's knees, getting them to jump out of the way where they've got a shot at getting out of the way. When you throw at somebody's head, you could really kill somebody. That's not really what you want to do. It's going to happen; I mean, I'll throw at somebody once in a while by accident, but when you're doing it intentionally, and for a purpose, for me it's better to just go hard in by the hip area."

Perhaps another reason Martínez hits batters from time to time is, as Smith noted, "because he has so much movement on that ball—it's live, man. And I don't think he's actually throwing *at* guys, but you can't let a hitter dive at the ball. Half of these guys got all the body armor on and they're diving, covering the whole plate. A pitcher has to have one part of the plate. I mean, if a hitter's going to hit the fastball in, *and* the fastball *and* breaking balls away, then there's nowhere for me to make my money, you're not going to be around that long. You have to have one side of the plate, but I don't think you have to hit somebody in the head or chest.

"If you keep the ball down and you brush somebody in or hit them in the backside or the thigh, they don't mind that—they respect that." The problem occurs when pitchers go up by the chin or even throw behind a batter, and Smith commented, "I know Pedro, and I don't think he's the type of person who would actually try to hit somebody in the head. But you've got to come in tight. It sends a message; plus, it lets a guy know, 'Hey, you can't cover both sides of the plate.' That's a pretty good message to send, and I think they heard it."

Another pitcher who wore a Fu Manchu and a withering scowl was reliever Al "The Mad Hungarian" Hrabosky. Once, his manager told him he'd have to shave off his facial hair. Hrabosky snorted, "How can I intimidate batters if I look like a damn golf pro." To him, shaving was tantamount to allowing Delilah to perform her strength-sapping barber act.

On the mound, Hrabosky seemingly had a version of a self-hypnosis that frequently featured him stomping several strides off the mound toward second base to meditate. He snapped out of it by violently and crisply firing the ball several inches into his glove as he strode back to the rubber, steam figuratively spurting out of his nose like a deranged dragon.

Once, though, his tactic resulted in a famous stalemate of intimidation between him and Cincinnati slugger George Foster. Ken Griffey Sr., a Big Red Machine teammate of Foster's, recalled, "Every time George stepped into the batter's box, Hrabosky would go behind the mound and turn his back on him and rub up the ball. Then he'd slam the ball into his glove and go back up on the mound, and then George would step out.

"They did that for about ten minutes. The umpire told George, 'Get in the box,' then he told Hrabosky, 'You. Pitch.' I said, 'Look at these two out there arguing, and they haven't said a word to each other.'"

Gossage had a take on Hrabosky's mound antics as he prepared to pitch. He felt the pitcher *shouldn't* have been all that intimidating to batters: "I think definitely [his posturing] was an act." Smith said he felt "he was just psyching himself out." Regardless, Hrabosky did get in the minds of some opposing batters, often messing up their timing and upsetting them by taking his strolls behind the mound as he worked himself into a frenzy.

Then there's Randy Johnson. His facial hair and long, rather unruly hair jutting out from his cap made him similar to Gossage in a way. So did his hard throwing—and his imposing 6-foot-10 frame didn't hurt. By the time he took his long stride and made his pitch, the ball was headed toward the batter at a distance a lot shorter than the 60 feet, 6 inches from the rubber to the plate—and his fastballs, which could top

100 miles per hour, got upon them in a hurry. One such fastball struck a dove that was in the ball's path and completely pulverized the animal, which vanished in an explosive puff of feathers.

Gossage said, "I think he's very intimidating, although I don't think he really tries to be. I think that's just the way he carries himself out there—that and throwing *hard*." Buhner, who faced Johnson in the minors when his control was extremely wild, said, "Let me put it this way, you didn't want to dig in on him."

THE FASTBALL (AND LOCATION)

Trevor Hoffman, the all-time saves leader before Mariano Rivera, said, "Your margin for error is definitely greater if you throw harder. The batters have to make their decisions quicker, they don't have as much time to see the baseball, but strike one is still the best pitch in baseball, whether it's at 95 or 85."

The fastball certainly is the number-one tool for pitchers, one that frequently is thrown for strike one. It also sets everything else up and can sometimes even instill fear in batters. And hitters who are ready to flinch or bail out are hardly dangerous opponents—they might as well take a toothpick to the plate instead of their bat.

While it may be the game's best pitch, finding a pitcher who can throw it hard and with accuracy is no easy chore. Bob Feller had a fantastic fastball, and while he said nearly any pitcher can be taught how to throw a curve, he said, "you can't teach somebody to throw a fastball. It's like trying to teach somebody how to grow hair on a bald head."

Satchel Paige is said to have once warmed up using a gum wrapper for a home plate, hitting his minuscule target with three consecutive strikes. When he tried out for the Indians in 1948, having to prove himself due to his being a baseball Methuselah—he is said to have been forty-one then—he threw to player/manager Lou Boudreau, who was then perched atop the AL in batting. Paige fired twenty pitches to Boudreau, nineteen for strikes. He gave up no hits and easily persuaded Cleveland to sign him, making him the oldest player ever to break into the bigs.

Former closer Matt Mantei said it would never happen, but if he didn't have to worry about a batter swinging, he could throw strikes "probably eight or nine times out of ten. There's a lot of muscle memory involved, and a lot of mechanics are involved. You just gotta get that certain slot."

Former manager Grady Little went one step further. "A guy like Greg Maddux could hit it eleven out of ten times, and it doesn't matter if a hitter's in there or not. That's the biggest difference between major league pitchers and pitchers coming up or amateur pitchers. It's location of their stuff, not how hard they throw it, but where they can put the ball and how often they can do that."

So why can't more pitchers just consistently fire fastballs for strikes? Mantei chuckled. "I wish it was that easy. I tell you what, if it was easy, everybody would be playing baseball. I've watched games from the stands and it's like, 'This *does* seem easy,' but it's not. It's hard to throw a 95-, 96-mile-an-hour fastball where guys can't hit it. It's not just throwing a strike."

Former pitcher Dan Warthen liked sheer speed, but like Paige, he knew control was so important. "Major league hitters have no trouble adjusting to velocity. Pitchers have to locate the ball."

When Warthen coached for the Padres, he noted, "I didn't have a guy that *blazed* it, but the guy who could *pitch* was Hoffman." In 1998, all Hoffman did was chalk up 53 saves while blowing only one. Warthen sounded like a real estate agent, stressing the importance of "location, location, location." In Hoffman's case that was so true because by 1998 he no longer could throw the ball in the 95-mile-per-hour neighborhood.

One pitcher scoffed when his manager, Lou Piniella, got frustrated by his reliever's wildness. He visited the mound, and his only advice was almost childish: "Throw the ball over the plate." The pitcher said he felt like saying words to the effect of, "Oh! So that's what you want me to do. I never knew that. I thought you wanted me to walk them."

So, Is Speed the Key to Success?
Given how important the fastball is, does that mean speed is ultimately the key to winning, that a pitcher without blistering speed is doomed? As Little touched upon earlier, not necessarily.

The ideal is to throw hard *and* to unhittable locations. As Warthen put it, "It just happens if you throw 95 to 100 miles an hour, you get by with bad location a little more often."

In 2007 an ESPN broadcaster told a story about Jamie Moyer's son joking that his father drove his car faster than he could pitch a baseball. While the story was embellished, it did contain a great deal of truth, and Moyer did talk readily about how he wasn't a fireballing pitcher. "For me, it's all about results," he said. "You gotta have results, and it doesn't matter how hard you throw, I don't think. Not everybody believes me, but, I mean, if you throw 95, you throw 95, if you throw 80, you throw 80. It's all about getting results and being consistent."

When he finally retired after pitching in four decades, he had faced almost exactly 9 percent of every big-leaguer to ever play the game. He also became the third man to win one hundred or more games after his fortieth birthday. His season high for strikeouts was 158, but his control was fine—one year he walked two or fewer men in twenty-nine of thirty-two starts. It is fitting that his memoir bears the title *Just Tell Me I Can't: How Jamie Moyer Defied the Radar Gun and Defeated Time*. It was true—in 2012, for example, his average fastball was right around 80 miles per hour.

Lee Smith recalled that when Maddux and Moyer came up to the Chicago Cubs' parent club, many top team officials didn't have faith in them because of their lack of sizzling speed. Years later, and after Maddux and Moyer amassed a combined 624 victories, the Cubs realized the folly of their thinking.

Smith summarized just how horrendous the Cubs' viewpoint was. "We had a kid, a highly touted left-handed pitcher named Drew Hall— they thought more of that guy than they did of Moyer and Maddux. They thought Hall had a better chance of being the better pitcher because he was a big lefty and he was throwing 93, 94." Hall didn't pan out, going on to log a 3–4 record with Chicago.

Moyer, a twenty-five-year vet who last pitched in 2012 at the age of forty-nine (when he became the oldest pitcher ever to earn a win), took being underestimated quite well. "Everybody's entitled to their opinion. That's how I look at it. You could go back over the history of this game and look at organizations that made decisions on players and say, 'Well, this guy's career's over' or 'This guy can't play.' And you know what? From what I've noticed in baseball, a change of scenery is good for a player.

"I look back at when Joe Carter was traded from the Cubs to Cleveland and Rick Sutcliffe went from Cleveland to the Cubs and won sixteen straight games. I don't think Cleveland thought Sutcliffe was done, but they probably thought, 'We can do better,' and it probably worked out better for both teams. You could go to every team and find 'Why did they get rid of this guy?' or 'Why did they get rid of that guy?' Maybe it's the makeup of the club—there are a lot of variables that come into play with that."

In 2007, All-Star Paul Byrd, believed to be the last pitcher to ever employ the large, old-school, double-pump windup, said that if he were being scouted then instead of having already played for eleven seasons, he wouldn't have earned a second look because, at just over 6 feet and without an impressive fastball—one season, his average four-seam fastball was clocked at 86 miles per hour—he just would not have been what teams were looking for.

Byrd said, "I remember playing with Maddux, and he said, 'If I was coming out of high school today, I would not get drafted, but that's just the way it is. The guys are bigger, stronger, and throw harder now.'" Maddux was listed, perhaps a bit generously, at 6 feet even.

Byrd also used John Franco, possessor of 424 saves, as a case in point. "He was a great closer. He didn't have good stuff but knew how to pitch. He wasn't in the era where they were looking for speed. When he came in, it was, like, 88, 89 miles per hour was okay, whereas now, that doesn't even get you drafted."

Dave Adler wrote a 2023 story for the Major League Baseball website[2] stating that the average height for a big-league pitcher that season was 6-foot-3. Dating back to the year 2000, the average height of a Cy Young Award recipient was 6-foot-4. Without getting too detailed, and to summarize, Adler observed that there are successful exceptions to the rule, but in such cases there are extenuating circumstances involved, including where a given pitcher releases the ball in relation to the rubber—call it "release extension." Naturally, the farther away from the rubber a pitch is launched, the closer it already is to the batter.

For the record, the fastest pitch ever clocked belongs to Aroldis Chapman. Over the years, the methods used to record speeds have varied. Once, a primitive effort was made to time a Bob Feller fastball by having a rider on a motorcycle race at a certain speed for 60 feet, 6 inches, timing it so he zoomed by Feller at the same time his pitch was released.[3]

Determining the speed of a fastball depends upon at what point the speed is measured. In 2010, the speed was measured when the ball was about 50 feet from the plate, but now the estimated velocity comes at the release of the pitch. With that caveat, here are some fastball stats. The average fastball thrown in the 2015 season flew at 93.1 miles per hour. In 2022, that speed was up to 93.9.

The Major League Baseball website states, "The fastball momentum has remarkably increased over time with the introduction of new techniques and training. Initially, Aroldis Chapman's pitch measured at 105.1 in 2010 was record-breaking and is now [after recalibration to the current measuring Statcast system] at 105.8 mph."

It's ironic, then, that today's front offices, scouts, managers, and coaches tend to feel they are using the most sophisticated methods possible to evaluate talent, yet sometimes their tools still result in huge mistakes being made. Just ask Moyer.

In Byrd's day, some fans had the impression that scouting was so sophisticated that if a kid was good enough, a scout somewhere would find him and sign him—he would not go undetected. Byrd, thinking what Maddux had told him, replied, "No, I disagree with that, I really do. There's a lot of guys who have gone undiscovered from smaller universities. I had the privilege to go to LSU where there's a lot of scouts behind home plate with radar guns.

"All you need is one to like you, but you go to a junior college or somewhere way out and you don't have ten or fifteen scouts sitting behind home plate. If you have a great record and dominate at a smaller school, that doesn't always necessarily mean you'll get drafted.

"I remember Jarrod Washburn telling me the best guy he ever played with never got drafted and he had unbelievable statistics. He was left-handed, didn't throw super hard, but Washburn said he could hit any corner he wanted to. It's a shame." In fact, the prospect never even got a look by scouts. "Baseball people say, 'It doesn't matter if you're 11 and 1. You're at a D3 school; who cares?' So it's tough."

Byrd knew of a scout who said, "Unless you consistently throw over 90, and if you're right-handed, under 6-foot, I can't even turn your name in. You know, I'm under 6-foot, right-handed, and throw, like, 85. There's just a lot of people in the world, and not everyone can get a chance."

CURVEBALLS

Candy Cummings, a man who had a name sounding more like a burlesque dancer than a pitcher is widely credited as being the creator of the curve, coming up with his innovation in the 1860s. It's been written that Cummings got the idea for the new pitch when he tossed a clamshell and witnessed its sweeping flight.

It can be a devastating pitch. An old story has it that a young player made his debut in the minors and did well at first, feasting mainly on a diet of fastballs. Pitchers soon caught on to his weakness and the kid found himself calling home, saying words to the effect of, "Hey, Mom, I'm coming home—they started throwing me curves." The pitch is a great equalizer, to be sure.

Dave Burba won 115 games with a .569 winning percentage. He said, "The tighter you grip the ball, the less velocity you're going to get— the slower the curve will be. The looser the grip, the more whip—it frees up your arm." It all depends upon the pitcher, as Burba said: some prefer a hard, tight, "shorter break," while others like the opposite.

A sampling of artists with deadman's curves include Mike Cuellar, Bert Blyleven, Jack Billingham, Sandy Koufax, Dwight Gooden, Mike Mussina, Carl Erskine, and Nolan Ryan, men with curves that curled like popcorn shrimp. Musial paid Erskine what the Dodgers pitcher called a "left-handed compliment" when he told him, "You had the best curve I ever hit. I don't know how I hit it."

Around the late 1990s, Roberto Alomar chose his top curveball masters, listing the big breaking ball of Shawn Estes, Tom Gordon's bending ball, and "David Wells, who has a pretty good curveball."

Sam McDowell had a blistering fastball but was accused of too often throwing curves. He supposedly said, "It's no fun throwing fastballs to guys who can't hit them." However, years after he retired, he contended, "People always stereotype players, make generalizations. Very few people realize for my entire career every pitch was called for by my manager."

Interestingly, when Lee Smith was a minor league pitching instructor, he said, "We don't like to get kids that throw curveballs *and* sliders because it's hard for the kid to get it in between." One or the other, but not both.

SLIDERS

Ted Williams said the one pitch which revolutionized the game was the slider. He even conceded he couldn't hit that pitch very well—and this is a man who once hit .406 and who owned a lifetime batting average of .344.

The slider can disguise itself as a fastball until it takes a last split-second break. It travels a lateral and downward path (not breaking as much as a curve) with a speed between that of a fastball and a curveball, and is an easy pitch to learn.

Perhaps the greatest slider ever belonged to Steve Carlton, although many experts point to Bob Gibson and Randy Johnson. In 1972 Carlton won one of his four Cy Young Awards when he went 27–10 for a hapless Phillies team that posted a record of 59–97. That meant he accounted for close to half (46 percent) of all his team's wins.

Smith discussed one specific pitcher he worked with: "We have one kid who has a decent curveball, but it's sort of a looping curveball, a lollipop curve, so the hitters can pick it up real quick. You can get away with it, I mean, he kicked butt; he was like 16–4 in 'A' ball. But when he came to 'Double-A,' he got *his* butt kicked in a league with some good hitters.

"But he's got a good fastball, so we're teaching him to throw a slider now. When we got him the slider, I think he won fifteen games. I tell him to throw more sliders than curveballs. Some guys pick things up quicker than others—it depends on the individual."

Smith said that next to his burning fastball, "my second best pitch was my slider [and sometimes his forkball]." When he dropped down and threw a slider from a sidearm slot, it got positive reactions. Smith smiled, recalling an announcer who described his delivery by saying, "Big Leroy, throwing from El Dorado."

Forkballs, Splitters, and Spitballs

There can be no question that a new pitch, once perfected and added to a player's repertoire, can turn a career around. One prime example is the family of elusive, diving pitches that includes the spitball, the forkball, and the split-finger fastball or splitter.

Hall of Famer Gaylord Perry possessed the best and most talked about spitball ever. Although the pitch is now illegal (it was banned in 1920 and was last thrown legally in 1934 by Burleigh Grimes, one of the pitchers who utilized it thanks to a grandfather clause), it's been in use since the earliest days of baseball.

Even though everyone from the rawest rookie to the sage veteran umpire knew Perry loaded the ball up with foreign substances, when accused of throwing spitballs, he denied it—although often his denial was accompanied by a sly grin. He even entitled his autobiography *Me and the Spitter*. He often said his pitch, which dipped low at the last moment, causing batters to swing over the ball, was nothing more than a legal forkball.

Perry said of his "splitter" (translation: his spitball), "It's fairly easy to teach it. Each guy throws it and grips it differently, though. I learned it from Lindy McDaniel, but I learned from watching, not talking to him about it."

Like many others before him, Perry relied upon the pitch because he *had to*. When asked if it took a long time to master, he replied with a chuckle, "Not when your record is 1–6, but for some people it is hard to control." Perry adopted the new pitch as a struggling young pitcher, learning his new pitch out of desperation, fearing that a pitcher who, in just his second season, had already lost six games versus one win, was one bad outing away from a swift trip to the minors.

Another Hall of Famer, Bruce Sutter, became a master of the pitch called the split-finger fastball, which, like the philosopher's stone, possessed the power to transform him into a solid gold Hall of Famer.

Like Perry, Sutter groped for help. In his case, desperation came after suffering a pinched nerve in his elbow after he had pitched in a mere two minor league games for the Cubs organization. Having lost his fastball, he sought the guidance of pitching instructor Fred Martin. After he spent a few years—and much toil—refining his pitch, he made it to the majors. There, he won the Cy Young Award in just his fourth season.

Hall of Fame manager Dick Williams said, "Pitching coach Fred Martin taught it to Bruce Sutter and Sutter began the new era of the split-finger fastball. Hitters try to lay off the pitch, but if he got a strike on you, he'd keep throwing it."

The success of men such as Sutter (300 saves, 2.38 lifetime ERA), considered to be the first pitcher of note to rely heavily on the splitter, led to a slew of followers, including Roger Clemens (who added the pitch to his already impressive arsenal), Jack Morris, and Dave Stewart, to name a few. The pitch is still used effectively, as pitching/hitting sensation Shohei Ohtani can attest.

Former big-league pitcher Mike Krukow remembered, "Everyone wanted to throw it after [Sutter] did. Everyone wanted to talk to him about it. He was the magician. He was throwing something no one had ever seen." He added, "If it wasn't for that pitch, Bruce Sutter would be tending bar in Mount Joy, Pennsylvania. A lot of guys tried to throw [the splitter], but no one threw it better than Bruce. No one."[4]

Back in the 1980s, Hall of Fame manager Tony La Russa said his pick for the pitcher with the best split-finger fastball was one of his own Oakland A's players. "I'll take Stewart," he said. "He throws the splitter different ways. He changes speeds and he changes directions. He does everything with it."

Meanwhile, Stewart, not unlike Clemens, said the split-finger pitch was not his main tool: "The splitter is my second or third pitch depending on the lineup I'm facing."

Stewart disagreed with Perry concerning how easy the specialty pitch was to develop. "It's not an easy pitch to pick up. It takes a lot of hard work. I learned it during the season with Sandy Koufax."

Of course, Koufax may have helped Stewart, but he did not throw a splitter. He probably agreed with something Bob Gibson said once about the baffling pitch: "I never had a splitter. The main reason was I can't spread my fingers that far apart, so I didn't mess with it." Then, his fierce and justifiable pride kicked in and he added, "I didn't need it!"

Gibson praised Sutter's split-finger fastball. "He had good control of it; that's one key to throwing it with success. If you took the pitch, the ball would drop out of the strike zone for a ball, but when you're trying to hit, the only way to hit is to be aggressive—you *have* to go after it. It's easy for announcers to say just lay off it, but it's not that easy."

The pitch's roots go way back. Credit not only goes to Martin, but to another coach/manager who popularized the splitter. Len Barker, who once threw a perfect game while he was with the Indians, gave credit to Roger Craig, calling him a "good pitching man, a good teacher. Before Craig, lots of guys threw the splitter, but he got the best results." In fact, in 1984 his World Series–winning staff had four of his disciples who used his split-finger pitch: Jack Morris, Milt Wilcox, Dan Petry, and Dave Rozema. They combined for 61 of Detroit's 105 wins.

Popular broadcaster and former big-leaguer Duane Kuiper said what made Craig special was that "he didn't force it on his players; if they can't control it, he wouldn't force it on you."

Kuiper dug deeper for the origins of the splitter, saying that some pitchers before the time of Martin and Craig actually threw more of a forkball. Kuiper pointed out, though, that pitchers such as Morris "threw the splitter a lot harder than the forkball."

Perry was one who saw little if any significant difference between a forkball and a split-finger fastball. "I changed speeds on my pitch and used it for a good off-speed pitch, but they called it a forkball back then." The forkball is held—actually jammed—with the baseball planted deep between the index and middle finger, a feat not everyone can (or would want to) do.

When Perry first heard that the splitter was being called "the Pitch of the 1990s," he laughed derisively. "The pitch has been around so long; it used to be called a Cuban forkball until they stopped getting guys from Cuba who threw it. Then they just called it a forkball."

Elroy Face was a pitcher whose forkball was so good it helped him set a record in 1959 for the highest winning percentage in a season ever—.947—when his win-loss record was a nearly unblemished 18–1. And that wasn't all. He recalled, "I won my last five in '58 and the first seventeen in '59 for twenty-two consecutive. I don't think anybody's ever going to do that again—I don't think anybody's going to be 18–1 again." Eleven of his wins came in extra innings, and he said that from May 30, 1958, until September 11, 1959, "I was in ninety-seven games in that stretch without a loss."

For the record, Dick Williams said, "Face is the pioneer of the forkball, but probably some guy threw the forkball before him." He's correct—there was at least one pitcher who used the pitch before Face came along. Ernie "Tiny" Bonham used it to go 103–72 lifetime with a 3.06 earned run average (ERA) from 1940 through 1949.

The 5-foot-8 Face, who weighed just 155 pounds, said he used to take a baseball and cram it between his index and middle fingers "to stretch them when I first started, but not later. I can still get the ball in there now." Amazingly, he made that claim during a 2019 interview when he was ninety-one years old, fifty years after he pitched his last big-league game.

The splitter/forkball may be difficult for most pitchers to throw with pinpoint precision, but Face controlled it like a maestro—one season he averaged just one walk per nine innings. His control with the forkball was so fine that pitcher Tom Cheney said Face could aim for and hit a gnat in midair with his specialty pitch.

"Actually, all I ever tried to do was throw it to the middle of the plate and let it break where it wanted to," said Face. "When it got to the plate about belt high it would normally sink. If a hitter was looking for a forkball, it made my fastball even more effective.

"If my forkball was working on a particular day, I'd go with it 75 percent of the time. If not, maybe 10 percent." By contrast, some say Sutter was known to throw his splitter up to 90 percent of the time.

One of Face's catchers said, "I never had a chance to bat against him, thank God. He had that forkball, and when he had it working, nobody was going to hit it. He was determined when he came into a game, 'Wrap it up, boys, it's all over.'"

Four time All-Star and 1970 AL MVP Boog Powell, thinking back on his career, which spanned from 1961 through 1977, commented, "Not many pitchers were around with a splitter when I played. But I batted against Elroy Face, who threw a forkball; his was a tough pitch. He threw it different than many pitchers. Bruce Sutter threw it hard, but Face threw soft.

"I was with Los Angeles, and I was looking for the forkball against Face. He threw it hard, then softer, and softer. I looked bad—it really is a tough pitch to hit. It acts like a splitter; the bottom just comes out of it. It drops like a spitball, and you can't tell the difference."

Which again brings Perry to mind, as that illegal pitch is exactly what everyone says he relied on for years and years. Once, when asked about his spitball, he said with pseudo-incredulity, "What? You mean the pitch I didn't have? It's the pitch they *thought* I threw, but I never did." He persisted in his claim that his spitball was really just a filthy forkball.

Sometimes he would go through theatrical motions, as if he was touching spots where he had petroleum jelly secreted away, but it was a ruse to fool hitters—to get in their heads. And he said it worked, as they became more concerned about the upcoming pitch than really focusing on the act of hitting.

Incidentally, at an Old Timers' Game in Cleveland in 1991, Perry, who was then fifty-three years old, took to the mound. When he faced A's bullpen coach Art Kusnyer, he struck him out. As Kusnyer slowly made his way back to the dugout, he was heard to mumble in disbelief, "He threw me a spitter!" Knowing Perry, that should have come as no surprise.

Mike Cubbage, who spent eight years as a big-league player and went on to coach and manage, also knew firsthand about Perry's valuable spitball. "When the Texas Rangers traded for Perry, Jim Fregosi walked up to Gaylord to greet him. He handed Gaylord a small tube of Vaseline and asked him, 'What's this?' Gaylord looked at him for a moment then said, 'That? That's a two-hit shutout.'" Actually, though, Cubbage revealed Perry's true weapon of choice: "Gaylord was more of a K-Y Jelly guy."

The bottom line on the forkball/splitter (and spitball) issue was reduced to one sentence by former Rookie of the Year Mike Hargrove: "It may be easy to teach, but it's hard to hit"—so difficult that experts confidently asserted that the split-finger fastball was a revolutionary pitch.

KNUCKLEBALLS

Major League Baseball first came to Canada in 1969 when Montreal, Quebec, was awarded an expansion club. Quebec is the only Canadian province that has French as its only official language, and even today about 70 percent of those who live there speak French as their first language. Because of that, the Expos scoreboards featured baseball terms such as "balls" and "strikes" in both French and English. For example, *la balle* means the ball, and the catcher is *le receveur*, and any fan could probably easily figure those terms out.

However, the French word for knuckleball needs some explaining. *La balle papillon* does mean the knuckler, but *papillon* itself translates to "butterfly." That's fitting, as that particular pitch flitters and flutters its way to home plate. It is easily baseball's most evasive and frustrating pitch because pitchers have little control over the flight of the ball, and batters are befuddled by its late, erratic, and multiple movements.

Trying to track the path of a knuckler can be impossible, and not just for batters. Catchers can testify to that. Bob Uecker once said, "The best way to catch a knuckleball is to wait until it stops rolling and then pick it up." Tim Wakefield, who had a great knuckleball, said the best way to judge how well the pitch was working was to see how clumsy the catcher looked when trying to corral it.

Willie Stargell saw the *papillon* analogy: "Throwing a knuckleball for a strike is like throwing a butterfly with hiccups across the street into your neighbor's mailbox." Richie Hebner, one of Stargell's teammates on the Pirates, said that trying to hit master knuckleball artist Phil

Niekro's specialty pitch "is liking eating soup with a fork." Hitting guru Charley Lau concluded, "There are two theories on hitting the knuckle-ball. Unfortunately, neither one of them works."

Travis Fryman, a five-time All-Star who played from 1990 through 2002, said, "In my career there's always been one guy, usually an older player, a Charlie Hough, the Niekros [brothers Phil and Joe], [or] Tom Candiotti, who were knuckleball pitchers. Right now there's Tim Wakefield and Steve Sparks."

Fryman pointed out it makes sense for an older guy to experiment with the pitch because in quite a few instances learning to throw one marked the difference between lingering in the game and a sudden departure from it.

However, he observed, "it's a tough pitch to master. The old adage is: 'There's nothing that goes further than a knuckle that doesn't knuckle.' I think that scares some people away from trying.

"Oh, it's a great pitch, very effective to those who have mastered it, but it certainly has some tremendous downsides as far as wild pitches and inconsistency. It's difficult not only for a catcher to catch, but also for an umpire to see effectively. And weather conditions have a tremendous impact upon the effectiveness of the knuckleball as well. So not every-one's willing to take that chance."

Trevor Hoffman was never tempted to add a knuckler to his reper-toire. He knew how it could be an effective pitch, but it was not often used in baseball history. "At best, we've seen fifty pitchers who have thrown the knuckleball. Charlie Hough lasted twenty-five years, which is a credit to him, but for me, it's a pitch that's uncontrollable, even to the pitcher. We've seen a lot of knuckleball pitchers, and they're either really on or they're really off, and in the closer role, I don't think there's a place for it."

When Tony Gwynn, who had a firm approach when he faced any type of pitching, faced a man like Phil Niekro or Candiotti, he admitted, he had to change his way of thinking. "The knuckleball is the one pitch I can't stay back on enough. My swing is geared to guys who throw 80 to 85 miles per hour." When told that occasional Niekro knuckleballs were clocked in the upper 30s, he smiled. "I'm not geared to *that!*" Pitchers like Phil Niekro and Tim Wakefield usually threw the pitch around 50 to 70 miles per hour.

Gwynn also said that facing knuckleball pitchers can easily mess up a hitter's swing. One season he lamented, "Every time I've faced Candiotti this year, I've gone in the tank for three days after seeing his knuckler."

In the meantime, Chipper Jones explained his approach to the pitch: "You cut down your swing, just try and center the ball. The ball's moving all over the place, it's unpredictable. You go up there and try to hit the ball 400 feet, chances are you're going to swing and miss, so just cut down on the swing, take your base hits, and try and put pressure on him [working the count]." He agreed with Gwynn, saying that after facing the unpredictable, floating knuckleball, he always hoped it wouldn't mess up his swing for the next game.

He added, "Most guys against knuckleballs, and good sinkers, I will move up in the box. I don't like to move much; I like to stay in the same place, keep consistent."

CHANGEUPS

When a batter is looking for a fastball and instead sees a changeup taking its time getting to the plate—remember the tedious wait batters had to endure when facing a Bugs Bunny change of pace—the hitter's timing is, of course, thrown way off.

Hoffman made a lucrative living fooling batters with his changeup. In a 2002 interview, when he was thirty-four, he discussed how that pitch and his ability to spot it were so important for him: "I think that the guys who have the ability to transcend generations or eras have the ability to be a little more fine-tuned with their location. I would hope that my career is nowhere being close to the end [he didn't retire until 2010], but I've seen a difference in how I used to throw—I was in the mid-90s, and now I'm in, roughly, the mid-80s, upper 80s on some good days. But I still have the ability to be effective by location."

Furthermore, while his fastball didn't exactly hum anymore, it still had its place. "I think any type of pitch that you have that's referred to as an equalizer pitch, that's an out pitch—strikeout type of pitch—I think it's always set up off your fastball. So there's no difference to me. You locate your heater, you get ahead, and then you show them something they haven't seen."

Doug Jones possessed one of the game's greatest changeups. It had to be great in order for him to fool big-leaguers for sixteen seasons, make four All-Star squads, and rack up 303 saves.

His change was so vexing that in 2000 he whiffed Chan Perry on a pitch that barely exceeded a 55-mile-per-hour speed limit. Said Perry, "I never thought I'd strike out on a major league pitch going 58 miles per hour that wasn't a knuckleball. Now I can say that I have."

Hoffman chuckled, recalling the old line about Jones throwing "slow, slower, and slowest." He said, "I saw him pitch and there was no doubt that he had three different speeds and all three were probably under 85. But Doug was the master of changing speeds and keeping you off balance, and he had a long career with it."

Hoffman said that his own changeup evolved. At one point he wanted to slow it down a notch. "To be able to get a little more velocity off of it, I went to 'choking' it [holding the ball deeper in the palm of his hand]. The pitch is more like a palm ball than it is like a straight change.

"It definitely would be nice to have the ability to rear back and throw it by guys, but even so, early in my career when that was the case, . . . I'd get hurt with location. So location is more important than anything else, I think." Someone once compared his changeup to a baseball coming in with a parachute attached.

Veteran player and coach Merv Rettenmund brought up another pitcher with a great changeup. "If you let Pedro Martínez throw a fastball away for strike one, then that means you [will then] get his changeup, and I'll tell you what, Tony Gwynn can't hit his changeup, so I know that no one else in baseball can hit it. So you're done; you're a dead man right now."

At one point Travis Fryman struck out 17 times over 23 at-bats against Martínez. He marveled at the pitcher's ability. "I'm a major league hitter. I've faced the best pitchers in the game. I ought to be able to put the ball in play half the time."

Lee Smith said that a great one-two punch for a pitcher can be the fastball-changeup combo. Smith said that mix "is the best pitching, but it takes a good bit out of you to throw a changeup. A lot of guys think that when a pitcher throws a changeup, that it's effortless, but it's just as hard to throw one as a fastball. You try to have the same arm speed as your fastball when you throw a changeup."

SIDEARMERS AND SUBMARINE PITCHERS

Kent Tekulve has had his submarine style of pitching "ever since I was a kid when I played catch with my dad in the backyard." He said that aside from the release points, there is no difference whatsoever between the sidearm style of pitching and submarine: "Actually, if you look at video, of myself or any of the guys who threw that way, we're throwing submarine, but in reality what we're doing is we're throwing sidearm. We are still throwing sidearm, but you lean to the side at the waist. If you stand straight up, you're throwing sidearm, but because we're bending at the waist, the arm angle is down lower. It's kind of like a golf swing; we're swinging down through that area.

"But if you look at the arm from the elbow to the armpit down the side of the body, that's still at 90 degrees, just like it would be at sidearm. So, submarine is actually sidearm with a tilt. Physically you cannot throw the ball with less than 90 degrees from your elbow to the armpit to your body. You lose all your strength as soon as you do that."

Pitchers who throw using this method are pretty rare, and in 2003, Tekulve speculated about that. For one thing, he said, scouts tend to look more for pitchers with scorching stuff and for attributes they can gauge. Down-under throwers don't usually have those whistling fastballs. Tekulve continued, "I would say as a rule, yeah, but not necessarily so. I was probably one of the harder throwers from down there. I threw about 90 in my hay day. There were other guys that were in the low 80s. Dan Quisenberry was about 83, 84, and we both had a lot of success. When you throw down there, it's not velocity, you're not throwing the ball by anybody, it's movement and location—that's what you get from throwing down there. So nobody's ever thrown 97 or 98 from down there unless it was Eddie Feigner the softball guy."

He was referring to the pitcher of King and his Court fame, the underhanded (of course) hurler who hit 104 miles per hour on a radar gun, K'd more than 140,000 batters, including almost 9,000 while he was blindfolded, and engineered more than 900 no-hitters.

"Because of the movement that's created by the submarine motion, which is the overspin on the ball which causes it to sink, it's a natural sinking action. You don't have to turn the ball over; you just throw it and it sinks because of the way it's coming off your fingers. Because it sinks, and because the release point is down around your knees, it's easy to throw the ball around the hitters' knees, which is where you want to throw it for a sinker."

Tekulve contrasted his style to overhand pitchers such as "the Nolan Ryans of this world, the guys who throw it overhand and hard. It's easier for them to throw high in the strike zone than it is to throw low because you're letting go of the ball basically on the same plane that you want it to end up at, up high.

"So, in submarine, you're letting go of the ball low—and it's actually more difficult to throw it high than it is low. That's because your arm has to go so much further through to the release point to let the ball go." Of course, since a cardinal baseball rule is to keep the ball low, "if you keep the sinker down, obviously it's much more effective.

"I think scouting has become so technical that it's all stuff that you can enter into a computer. You can enter miles per hour into a computer, but movement and stuff like that, you just can't measure. When you look at somebody that throws submarine or sidearm or something that's abnormal, you don't really know what to compare it to, either. It's harder for them to evaluate, therefore, in a lot of cases they just don't."

Mark Grace said that when he had to face the rare lefty who threw sidearm, it was "never real easy. But most of the right-handers, for me as a left-handed hitter, are giving me a great look at it out there. It doesn't take long to get used to that arm slot. It's effective because it's something different, it's a different look."

Tekulve said that while lefties such as Grace may have liked the look of sidearm/submarine offerings and the angle those pitches took coming in to them from righties, he didn't care—he was determined simply to throw his sidearm stuff low, shooting for the knees, a target that would be tough on almost any hitter.

Grace commented, "That's what they're there to do, try to get ground balls. Dan Quisenberry, Kent Tekulve, those guys. They're putting sink on it and trying to get you to hit the ball on the ground. They're not trying to strike you out; they want you swinging."

Scott Hatteberg, a fourteen-year veteran, explained how he prepares for submarine throwers: "It depends on the guy and how hard he throws. There are some good ones out there. Chad Bradford comes to mind, and there are some lefties—Mike Myers has always been tough. It's just an odd angle you don't really see often. The ball is different than you're used to, so it's an adjustment. Usually they are the guys who are only going to face you once in a game, so it's tough to make an adjustment."

Further, there's nothing one can really do to get ready for them. Batters don't, for instance, tell their coaches to emulate a down-under style of pitching during batting practice. "That's what makes them special," said Hatteberg.

Chipper Jones said that when he faced a pitcher with an odd, funky delivery like that of a submarine artist, his preparation was all a matter "of mindset—you gotta know what you want to do with what they're gonna throw up there. The guys who throw submarine have good sinkers. You try and pull him, you're going to hit a ground ball to second base. So you have to stay up the middle and go the other way."

Tekulve spoke of the oddity about sidearm/submarine pitchers almost always being right-handed, such as Ted Abernathy, who pitched from 1955 through 1972. He said that prior to Mike Myers (who debuted in 1995) and Sean Runyan (who followed three years later but lasted only one full season in which he led the league in appearances, with 88), the only other lefty, low-to-the-ground pitcher he recalled was Ramón Hernández, who retired in 1977.

PITCHING STYLES

Relief pitcher Mike Stanton spoke about the wide disparity in pitchers' styles from Paul Byrd and his throwback to the Warren Spahn–era windup (one Bryd felt provided him with a starting point and some added momentum, contrary to the prevailing style of his 1995–2009 playing days), to Dontrelle Willis with his huge leg kick (a bit reminiscent of

Juan Marichal), to Mike Mussina's deep bow while working from the stretch. Does form follow function in these cases? "Absolutely," Stanton began. "You pick up mechanics. Usually there's some kind of mindset that goes along with it."

Stanton continued, "Heck, a lot of mechanics come from emulating someone you idolized as a child. Roger Clemens is a perfect example. His idol, the person he looked at more than anybody else, was Nolan Ryan, and you can see they're not the same, but you can see the high leg kick, the big leg drive. That's probably where mechanics come from more than anything else, just what you did as a child and how you got used to throwing.

"One of the reasons why major overhauls don't work is a lot of times when you're learning to throw, when you're a kid, your body develops that way. And by changing that when you get older, your body's not used to throwing that way, and that's where a lot of injuries come from."

He found it quite interesting that there are so many diverse styles, yet success can follow the variety of methods. "There might be guys who throw similarly, but if you have twelve pitchers on the staff, you have twelve different styles, and that goes all the way across—that's not just the major leagues, that's anywhere. I think that's where a lot of organizations and even some of the big college programs get in trouble—they try to make everyone throw the same, and that's just not physically possible."

When a pitcher who may have relied heavily on his fastball begins to age, he is wise to change his style and learn a new approach. Some pitchers go to a screwball or a knuckleball in their final stages, but Hoffman says there's another subtle way to change: "I think guys will have success later in their careers if they can apply the experience they've had, the amount of time that they've been on the hill, and realize that there's as much pressure on the hitter as there is on them—and to be able to locate a fastball and work off of that."

PITCHING THEORIES

At least some of Hoffman's success came from his approach to pitching. "I think I came up with the same mentality I use now: . . . I concentrate on one pitch at a time. That turns into one out at a time, that turns into one inning at a time, one year at a time—there are stepping stones.

"I don't think you can get to any particular point of success by looking too far in advance. If you think: keep things simple and control the one thing that you can control, and that's that particular pitch at that moment, then you can live with it."

When he entered games, accompanied by his theme song, "Hell's Bells" by AC/DC, his way of thinking was that "rhythm and momentum are the keys. If they get a couple of hits off you, you have to try and break that on your own and recognize that. If not, then you just keep rolling and hopefully you'll get some outs quick."

Bob Feller expounded on his theories of pitching. He said that when he had a comfortable lead in a contest, he'd take something off his pitches, not wanting to strain his valuable arm. "I'd pace myself. If I had a lead, I'd ease up. Then you can bear down on tough guys or save yourself for the next game. I didn't care about my ERA, but it takes time to learn this."

He said inflating his ERA was the price for being able to stay out there on the hill and help his Indians win. As he put it, "The bottom line is, did you win or lose? What's more important: having a low ERA, or a high one and win?"

Actually, Feller, who sounded like he could pitch effectively even on a leisurely cruise-control setting, enjoyed the best of both worlds. He won 266 games *and* maintained an admirable ERA of 3.25.

Atlanta's great pitching coach Leo Mazzone passed some of his theories on to a superb staff. In 2002, Braves catcher Eddie Perez said, "He keeps his pitchers in shape, doing what they need to do. And he makes sure they throw the right pitch in the right situation. He knows what they need to do every day when they're not pitching.

"And there's something I think that the Braves are the only team to do—when they pitch, the next [two or] three days they're throwing in the pen. They're not throwing 100 percent, but they're like 60 to 70 percent."

Perez said that routine is "something that the whole Braves organization does—even when you're in the minor leagues, they throw almost every day. The only day that they don't pitch is the day before they throw in the game. They do this in the minors, and it's been working great for them for the last ten years." That's an understatement, as the Braves—with stars such as Greg Maddux, Tom Glavine, and John Smoltz—enjoyed a stranglehold on their division, capturing a record fourteen consecutive titles from 1991 to 2005. Those three men ended their careers with a combined total of 873 victories.

THROWING STRIKES AND CHALLENGING BATTERS

Some theories on pitching are general ones, such as throw strikes and get ahead of batters. When the Braves were winning their division with almost ho-hum regularity, Perez said the pitching staff was so successful "because they throw strikes. They throw strikes all the time, and on both sides of the plate. They never throw the ball in the middle.

"The first thing [discussed] when we were doing a meeting was, 'Throw strike one to make this thing go. Get ahead of the hitters, and then they can do whatever they want.'"

Bob Gibson revealed one of his pitching theories: "On an 0-and-2 count, throw your best fastball or slider. Don't lay it in there when you've got 0-and-2 on the batter. Ninety percent of the time if you throw fastballs pretty good, down the middle, but with stuff on it, they'll foul it off. But pitchers are getting too cute and go deeper in the count now." Gibson, who clearly did not believe in wasting pitches, was unafraid to challenge batters.

Paul Byrd, the type of pitcher who did not rely upon speed, rarely blowing the ball by batters, expounded his thinking process. He said he stressed throwing strikes, so his pitches were right around the plate. He was aware, of course, that opposing batters knew this, too, but he felt he had to be himself and do things his way no matter what.

"I'm afraid to walk anybody, to tell you the truth," he said. "I give up so many hits, I'm actually afraid to walk anybody because if I mix in some walks I'd really be in trouble. I just try to make pitches, and even when it's 0-and-2, I want to throw a strike—I just want it to be a good strike. You know, when the count goes to 2–1, the odds get a little more in his favor, so I don't want to waste anything, I want to go right at the hitter and keep my defense ready because, as you can see, I'm a contact guy and I want them at their best."

He realized that his opponents, in return, were ready to tee off on his in-the-zone offerings. "I'm going to throw strikes, so I don't blame them for swinging early. I'm not overpowering. Your best pitch to hit is probably going to be your first, and I think it's a good strategy against me. I don't want to fall behind, and they know that, so I throw a lot of first-pitch strikes and usually they're not on the black, they're knee high.

"After that, I have a little confidence I can move the ball around and do what I need to do—at least that's my game plan." Thus, he hoped to get away with throwing a fairly hittable first pitch for a strike. Then, if ahead in the count, he could take command of the situation, being able to throw to his spots from there on out.

He made good on his philosophy of throwing strikes, going from April 26 until July 3 in 2007 before he gave up an unintentional walk.

Some pitchers are unafraid to challenge batters, even to the point of firing their best fastball in counts when hitters are sitting on a fastball. The result can be a satisfying strikeout. Of course, the result can also be serving up a pitch that is about to take off on a very long trip.

Hitters say, "I respect a pitcher for coming at me with fastballs, not trying to play it cute and hit corners or walking me," but you'd *expect* them to say that. Dennis Cook was fierce when it came to his mano a mano with hitters, and yes, he paid for that ferocity at times. As a starter/reliever in 1990, he gave up 20 home runs (#10 in the NL), but he shrugged it off, saying, "I don't like to give in to the batter. That's just my personality—I challenge them. If they hit it out, make it be a solo. I'll just try to keep the ball down. I can't let it bother me."

Dave Burba, a pitcher for fifteen seasons, remembered a 2000 game in which throwing strikes, even fat ones, paid off. "After I got that 9–0 lead," he said, "I threw batting practice. I didn't throw many splits. I didn't throw many curveballs. I threw batting practice." After fanning Rickey Henderson on a right-down-the-pipe batting-practice-type fastball, Burba wondered, "Why can't it always be this easy?" He wound up working seven innings, giving up just two runs (on ten scattered hits), and winning the 12–4 laugher for Cleveland over Seattle.

Bob Brenly, manager of the Arizona Diamondbacks from 2001 to 2004, gave his view on going right at batters: "I think it's all dependent upon game situations—who the hitter is, what the score is. There are a lot of determining factors, but there are a lot of pitchers out there—we've got a couple on our own staff—who'd rather throw a fastball down the middle of the plate on a 3–1 count and force that guy to put it in play than nibble around and maybe walk the guy, and now you give up a *two-run* homer.

"Curt Schilling gives up his share of home runs, Rick Helling gives up a lot of homers, Brian Anderson is a guy who gives up a lot of home runs," he said, rattling off members of his staff, "but fortunately, they don't walk a lot of guys, and most of the time they're solo home runs.

"We joke about the 'rally-killing solo home run'; after those, the other team has no one on base and they have to start all over again. But I think there's something to be said for challenging hitters in those situations.

"I think when you walk a guy, that opens up so many possibilities. The first baseman's got to hold the guy on first; now the pitcher's into the stretch, his stuff may be not quite as good in the stretch as it was out of the windup. And the catcher has to be concerned with what pitches he calls depending on whether that guy [runner who had just walked] is a threat to steal or not—is the batter going to bunt, are they going to hit and run, is he going to swing away?

"Runners on base lend themselves to opening holes in the defense, and, like I said, sometimes that solo home run is a rally killer. The runner on base certainly can be [a disruption] but sometimes that ball bouncing in the seats is disruptive, too, depending on the score of the game."

PITCHERS' ADJUSTMENTS

Rick Sutcliffe won the Rookie of the Year Award in 1979 and five years later copped the Cy Young Award. He said, "In the majors, the physical part of the game is over—it becomes mental. Baseball is a game of adjustments. Those who make adjustments are a success." He said that in order to adjust to the batters he had to face over the course of a game, a season, or a career, "you have to have a good memory."

Learning How to Pitch

There is a vast difference between throwing and pitching. Vern Law, the 1960 Cy Young Award winner, spent about three seasons in the majors and still didn't feel as if he had learned the true craft of pitching. With experience and maturity, that changed.

"In 1955, when I began to show a little bit more maturity, I threw eighteen innings of a nineteen-inning game," he said. "It was against the Milwaukee Braves—Hank Aaron, Eddie Mathews, and those guys, and I started to get people out."

What gave him his figurative degree in pitching was when a pitching coach "changed my style. That made all the difference in the world; instead of being a .500 pitcher, why, I was winning most of my ball games."

Learning versus Mastering a New Pitch

There's quite a difference between *learning* a new pitch and *mastering* one. David Weathers was good enough to stay in the big leagues for nineteen seasons. Over such a long career, a pitcher is bound to experiment with new tools. Weathers said, "You can learn a new one, but until you put it in play on the field it means nothing. It's two different worlds to work on a pitch and actually use it in a game."

Does this mean he wouldn't unveil a new pitch until he was absolutely confident he had full mastery of it? "Oh, no, no. I've been out there before and my catcher would come out and say, 'Hey, man, what are you going to throw here?' I said, 'Let's throw a split,' and I never threw a split [in a game]. There's times when you just got to be innovative, but you pick your spots—you don't do it with the winning run on third base.

"But a pitch that you'll use in a game when it means something? Absolutely, you know 100 percent you're comfortable with that pitch."

He also believes it is easier for an older pitcher than a youngster to take on a new pitch "because a lot of times when you try to teach a young guy a new pitch, they try to go all out and they get out of their mechanics. Whereas an older guy will say, 'Keep the same mechanics, the same arm slot, different grip.' You can focus a little bit more on the pitch itself and not worry about the mechanics of it." Plus, a veteran pitcher has more of a frame of reference than a younger one to relate to a new pitch.

FACING AN UNFAMILIAR HITTER

Closer Bob Wickman, a man who notched 267 saves, mused, "A lot of times you can tell by the way a guy swings what he's looking for. You look at the way his stance is and get about as much from the scouting report as you can. You're just basically feeling out the whole at-bat how a guy's reacting to the ball. Most likely early in the count he can hurt you, but once you figure it out—if you get deep into the count—you can usually sense what a guy's looking for."

Wickman relies on scouting reports, but also considers other factors, including some baseball superstition. "You don't want to face a guy who's 0-for-20 because you know what's bound to happen is he's going to get a knock [hit]."

SOME KEY COMPONENTS TO EFFECTIVE PITCHING

A Cy Young Award winner when he was with the Milwaukee Brewers, Corbin Burnes chimed in on this topic, and, probably surprisingly to many fans, his number-one key to effective pitching is mental, not physical. "If you broke it down into mental, physical, and then mechanical pitching-type stuff, I wouldn't say it's an even third [each]. There's definitely more that goes into the mental side of it, just because the mental side is something I'm working on every single day."

By way of comparison, the veteran ace of the Baltimore Orioles staff pointed out that the other two components get honed during "working out three to four days a week. Early in the offseason, you're only throwing three days a week until you get really ramped up and [begin] throwing five days a week. The mental side is something that, you may not be adding something new, but you're still working on it and kind of hammering it down [daily]."[5] Developing and sticking with a routine is crucial to his mental approach.

One can't argue his approach. Why? Well, in 2019 he went 1–5 with a balloon-like 8.82 ERA and a helium-like WHIP (walks and hits per inning pitched) of 1.837, but what followed was diamond magic. In

2020, he hooked up with a mental performance coach, a master of mind legerdemain named Brian Cain. Working together, they punctured his inflated ERA and WHIP, deflating them to 2.11 and 1.022, respectively. Burnes followed that up in 2021 by winning the Cy Young Award after posting a league-leading ERA of 2.43 and his lowest WHIP to date, 0.940.

Focus is another aspect of the mental side of pitching. Dennis Cook said, "I'm a guy who's a location pitcher. I throw fastballs, but I'm not overpowering by any means." Because of that he said he had to concentrate, "I'm a guy who has to hit my spots."

He spoke of the time he lost his focus and it cost him dearly. Cook was an All–Southwest Conference outfielder at the University of Texas who hit .306 in 1990 in NL play. "I hit a home run versus Fernando Valenzuela, a three-run shot. I got around the bases real quick. I was pretty excited. I was *so* excited, I went out the next inning and got shelled. I went out there thinking about the home run and not enough about pitching."

PITCHERS' ATTITUDE/CONFIDENCE

Successful pitchers must possess an air of confidence—even after failing, he must feel as if "I'll get them next time." Star reliever Billy Wagner, for one, discussed this, and did so one day after he had dished up a grand slam to cost his Houston Astros a game in Pittsburgh. He faced the media as if nothing had taken place the night before. In fact, he answered questions with the same equanimity as if he had earned a save just hours earlier.

"It's obviously easier sometimes than others to earn a save," he said. "If you make good pitches and you don't get the job done, that can be tough, but if you go out there and you hang a pitch and it gets hit hard, that can be just as hard. It's something that you have to develop if you're going to have any success in this game—to be able to not necessarily put it *behind* you, but get past it. No one forgets. If anyone tells you they forget about it, that's a lie. You just learn how to get past it and move on."

PITCHERS' VERSUS HITTERS' PREGAME ATTITUDE

There are vast differences in players' pregame intensity levels. Jermaine Dye was successful enough to pelt 325 home runs and make two All-Star teams. He had his pregame routine down pat, and it was far from being intense. "You just go out there and try to get ready for the game any way you can. Try and get out there and get some stretching in and get some running in to get your heartbeat going a little bit. That's basically the approach I try to get every day."

He wasn't even into watching videos much. "I look forward; I try not to look in the past. I take it day by day and, every now and then, if I'm going bad and I know I had a hot streak somewhere, I might go back and look at my swing. Other than that, I try to stay away from that."

As a rule, the everyday players don't get too hyped up over a given game. After all, the 162-game schedule pretty much precludes players from getting overly excited about individual games, especially so-called meaningless ones. Legendary Orioles manager Earl Weaver summed it up by saying of the relaxed rhythm of baseball's seasons, "This ain't a football game; we do this every day." Baseball players are certainly unlike football players, who have been known to get so wired before a game that it was as if throwing up were part of their pregame regimen.

That's not to say baseball players become complacent, but they may border on being rather blasé in the clubhouse prior to the cry of "Play ball!" However, Ken Griffey Jr. says they do take things seriously: "We're baseball players, professionals. We know how to get ready." He added that players need some time to unwind before a game. He said, "Once you have your clothes on, it's easy to relax in the clubhouse."

During a rare interview, Albert Belle said he relaxed and prepared himself before games by playing cards, stretching, getting treatment, putting in extra outfield work, or taking early hitting. After games he wound down "watching videos of the opposing pitcher [for the next day's game] or watching my at-bats. The more you see a pitcher, the more comfortable you are. I'll get a picture of how [an upcoming starter] will face us. After a game I also tend to stay and lift weights."

Griffey said, "I read *USA Today* every once in a while, and the *Sporting News* comes to the park and I grab it sometimes. If I happen to come across or hear about an article [on himself], I read it—true or not."

Belle, on the other hand, often got a lot of bad ink, prompting him to say, "I prefer *not* to read the local paper. I usually don't. They tend to be more negative." No player needs negative vibes before taking the field. Carl Erskine, who spun two no-hitters, remembered Jackie Robinson sometimes being sensitive about what he read, "and he read every edition of every paper."

Many pitchers are quite different from their more laid-back teammates—but not always. On June 16, 2007, Cleveland's Paul Bryd and Atlanta's John Smoltz were preparing to square off against each other. In the Braves clubhouse, one would never have guessed it was Smoltz's turn to throw. A teammate told Smoltz he had recently pulled a muscle. Smoltz joked that that was nothing: "*You* could do that getting out of a cab."

Across the stadium in the Indians locker room, Bryd found relaxation and concentration off by himself with his locker being his Fortress of Solitude. With teammates on the field for pregame workouts, he sat in the clubhouse listening to his iPod.

Approach most pitchers on the day of a start, and you might be greeted by silence, a scowl, a snarl—or worse. Writers know not to approach the day's starters prior to their outing. However, a young writer once found Nolan Ryan alone in the clubhouse and thought it was a great chance to do a one-on-one with the pitching great.

The writer, who had forgotten the etiquette of not bothering the starter, approached Ryan and asked if he had time to answer some questions. Ryan was totally unperturbed, unconcerned about isolation and privacy—he had been there before. The laid-back Ryan, who would end up starting 773 times, knew he could relax and prepare for the game even while cooperating with the writer.

He and Smoltz were exceptions, though. Scott Pose, who was with the Yankees in 1997 when their starters were Andy Pettitte, David Wells, David Cone, Kenny Rogers, and Dwight Gooden, commented, "More often than not, the pitchers usually stay by themselves, and everybody's kind of wary about talking to them. But regular players, we play so much that it really doesn't matter, it's not as big a ritual."

He added that some players avoid the clamor of the press by hiding out in the trainer's room or other areas that are off-limits to the media: "In New York, guys had to go to the players' lounge just to get some time to be by themselves."

Justin Verlander, who fashioned three no-hitters, said he "can't be that guy that rolls in on start day and is loosey-goosey and having fun with the guys and then try to turn it on when I take the field. It doesn't work for me. I have to stay focused."[6]

THE BULLPEN

From the setup men to the kings of the hill—the bullpen hill, that is—relief pitchers are more important now than ever before. The trend for years now has been that the number of innings pitched and complete games has spiraled down for starters, and relievers' innings have therefore soared. A starter nowadays can lead his league in complete games, with a total as low as two. The modern-era record, set by Jack Chesbro in 1904, is 48 (more than his win total that season). Through 2022, only three active pitchers had as many as 25 *career* complete games, and in 2022 there were only 35 total complete games pitched.

Reliever T. J. House was a student of his craft and its workload. "I think it's different having to pitch multiple days in a row," he said, "but I think the hardest thing is having a long rest period and trying to come back again and throw. After not being on the mound for three or four days, it's tough to kind of get your feel back. You can throw bullpens all you want, but when that guy steps in the box, it's a whole different game."

Lee Smith's story was different. Initially he was groomed to be a starter, but he said any chance of that role continuing ended "when they found out that I could throw four, five days in a row. Joe Torre was one of my favorite managers. He'd just say, 'Hey, Smitty, you need a day off?' I'm like, 'Yeah, I'll take one off in November. I'm playing the game, man, I'm ready to play. That's why I come here for. I don't come here to watch the game—I could sit in the bleacher to do that.' I liked to throw a lot."

Scott Stewart spoke for relievers everywhere when he candidly stated that when it comes to the amount of rest it takes for the pain to depart after a day spent on the mound, "it never goes away. As a reliever it never goes away—once you start hurting, usually you're hurting for the rest of the year. But it's not really a hurt; it's just an aching because you're throwing so much."

Bullpen denizens now are used quite differently than they once were, with closers, for instance, working only the ninth inning. Long ago, if there was a threat brewing and the starting pitcher no longer had it, a closer would often enter a game early, even as early as the seventh inning, and go on to finish the contest.

Occasionally, in certain types of games, a star reliever might enter, say, an important extra-inning game, work his typical one-inning stint, then exit the contest, with managers opposed to sending their closer out for another inning. That was not the case in earlier ironman eras of the game. "I usually pitched 100 to 120 innings in, maybe, sixty to sixty-five games," recalled Elroy Face.

Finally, here's a random sampling of some of the best flame throwing relievers of the late 1900s and into the early part of this century. Let's begin with John Wetteland, who threw up to 96 miles per hour. Former manager Jim Lefebvre said, "He goes out there and, 'Here it is, man.' He comes after you hard with his fastball." However, Lefebvre added, there's more to a reliever than heat if that's defined by sheer speed alone. "He comes at you with his slider, too. If you're going to beat him, you're going to have to hit his best stuff."

When Dan Warthen was the Tigers' pitching coach, he said Billy Wagner "doesn't look like he's throwing as hard as he's throwing," which was over 100 miles per hour at times. "You use the term 'sneaky' fast, but how can you say 96 and 97 is sneaky? But it's just easy for him—the great leg drive, very quick arm through the zone, and smooth. He's a little guy [listed at 5-foot-10 and 180 pounds], but he gets that hand through the zone."

In 1999, he had more saves than hits allowed (39 to 35), an incredible feat that only Dennis Eckersley, Trevor Hoffman, and Mariano Rivera had ever before accomplished.

When Wagner's Astros were knotted, 0–0, in a July 12, 1997, game the Pirates eventually won in an eleven-inning combined no-hitter, Wagner hit 101 miles per hour. He felt that a pumped-up pitcher could increase the speed on their fastballs. "I think tight games have a lot to do with it," he speculated. "I don't think necessarily the hitter [is the key factor]. Once you kinda get established and you've been through it a little bit, you don't really sit there and go, 'Hey, this guy is tough.' I don't throw any harder against Barry Bonds than I would do against Jason Kendall or Brian Giles."

Warthen mentioned a handful of other men who threw hard, including José Mesa (321 saves) and Todd Jones (319). "You also have Armando Benítez [289 saves] who throws the ball very hard, up to 100 miles an hour."

And reliever Steve Karsay said, "I like Troy Percival's fastball out of the bullpen, and for a young kid, Billy Koch." Percival wound up with 358 saves, but arm issues held Koch to 163 saves over just six seasons, with a high of 44 in 2002, when he led the AL in appearances and games finished.

Karsay saved the best for last: the all-time leader in saves with an astonishing 652, Mariano Rivera. During his years as the Yankees closer, for seasons in which he toiled fifty or more innings, he averaged 40.9 saves each year. Even in his final season, at the age of forty-three, he racked up 44 saves, fourth best in the majors. Karsay said Rivera threw around 96 miles an hour, tops, but added, "I think he has a very good fastball. His ball moves and cuts."

Veteran reliever Paul Shuey added, "He's just hard to hit. He doesn't have many pitches—he's just got, like the one pitch [the cutter], but he gets people out with it all the time. I probably throw a harder fastball than he does, but his is more effective. So he's got a better fastball than mine."

A key to Rivera's superlative cutter, said Shuey, is that "he's got such a nice, easy, relaxed motion that when it comes out, it comes out on top of you. Whereas mine looks like I load up. His is sneaky fast."

Meanwhile, from the hitters' point of view, Roberto Alomar pointed out one good thing—perhaps the *only* good thing—about batting against Rivera: "He's a reliever, so you don't face him a lot, but he's nasty."

SAVES

The rules concerning pitchers' requirements to earn a save have changed over the years. From 1995 through 2012, Billy Wagner was a gunslinger who was sometimes called "Billy the Kid." When he literally was a kid, he broke his right arm, which was then his pitching arm. Undaunted, he taught himself to throw as a lefty, transforming himself into a stud who earned 422 saves (#6 all-time).

When asked what he thought about relievers who get easy saves—for example, under certain save rules, a pitcher could come into a game with a three-run lead, pitch one inning, and record a save—Wagner said, "They can say it's easy, but I can prove you wrong. It's not that easy [usually]—you can't go out there and face Mark McGwire in a one-run ball game."

Asked if a pitcher deserved a save when, for instance, he faces the bottom third of a batting order and mows them down with ease, Wagner continued, "It comes with the territory because you can't go in and say, 'You know what? I'd rather have it as tough as you can get it, so bring on [three superstars].' You can't do that. You have to say, 'It's my job; I'll do it.'

"It's like when a guy comes in and he's throwing 88 miles an hour and Baggy's [Jeff Bagwell] up there thinking, 'Mmm, you know I could hit a home run off this guy, but I'd rather not. Too easy. You know what? Bring in the guy that's throwing 110.' It's just the way it goes." Wagner also felt that things even out—sometimes a save is a bear to get, while others really are *relatively* easy.

One sidenote: with luck, sometimes relievers take a win away from starters. Vern Law said that in 1959, "Elroy Face got seven wins of mine. I started off the season 0–5 with an ERA of 1.50. We just were not a good club at first. He ended up at 18–1 for the season."

Former third baseman Ryan Minor, who replaced Cal Ripken Jr. in the lineup the day his streak of 2,632 consecutive games played ended, gave his point of view from the perspective of a regular, not a pitcher. Even he agreed with most pitchers that the save rule is fair. In a 2001 interview, he said, "I don't think it's too easy to get a save, the way the hitters are hitting now. You see a lot of late-inning comebacks, and you've got to have a guy out there that's going to be able to stop that. I think that's what closers are getting geared to now.

"Years ago, closers would come in for two, three, or four innings and finish a game, but now there's more of a specialty kind of pitcher that goes out there and they gotta get those guys out [to end games].

"A three-run lead is nothing nowadays. If you're up by three, they've got three hitters coming to the plate—so that's three chances to, say, hit home runs. Or you have a one-run lead in the ninth inning, you never know what's going to happen the way balls are flying out of the parks.

"The way guys hit, there's not an easy save—they can all hit balls out of the parks nowadays. You got shortstops that used to be able just to bunt and get on base, but now they're hitting home runs. Middle infielders are doing that. Guys are getting bigger and stronger, and the ballparks are getting a little smaller."

Naturally, pitchers from a time period when the save rules were more stringent see things differently—and they do have valid points to make. Elroy Face remembered, "Back when we got a save, you had to face the tying or winning run, or they had to be on base, and you did it from the seventh inning on, you didn't wait until the ninth inning like they do now."

He noted, too, that relievers now often enter the ninth with nobody aboard, or they "come in with one out and get two outs for a save. I went five innings one time in Chicago and won the game in the fourteenth inning."

In Face's day, it was more the norm to enter a game only when there was danger, a blaze to be extinguished: in perhaps the eighth or ninth inning, with only one out, bases loaded, game on the line. Hence the term "fireman" was used for relievers back then. "I enjoyed it that way, rather than come in with nobody on base. I'd rather have a bigger challenge. Then there was a little more pressure on the hitter, too." To men like Face, today's closers may, in fact, close out games, but they are no longer the brave firemen who rush from the bullpen and into danger.

A look at the evolution of the single-season record for saves reveals how much tougher it was to record saves long ago. In 1973, John Hiller took the season record for saves up to 38. In 2008, Francisco Rodriguez had 38 saves *at the All-Star break.* He wound up with what is still the record, 62.

BLOWN SAVES

Closers love nothing more than compiling saves to help their team win— and elite relievers chalk up as many as about 80 to 90 percent of their save chances. In fact, one bullpen dweller, Eric Gagne of the Dodgers, saw no reason to blow *any* saves. In his Cy Young Award–winning 2003 season, he had 55 saves in as many opportunities.

Combine his stats from the end of the 2002 season with his start of 2004 numbers, and Gagne went a phenomenal 84 straight money-in-the-bank games without once blowing a save, still the all-time record. He converted 91.6 percent of his save situations over his nine-year career, including a three-year stretch at 96.2 percent. In his final season he blew seven saves. Prior to that, going back over his last seven years, he had only blown ten.

A few other notable relievers and their success rate: baseball's only unanimous Hall of Fame inductee, Mariano Rivera, 89.1 percent; Trevor Hoffman, who ranks second for career saves with 601, 88.8 percent; Billy Wagner, 85.9 percent; Dennis Eckersley, 84.6 percent; Bobby Thigpen, who once held the season save record with 57, 79.4 percent; and the current single-season save record holder with 62, Francisco Rodriguez, 85.6 percent.

FEAR ON THE MOUND

Bob Wickman and other relievers try to avoid any sense of fear when entering a tight game. "We study the game pretty darn close because anything can happen in the ninth inning—you think the game's over with, but, you know what, the game's never over until that twenty-seventh out occurs."

By the very nature of their job, relievers have to be unflinching, or as close to that mental state as possible. Matt Mantei, who had personal high seasons of 32 and 29 saves, said that a bad outing leaves a lasting impression on a player: "When you go out there, put in a long day, and struggle, it makes it real frustrating. You go home and sleep on it—this is our livelihood."

As for fear, he said that for him (and many others), one of the biggest motivational factors is, in fact, the fear of failure. Mantei dreaded the concept of failing. "I think more than anything else, we have an emotional roller coaster. Everybody wants to succeed every time out there, and you know that's not going to happen, but you got to learn how to take failure, and you got to learn how to go through the ups and downs."

Wickman said, "I wouldn't say that I'm fearless; you still have some fear, but your chances of going out there every single day [exists]—you still have a chance, so you have to get yourself prepared to go out there. On the mound you have to have a short memory—something happens to you, you gotta run back out there the next night."

The fear aspect comes into play in that professionals, playing the game at the highest level in the world, don't want to, as Wickman put it, "embarrass yourself and your family and your organization. A lot is for the team, you let the team down. And you got people at the game.

"There were a couple of games with my son [watching], and I basically have blown the game, and he's felt terrible for it. Fans start yelling, like they should—they paid money to see the game, and I gotta explain to him. It's like, 'Just remember the good games that you have when they're all cheering for us when we come off the field.'"

Even as a kid, Wickman had bouts with fear and came away from them knowing that one must cope with occasional failure. "I missed an extra point that would've tied a game and we would have had a chance to go to the playoffs that year in high school—I screwed it up big time."

Trevor Hoffman didn't fail very often, but he did speak about the self-doubt players sometimes experience. "I don't think something like that ever really goes away. I think you have confidence in yourself, but there's always a sense of negativity that creeps in your head, that you have to address and flush out with some positive thoughts.

"I don't care if you're one day in the big leagues or ten years, you're going to have doubt in your ability at times. It's just how you handle that and know that your stuff *is* good enough to keep getting guys out. The ability to do that and visualizing quality pitches is being effective."

Then there's the fear of being drilled by a wicked comeback shot. Pitchers, who are closer than 60 feet away from the batter once they release the ball, are in a very vulnerable spot. Many a pitcher has been struck with a batted ball, and some (e.g., Dizzy Dean and Herb Score) have had their careers altered due to the vicious impact.

Wagner said that the idea of getting hit is really planted in pitchers' minds "once it happens. There's always a fear factor out there, but you talk to a hitter, and they have that fear factor as well, with a pitcher hitting them. Any sport you play, there's a fear factor. I think if you're wanting to do anything in life, there's going to be fear, and you've got to be able to kind of just accept that and go on or you'll be scared of everything."

But yes, he says, before facing a hitter who perhaps is known to crack the ball back through the box at times, the thought of getting hit is present. "Once you've been hit, there's always that, but if you love the game, and you're willing to go out there and say, 'You know what? This is my job, this is my livelihood, I've got to do it.' So you go out there and do it."

THE CHALLENGE OF PITCHING

Adam Wainwright, an eighteen-season veteran who spent his whole career as a Cardinal, said he loved the interplay between pitcher and batter. "That's my absolute favorite thing about baseball—the one-on-one, me-versus-you battle." In a 2023 interview, he elaborated, calling the challenge a case of "your execution versus my execution. That part of baseball, and sports in general, will never get old to me. The mind behind that one-on-one battle is such a fascinating thing and the preparation behind digging into a hitter's weaknesses still excites me more than ever. I love breaking that stuff down and engaging in the battle."[7]

PITCHERS DISCUSS SELECT STAR HITTERS

Sam McDowell was a fireballing pitcher from 1961 through 1975, mainly with the Cleveland Indians. He led his league in strikeouts five times and twice fanned 300-plus batters, reaching an astronomical total of 325 K's in 1965. His career ended before Tony Gwynn came along in 1982, but McDowell theorized about how he'd pitch to that member of the 3,000-hit club: "Well, in my particular case with my fastball, and knowing he has a weakness up and in, I'd throw him hard fastballs up and in. Oh, I'd keep him honest, too, with changeups away."

Another pitcher who preceded Gwynn was Carl Erskine. He said about the only specific way he could think to even try to curb Gwynn was "a basic standard in pitching—pitch high and tight and low and away. You also change speeds." In other words, when facing such stars as Gwynn, good luck. Holding him anywhere below his career batting average of .338 might have to be considered a success.

Most hitters are uncomfortable with two strikes on them, but Chipper Jones called Gwynn the game's "best two-strike hitter."

As for an analysis of the game's most famous figure, Jim Palmer said, "I think you pitch Ruth like you pitch Barry Bonds or you pitch Harmon Killebrew—you don't let them beat you if you can. You're not going to let him beat you, and you hope to get the guys out in front of him and behind him, so if Babe Ruth is going to hit home runs, you don't want anybody else to be on base and, obviously, you always know who's up and who's on deck. You're not going to miss Ruth in the on-deck circle, so you pitch him carefully, and it's a matter of trusting yourself. And if you're going to let Ruth hit a single, it's a lot better than a home run or a grand slam, because you're able to get the other guys in front of him."

Fielders

INFIELDERS AND ERRORS

Fielding percentages can be very misleading, and newer measuring sticks now have more credibility than that old statistic. Likewise, the number of errors a player makes is also a stat that requires deeper consideration. For instance, young players' error totals aren't always an indicator of ability or potential. Many players who went on to become all-time greats often had fielding woes and less than stellar numbers early on.

Consider, for example, shortstops such as Detroit Tigers star Alan Trammell, who had 26 errors when he was twenty-one. Then there was future Hall of Famer Robin Yount. During the season he turned twenty, some observers thought he was a butcher—he was guilty of committing 44 errors. Toss in Derek Jeter, who made a mind-reeling 56 errors one year in the minors!

Trammell said, "You're gonna boot some balls; that's the way it is. But if you eliminate the careless errors, you'll be okay." He stressed that careless errors often come on poor, casual throws like those that pull the first baseman off the bag. Improvement in areas such as those bad throws comes with age. "You get more comfortable as years go on. Infielders get around 15 errors a year—that's pretty good. When you get up to 25 errors, a lot could have *not* occurred."

Jesse Orosco, a valuable southpaw reliever who appeared on the mound in more games than any other pitcher ever (1,252 over a sterling twenty-four seasons), was well aware of how errors and fielding percentages must be analyzed deeply, going beyond quantity. "A guy that makes errors is [sometimes] a guy who gets to a lot of balls that other guys can't get to, and most of the time his errors aren't going to be caused by trying to make the play—it'll be trying to make the throw and it got away. Every once in a while a ball goes through your legs, but that's going to happen."

Yes, everybody muffs some easy ones, but Orosco observed that great infield glove men such as Roberto Alomar and Omar Vizquel usually make their errors "on plays you could never imagine them making, and then he tries to make an unbelievable throw and maybe throws it in the stands or something like that. As a pitcher, you appreciate that effort—you love the idea."

When Orosco was with the Orioles in the late 1990s, he praised a record-setting teammate: "Mike Bordick has saved me a number of times, and that's how you win games. You have to have defense behind you."

FIRST BASEMEN

Hall of Famer Billy Williams said, "The measure of a good first baseman is when he makes that 3–6–3 double play. You have to be quick, you have to concentrate on picking the ball up and making a good throw to second base, then you got to get back to the bag. You have to have good agility over there."

Having played some first base, Kevin Rhomberg has fond memories of the position. "It's a great place to play," he said. "You're almost like the catcher; you're in there on almost every play. Every ground ball you've got to do something, and you're the cutoff man on [plays at the plate], you've got relays, you cover bunts. I mean, first base is a place where all the good athletes can go and do well at the end of their career or when they need to slide over there. When you get there, you really enjoy it."

However, the position can be demanding to a newcomer. "It's not only how difficult it can be, but learning the position—you have more than just your responsibility. There's covering bunts, and PFP [pitchers' fielding practice] with the pitchers is a lot of extra work, too."

Rhomberg said that even veteran first basemen sometimes may find that a so-called easy play can be more difficult than expected: "The play that still gets me at first base is if you have a runner on first, or first and second, or bases loaded, and there are two outs. When the first baseman gets a ground ball, even if it's to your right, they often get it, they stop, they turn, and they hit the pitcher on the run at first base, but with two outs all you've got to do is flip it to second. You don't see enough of this, especially at the amateur level—it's so easy. 'Hey, on a ball hit to my right, I'm coming to you at shortstop.' It's easier than trying to hit the pitcher on the run to beat the base runner."

Ron Blomberg played first base at times for the Yankees. "People think you just catch the ball there, but it's totally different," he said. "You have Graig Nettles who throws you a ball that sinks, then you've got Gene Michael and Bucky Dent who threw balls that moved all over the place, and you have Willie Randolph at second base who threw such a light ball, it just took off.

"A lot of guys have a hard time playing first base. You have to adjust to everybody who throws, and often the ball doesn't come straight—the ball rises, it sinks, sometimes it knuckles a little bit."

Even pickoff throws can be a challenge. "You've got to watch the runner at all times, something I had never done before as an outfielder, and then you have people like Sparky Lyle or Mel Stottlemyre who threw such a heavy ball, and they'd sink every time. Then you had Catfish Hunter, whose control was so great, but then you have some rookies who want to get somebody out at first base, but nine out of ten times you don't catch anybody off first base.

"You don't pick off many guys at first base. The only time you do is when the guy's taking off [starting to break for second base]. Do you think people could pick Mickey Rivers off a lot? No. Rivers was fast *and* quick. But the pitchers throw it hard. Just picture yourself going 60 feet away and somebody's throwing bullets at you. It's not easy.

"And that's especially true when it's raining and there's moisture on your fingers and on the ball. And sometimes a lot of pitchers, when we played, scuffed up the ball, and that makes the ball move funny."

Middle Infielders

Even though he played his last game more than fifty years ago, Bill Mazeroski is still the gold standard for second basemen. Alex Grammas was around the game as a player, manager, and coach for an eon, and he said of the eight-time Gold Glove winner, "He could make the double play as good or better than anybody ever will—quicker—and he had as good of hands as anyone. He was as quick as I've ever seen getting rid of the ball."

Mazeroski's double play partner Dick Groat said, "It was like his hands never touched the ball. As soon as the ball would reach his glove, it was on its way to first base."

Grammas also said, "He used the bag for protection, oh, yeah. He was built real well, too, from the waist—well, from the head down, he was pretty good size, but he had strong legs."

Experts said it was as if runners would bounce off Mazeroski's tree trunk legs and absorb the punishment, not Maz. All-Star second sacker Junior Spivey said he could relate to such durability and strength. "I like to be tough around the bag because I played football, and I can endure contact; it doesn't bother me at all. I've been taken out quite a bit, but I know how to get out of the way as well, but I'm also going to hang in there—I have the scars to prove it."

Then, as if displaying a bunch of badges of courage, he thrust out his left leg—the one exposed to runners coming in with spikes high—rolled up his pant leg, and revealed his war wounds.

"I like to hang in there, and I can jump and get out of the way. I'm athletic enough to get out of the way. So it doesn't scare me. You just can't be afraid of being taken out if you think you'll be a good guy around the bag."

Even though his scars, like the notches on an Old West gunslinger's pistol, came in his minor league days, he said he had "never been spiked; I've just been scraped, never been taken out that bad to where I had to use stitches. I'm not the traditional second baseman because I'm 200 pounds and I'm not scared of anyone.

"If a guy takes me out, he just takes me out. I'll brush myself off and get up right away. Now I know how to maneuver myself and basically avoid a collision, avoid being taken out." To him, his legs were the key because "they're strong enough to jump and get out of the way, and you have to have quick feet."

Matt Kata was a five-year big-league veteran who, coincidentally, at one time or another had played for all four of the teams who played in the 2023 NL and AL Championship Series. He critiqued what makes a good second baseman by citing two of his contemporaries: "I like the way Bret Boone gets rid of the ball—the turn around second [on double plays] is just 'sick.' I mean, his footwork is just great around the bag, and he knows when he needs to be quick and when he doesn't."

Kata said the same held true for Fernando Viña. "He gets rid of the ball quick on the turn and you're always seeing him ranging to the left, to the right, coming in on balls and making smart plays when needed."

Kata also broke down keys to a successful twin killing. "Number one, you look at the hitter and see what kind of speed he has. If he's a guy who can run, then you know that on a ball hit to your left, you're going to have to be a little quicker, so you may have to do the spin move [to make the throw]. If possible, you want to help that pitcher out, and you want to turn every ball that you think you can turn realistically."

If the hitter is left-handed, Kata said, he may have to hurry a bit "and use a different turn," knowing the batter can get out of the batter's box quicker than a right-handed hitter.

The bottom line, though, is relatively simple: "Most of it's just reaction, but [factors] do go through your head before the ball is actually hit." All good players routinely go through a mental checklist before the ball is put into play. As Kata put it, "Hey, if it's hit here, here's what I'm going to do."

Of course, another huge factor is knowing one's own limitations—a player knows how wide his range is and that on certain balls he will have to be content to "get the out at second—you probably are not going to be able to turn it."

Pitchers love shortstops who steal hits away from opponents the way Willie Sutton robbed banks. An Ozzie Smith, for example, is, like the double play ball itself, a pitcher's best friend.

Craig Biggio played second base for fifteen seasons on many different fields. "They look beautiful and manicured from the stands, but when you're on it, they're all different," he said. A case in point is the grounder that finds an errant pebble and take a bad hop.

One thing that hasn't changed with the fields, though, is their tailoring by grounds crews. Biggio said, "I think the fields now are more designed for certain teams. If you really want to slow it down, you can make it slow and soft. If you have a fast team, you can speed it up and make it quick."

One trick middle infielders occasionally yank out of their tattered bag of tricks is the decoy. Roberto Alomar analyzed the "deke," saying, "If the guy's running and the batter hits the ball behind the runner, I can try to deke him that I caught the ball and that I'm going to throw it to the shortstop." He pantomimed a phantom catch and throw.

"The shortstop makes it look like he's going to make a double play, so the guy thinks I caught it and he's going to slide. So now he's not going to make it to third base on the ball to right field.

"Now, if there's a fly ball to right field, and he's running and doesn't know where the ball is, we're going to try to deke him, see if we can make him look for the ball. If he doesn't know where the ball really is, many times the right fielder has already caught the ball and he can throw him out at first base for a double play."

Alomar also said it takes infield communication to make such fakes work. He also recalled decoys where a confused runner, held up by the deke, is slowed down going to second. If an outfielder quickly gets to a ball that has dropped in for an apparent single, the runner from first can be forced at second by the outfielder.

A good base runner can avoid such embarrassment, said Alomar, if he "peek[s] to home plate. If he doesn't do this, and as an infielder you can see that, then you know the runner doesn't know where the ball is—he has no clue. Now he's got to look at the coaches, but some of the guys can't hear them—it's not easy out there, it's so loud. If he doesn't look at the coaches and doesn't see what's going on, you try to decoy him, and we can get a double play. Maybe it's going to work 5 percent of the time, maybe 2 percent, but it could be good." In other words, it's worth a try.

Slick-fielding Royce Clayton spoke about positioning: "A lot of it is instinct. Scouting does help as far as pitching reports about what a guy's throwing and tendencies, but as far as positioning out there, a lot of it's [that] I have to go off my pitcher. You can't position a guy to pull if my guy's throwing [a] 99-mile-an-hour fastball. Certain pitches—guys will roll over a slider, so I just go off of that for the most part. A lot of it depends on who's pitching and the hitter and the situation."

John McDonald lasted for sixteen big-league seasons despite carrying a lifetime batting average of just .233. Why? He was a dexterous glove man at second, short, and third. In Cleveland, where he broke in (1999), he was behind Omar Vizquel at shortstop and Roberto Alomar at second base—translated, that means that as talented as McDonald was, he was destined to be chained to the bench, watching Vizquel, who would end up owning eleven Gold Gloves (more than any other shortstop except Ozzie Smith, who had thirteen), and Alomar, who earned ten Gold Glove Awards, more than any other second baseman ever. McDonald only played the field in thirty-seven games from 1999 through 2001, but he was a fantastic insurance policy sitting in the dugout.

For McDonald, observing the men ahead of him paid off, but he also qualified that point: "It helps to watch a lot of ball games, but it's being out there and seeing it firsthand—seeing how the ball comes off somebody's bat. I mean, that's the best way to learn, but sometimes it doesn't happen. You get a good feeling by looking at the charts and the way you see where a guy normally hits all his balls, but until you get out there . . . ," his voice trailed off pensively.

Vizquel's instructions for McDonald helped greatly. "He's taught me a little bit about being fearless, about how you have to know your limitations, and you have to know your strengths. And the only way you can find those things out—that's not in practice—you need to find those things out in a game. What can I do in a game? It's something if you can do it in practice, but if you can do it in a game, it can take you to a whole other level—like barehanding the ball like he does.

"You have to be willing to try it when you're out there playing, not just in practice. Anybody can do it in practice, but to do it in a game when you've got people moving around is different."

As mentioned, fielding percentage isn't the greatest gauge for fielding proficiency, but McDonald's career fielding percentage of .989 at second base was actually better than Alomar's .984, and McDonald's percentage at short wasn't shabby, either.

McDonald spoke of what it takes to be a good defensive shortstop: "Footwork. I think everything on defense starts with your feet. If you're balanced and your feet are in good position, it allows your hands to get in a good position. If you try to do it the other way around, try to catch everything and have your feet not in good position, you're not going to be in balance and it's going to make everything hard. It's going to make fielding the ball harder, and the way you get in position to make a throw is going to be slower, and you're not going to be able to get as much on your throw."

Spivey ran down his checklist of key skills for middle infielders, beginning with a quick first step and wide range. "I think it all goes hand in hand. I think if a guy has good instincts and he has a good first move, first step, I think that's the key to getting to balls and being able to have great range, take away hits, as well as having the ability to position yourself. It's what separates you from the rest of the pack."

McDonald also studied the nuances of that art of the double play. "The quick pivot. Anticipating without getting ahead of yourself. I think you always have to anticipate where the ball's going to go and then be able to react to a bad throw. Again, the pivot is with your feet. If you're a shortstop, being able to hit the back corner of the bag [is crucial], and not catching too much of it—being able to hit the corner of the bag and making it so your feet are in line to throw to first base."

McDonald said that even when an infielder completes a twin killing by stepping on the bag then moving into the grass part of the infield before making the throw, the key is still footwork: "It's being able to jump to the other side of the bag real quick to avoid the runner. If you get a throw that takes you that way, you still get your feet in the position to throw."

He itemized some of Vizquel's and Alomar's biggest assets, beginning with Vizquel. "He has the ability to change at the last second, to drop his hands into a better spot for that ground ball. If the ball is going to take a bad hop, he just moves his feet real quick, and all of a sudden, his hands slide into the spot where he wants them. Great hand-eye coordination. He's got the whole package."

Between innings when infielders take practice grounders from the first baseman, Vizquel occasionally performed stunts, as if handling grounders the normal way might make him yawn. He would let the ball roll into his glove, then let it continue up onto the heel of the glove, and then on up his wrist before finally securing it. Other times, when the grounder reached him, he would kick it upward, soccer style, then grab and throw the ball—a great display of dexterity.

As for Alomar, McDonald said, "He has tremendous arm strength, so he doesn't always have to get in front of the ball and get set. He could throw off-balance a little bit more because he had such good arm strength and anticipation of where the ball's going to be hit.

"It's from studying the hitters, knowing your pitchers, knowing when you see a bat go a certain way where the ball's going to go off of it. But before you see where the ball's going, you're already taking a step in the direction of where it's going to go, before it actually leaves the bat.

"I think Omar and Robbie are so consistent, they make every routine play. I think that's what sets them apart more than anything. Yeah, they can make the great play, but they make *every* routine play."

They could make the electrifying plays, too. "That was one of the best combinations ever," admired Spivey, "as far as both of them being flashy. I mean, they were unbelievable together; they were definitely fun to watch. They kind of brought that middle-of-the-infield position back to where it used to be when you had Alan Trammell and Lou Whitaker—those two were the best in their era.

"And I would say that Alomar and Vizquel were the best at the time that they played together. That brought that sense of, I guess, 'urgency' to the middle infield. It was like Magic and Bird to me."

Spivey called Alomar "a magician in the field. He makes all the routine plays as well as the great ones, and that sets him apart from most of the second basemen in the game. That's what I respect about him. He also brings a bat with him, so to get that in a player, you're getting everything." With Alomar's power, speed, and switch-hitting skill, Spivey said, "he kind of changed the game at that position. He has the complete package, no doubt about it."

The Hot Corner

When it comes to third basemen, two names instantly pop up: Mike Schmidt for his offense—no wonder, he launched 548 homers—and Brooks Robinson who won more Gold Gloves, sixteen, than anyone but pitcher Greg Maddux, who won eighteen. (Pitcher Jim Kaat also won sixteen.) Robinson's trophies came sixteen years in a row, from his second full year on the job in 1960 through his last full season in 1975.

Cleveland announcer Matt Underwood was with Gold Glove winner Travis Fryman when the team had a private tour of the Hall of Fame in 2000. Underwood said, "Being a third baseman, he was interested in Brooks Robinson's glove. We looked at it, and Travis said, 'Look at that beat-up old piece of leather.' Those guys didn't have a new glove every day; some of these guys today don't use the same glove for more than a couple of weeks at a time. In the days of Brooks Robinson, they probably used the same glove most of their career." It didn't matter—it was the man and not the glove that made the difference.

Pitcher David Weathers did say that quite a few third basemen wear rather large gloves. "It's just to have a little more range on the line," he noted. "I mean, sometimes an inch and a half extra on a glove is the difference between a double or an out."

Scott Hatteberg added, "I think before, the only reason you had a smaller glove was you were able to get the ball out of it quicker, but I think some guys are still finding the ball in bigger gloves now—they're not having trouble turning double plays, getting the ball out. Having a bigger glove, you're going to get more range and be more consistent."

Had it not been for Robinson, Clete Boyer would have won numerous Gold Gloves. It wasn't until he was traded to Atlanta, in the NL, that he won his Gold Glove Award, in 1969 when he was thirty-two. He had already led the AL in a handful of defensive categories, including a statistic known as range factor, which he led five times.

With all his expertise and experience, Boyer came up with a rule of thumb on judging hot-corner defense: "I figure about one error for every ten games [is what to expect] for a third baseman."

He also said the best men he ever saw at third were "Robinson, who really worked hard on his defense," Eddie Mathews, Wade Boggs, Carney Lansford, and the very best, Mike Schmidt.

Although there are some similarities between playing first base and third, Jeff Bagwell, who began as a third baseman, noticed a mirror image factor: "At third base your glove hand has more plays, and at first base it's your back hand."

Todd Helton was a very smooth fielder, but he said his biggest weakness was pop-ups. Bagwell said that for a third baseman (or any infielder), "pop-ups are difficult at times, just because of the sun, you're going backward, and when you're on a corner, you're going toward the stands or the dugout, and things like that."

There can be more to playing third base than coming up with sizzling grounders and making the long peg over to first. Matt Williams, a four-time Gold Glove winner, pulled off the ol' hidden ball trick a few times. His Cleveland teammate Sandy Alomar related one instance in a game against the Kansas City Royals: "He told the [base runner] Jed Hansen to get off the base so he could clean it. He was a rookie. Williams tagged the guy and he was out; they were pretty upset about that." The Royals were so upset, in fact, that when Williams came to the plate in the next inning, he was hit by a pitch.

OUTFIELDERS' FUNDAMENTALS

Even though major leaguers are the best players on the planet, there are some outfielders—successful ones—who don't follow the fundamentals of the game. In a 2003 interview, five-time All-Star outfielder Luis Gonzalez said, "I enjoy watching a guy like Andruw Jones and Ken Griffey Jr. play center field. They make everything so easy. My only drawback to Jones is his way of catching balls, very nonchalant. To me, that sets a bad example for younger kids. We're playing in the big leagues, and he's got God-given ability and great talent—he's one of the best outfielders in the game—but I'd like to see him use two hands or catch the ball up high instead of down by his waist sometimes."

Likewise, when Barry Bonds made a catch with a downward swipe, a snatching motion—which seemed to have only one purpose: displaying a showboating attitude of "Look at me!"—it bothered Gonzalez "a little bit, because I'm one of those guys that I always feel like there's young kids watching you out there and that's how kids learn—when they see big-league guys doing things like that. That's where they get those examples to say, 'Hey, if he does it, it should be OK for me to do it.'

"Maybe it's because I'm old-school and I don't believe in a lot of stuff like that. I just enjoy going out there and grinding things out. I'm not one of those guys who had things handed to me. I've had to work for it, and I believe that you gotta keep working hard and that's the only way to get better."

Of course, Hall of Famers Willie Mays and Roberto Clemente were known for often making basket catches, and Rickey Henderson often made snatching catches with a flair long before Bonds.

Now, for those who adhere to the fundamentals, Gabe Kapler, an outfielder who became the manager of the San Francisco Giants in 2020, said he checked on even minute details to help his game: "I even like to throw balls off certain outfield corners to see how the ball bounces, and to 'learn' the wall. You get a sense during BP how the ball is going to come off the wall. [Is] a line drive . . . going to die on the wall, or is it going to hit the dirt and roll around?

"Certain places like Kansas City, you know if it stays on the line you can't let the ball get by you because it's going to roll all the way to center field. It depends on the ballpark. Some are pretty standard." Parks that fit that description include the numerous cookie-cutter parks outfielders used to cope with a lot, such as Three Rivers Stadium in Pittsburgh and Riverfront Stadium in Cincinnati.

Kapler went on, "Once I've played in a ballpark two, three times in one series, I feel pretty comfortable. It's the first time in each ballpark that's a little bit tricky."

He said outfielders even have to analyze and consider such factors as domes, which "sometimes have the roof open, and a closed roof is a factor depending upon the ballpark like SkyDome." Knowing how the ball carries in different parks is an important fielder's tool. The knowledge of the great glove men often provided abundant benefits to their teams, ones that remained hidden to the average fan.

Matt Diaz, a vet of eleven seasons, played alongside Jones in Atlanta. In a 2007 interview, he said that like Mays, Clemente, and Henderson, Jones provided potent offense, too: "Last year every time we needed a clutch hit and he came up, he delivered." Jones, who was coming off a season in which he led the NL with 51 homers and 128 runs batted in, added 41 home runs and 129 ribbies that year.

As for defense, "he makes my job easy," said Diaz. "He covers so much ground out there. He makes the outfielders around him better."

According to star outfielder Billy Williams, there are several keys that mark strong, fundamental outfield play. He began with an excellent model, calling the speed burner Henderson "one of the best left fielders ever." Williams said that in his final season (1976), "I was out in Oakland when Rickey played left field. I've seen guys get to the line quick, but there was *nobody* quicker than Rickey Henderson taking away doubles."

In addition, there is more to outfield play than raw speed. Williams said, "When you look at Barry Bonds playing the outfield, he's worked hard. He doesn't have a strong arm, but he charges the ball and he makes great plays in the outfield. I think with his experience, knowing where hitters hit the ball, he gets himself in good position to make the plays. He's just become a great left fielder."

Former Orioles manager Sam Perlozzo said, "There's a lot more to it than a strong arm. I've seen some guys with average arms who charge the ball really well and are really accurate who are better than most outfielders." One example was Paul O'Neill: "He's just an all-round good outfielder; he doesn't make many mistakes, he's very accurate, he never misses a cutoff man, and he has a pretty good arm."

As for the strongest outfield arms, players from Carl Furillo and Roberto Clemente to Ronald Acuna Jr. and Fernando Tatis Jr. are often nominated. Bob Feller argued for Rocky Colavito: "I saw him stand 10 feet to the right of home plate in Washington and throw a ball two-thirds of the way up into the right field stands in Griffith Stadium."

When Trot Nixon was with the Red Sox, he played alongside Darren Lewis. "He always wanted to put himself in a good position to catch the ball when fielding a ground ball or a fly ball.

"I learned a lot from him. He was one of the most respected guys in this game when he was playing, and I still put him in that status."

When Lewis broke in with the A's, he started a record-setting stretch of errorless play that ran from his debut on August 21, 1990, until 1994. The unblemished fielding streak covered 392 contests. In all, he handled 938 straight chances without once being charged with an error. Over his thirteen-season career, he made a mere 16 errors with his magnetized glove.

"If I had to have somebody work with me in the outfield—I mean there's some great people like Dwight Evans—Darren Lewis was *the* best," continued Nixon. "He had a great approach. He knew how to read what pitchers were doing on the mound—are they hitting their spots, and if they're hitting their spots, you move from side to side. He wasn't flashy *at all*. He played the game the right way; he respected the game and he took a lot of pride in his defense. Whether he had to go all out for a ball to throw somebody out, or go get a ball in the gap, he just did the basics—watch the ball go into your glove, and don't allow your at-bats to dictate how you play in the field.

"I learned [from Lewis] that playing defense is just as important as trying to go up there and hit the ball as well as base running. You can win ball games [with defense], but that's overlooked a lot—I think because the media hypes hitting all the time.

"I try to take pride in my defense. I'm not a megasuperstar at the plate, so I've got to do certain things that are going to help this team win ball games, and playing defense is one of them."

In a 2007 interview, Nixon also said that an outfielder without a howitzer for an arm can still excel by compensating, as Lewis did. Such men need to put "themselves in the right position and make the throws they need to make, and made them accurately, and get the throws out quick, and get the outs."

Nixon praised Ichiro for doing things the right way and having "a special blend [of skills]. He's a special ballplayer because he's got a canon for an arm and he keeps the ball low. I'm someone who's got to rely on strictly getting the ball out of my glove as quickly as possible and with enough momentum going toward home or third to throw somebody out."

Another standout who did it all was five-time Gold Glove winner Steve Finley. Teammate Matt Kata reeled off Finley's talents: "I've seen him numerous times go back on balls, cut balls off in the gaps, and come up making good solid throws to the cutoff men and to the bases."

Like Finely, Hall of Famer Al Kaline had a teammate who was well aware off his tremendous skills as a right fielder. Willie Horton said that Kaline owed his greatness to "knowing the game, being a student of the game, knowing his job, knowing when he'd come to the ballpark what he had to do, and taking on his responsibilities. He had a great arm and a very accurate arm—he set the example for all of us in the outfield."

Horton said Kaline, who won a whopping ten Gold Gloves, kept his throws as low line drives, not missing his cutoff man: "No, no. All the time his throws were right there." Further, he said that while Kaline wasn't speedy in the outfield, "he wasn't slow, either. I think it's instinct. He had the feel and the instinct of the game—when to do things.

"He knew how to read the pitcher real good. We learned our pitching staff and we'd play our position [accordingly], and pick up the ball off the bat, so you didn't have to do the one-hand [stretching] catch."

OUTFIELDERS TAKING HITS AWAY

Tony Gwynn collected a slew of his 3,141 lifetime hits on slashing line drives and bloopers to left. Why, he was asked, didn't more teams play him more shallow in left? "It's funny," he began. "Every team is different. Some try to take hits up the middle away from you, or take away something else. Barry Bonds tries to take left field away from me, but it takes guts and talent to do that. Bonds is the only left fielder in the

National League who has the guts to come in and say, 'I dare you to hit it over my head.' In my career [through mid-1992], I only did it once.

"I kid him all the time, 'I'm gonna burn you.' Three years ago off Doug Drabek I hit one over his head. It took me going off the wall to burn him. If I don't hit the wall, he'll catch it."

Though Bonds is widely reviled for his nasty personality and his tainting of Hank Aaron's pure career home run record, he was nevertheless an outstanding left fielder. Sparky Anderson called him the best in the game.

The most dramatic outfield play, one that takes fans' breath away, is the one where an acrobatic player robs a homer. Ken Griffey Jr. observed, "Probably the *toughest* play is going over and robbing somebody of a home run. It's just the timing of it—everything else is a matter of just try to get the ball and get rid of it, get it back to the infield."

All-Star outfielder Preston Wilson said that some fans think outfielders can best rob a home run by getting to the wall quickly, getting his back to the fence, waiting for the ball, then timing his leap. Not so. He said an outfielder should "run at an angle [to where the ball is heading]. If you run straight back, you're running this way [he indicated an awkward defensive style]. You have to run at an angle and hope that you get it." Therefore, his last few steps before liftoff were not taken from, say, the deepest grass areas of the outfield just in front of the warning track, but on the track, parallel to the wall.

DIFFERENCE IN OUTFIELD POSITIONS

While everyone speaks of how defense up the middle is vital in baseball, thereby indicating that the center fielder is the key to the outfield, many experts surprise the average fan by saying playing there is easier (not less important, but easier) than the corner spots. Chipper Jones, who played 356 games in left and 9 in right, said, "Left and right are definitely harder than center because most of the time the guy in center has the best angle on every ball that's hit. They can see where the pitch is going to be; they can anticipate where the ball is going to be hit.

"In left and right you can't see where the pitch is coming, and you don't get as good of jumps as you do in center. Obviously the ball is hooking or fading from you more in left and center—it's just different."

Former Manager of the Year Johnny Oates added, "In some ways center field is the easiest field to play because out there you can see the ball make contact with the bat." That makes it easier to get a real good read and jump on the ball.

Still, center fielders are the ones who usually impress Gold Glove voters the most, but right fielders can gain a lot of kudos (much more than left fielders). The outfielders with the most Gold Gloves on their shelves are Willie Mays and Roberto Clemente, with a dozen each, followed by Ken Griffey Jr., Al Kaline, Ichiro, and Andruw Jones, each with ten.

Another right fielder, Hank Aaron, won three Gold Gloves but deserved more, partly because he was somewhat overshadowed by Clemente, who played right field in the same era. From 1957, the first year the award was given out, through 1960, an award was given to one right fielder, one center fielder, and one left fielder, which hurt Aaron's cause.

Clete Boyer had another reason Aaron was underrated as a defender: He made it look too easy. "You take two cars, a Rolls Royce and a Volkswagen; both go down the highway, but the Rolls is smooth—that was Aaron. He was a Rolls Royce. If it hadn't been for Roberto Clemente, Aaron would have won all the Gold Gloves."

Boyer also named his top outfield arms in Clemente, Kaline, Roger Maris, and Carl Furillo.

CATCHERS IN GENERAL

Jason Kendall made more appearances behind the Pirates home plate than any catcher in the long history of the Bucs. When asked what was the *single* most difficult part of his job, he replied, "Everything about it. You can never be satisfied. You gotta keep working and keep doing what you can to do better."

When PNC Park in Pittsburgh opened in 2001, some members of the media pointed out that the backstop, with its irregular stone surface, could drive a catcher crazy on wild pitches. Kendall dismissed that facet of a catcher's problems: "Nah, everything's different, those things sometimes come into factor, but you can't worry. You check them out, but you can't do anything about it." Since the way a ball careens off such a surface is mostly a matter of chance, he felt it was futile to analyze pitches' reactions to hitting the backstop. "That's just the way they built it," he concluded, discarding it as a catcher's obstacle.

In 2009, Detroit catcher Gerald Laird led the AL by gunning down 42 percent of would-be base stealers. He said that footwork is a key for catchers, so he prepared a great deal in the offseason, but added, "I do a few things during the season, but here toward the end of the season I kind of get my workload down a little bit because I've been playing every day, and you're going to need that energy for the game. For the most part it's staying with routines and working with the strength coach and conditioning guys and keeping yourself in shape—just doing maintaining things so you can keep your quickness during the season."

Not unlike a prizefighter, who also relies upon quick feet, Laird jumped ropes, and said, "I do cones, I do step-ups, hops," plus exercise training, which helps produce fast and powerful motions, "just to keep my footwork as quick as I can."

In one area, though, being quick can be bad: "When you try to be too quick. Even in the big leagues, when you try to do too much and you see base stealers getting good jumps and you try to make up for that time, that's when you tend to be off a little bit—your throws tend to be wide.

"You just have the same footwork and the same transition as any time, and make the same accurate throw, and you're going to be more successful." When, for example, a catcher's throw tails, Laird said, it is "because you're out of mechanics, you try to do too much. The next thing your stride gets too long and your arm falls and the ball tails on you and takes off. It's just one of those things where I just try to make the same throw every time, and if the pitcher gives me a chance, usually I get him."

The old stereotypical image people had of catchers, especially at young levels of play, was one of squat, even chubby, lead-footed men—and some players, like the 230-pound Ernie Lombardi, did fit that bill. Even Yogi Berra had a dumpy appearance. Over the years, movies such as *The Sandlot* kept the stereotype alive.

All-Star Gregg Jefferies, who led the NL with 40 doubles in 1990, expressed how he saw the catcher's position: "Catchers are becoming more like shortstops; they're not the big, bulky guys—they're really the good athletes: the Mike Lieberthals, 'Pudge' [Ivan Rodriguez], Brad Ausmus, Charles Johnson, Jason Kendall, guys like that. [Kendall reached a personal high of 26 steals in 1998, 12 shy of John Wathan's season record by a catcher in 1982.]

"You look at those guys and they're not real big power guys, body-wise, like they used to be in the 1980s, like Gary Carter and Lance Parrish. Now you got some catchers that can steal bases."

The 6-foot-2, 215-pound Charles Johnson was special. He won four Gold Gloves in a row, beginning in his rookie season of 1995, and only two men ever caught more than his handling of three no-hitters. The Marlins' first number-one draft pick in their initial draft of 1992, he once gunned down 48 percent of would-be base stealers. He listed two attributes great receivers must have: "Instincts really make you good at what you do, and good footwork. Those are the big keys."

Johnson pulverized a thirty-eight-year-old Yogi Berra record of accepting 950 consecutive chances as a catcher across a career without an error by handling 1,294 errorless chances. In 1997, he also broke the record for the most consecutive errorless games behind the plate in a season (123) and yet another single-season record of handling 973 chances flawlessly. Tom Verducci wrote that Johnson "had more E's in his first name than on his stat sheet."[1]

Only one passed ball in 1997 prevented him from becoming the first catcher ever to go an entire season without an error or passed ball. Ironically, he committed an error in the season opener of the following season. Overall, he had gone 172 games without a miscue.

His training as a youngster was rigorous, leading to many bruises and worse. He worked on blocking balls in the dirt diligently, learning how to position himself. His father even taught him not to flinch or blink. The lesson wasn't learned easily—his father used a pitching machine to propel myriad balls against his mask (and his chest protector, and at the ground in front of him), often from close range.

Johnson said, "As a catcher, you look at other guys—their setups, their unique ways of doing things. There are a lot of guys I respect." He mentioned Jason Varitek, who is tied for having caught the most no-hitters ever (with 4), John Flaherty, and Jorge Posada as "solid catchers. I like a lot of young guys, too, like Bengie Molina."

Bengie drew this praise in a 2000 interview, four years before his brother Yadier joined him and a third catcher of the family, José, in the majors. What a bloodline: Yadier starred for nineteen seasons, José for fifteen, and Bengie for ten. Bengie won two Gold Glove Awards, while Yadier turned heads, winning nine, plus four Platinum Gloves. Only Ivan Rodriguez (thirteen) and Johnny Bench (ten) have more Gold Glove trophies on display than Yadier Molina.

While pitchers don't want fat, immobile catchers, seven-year veteran sidearm hurler Mike Koplove said, "I prefer a larger guy back there—big targets are obviously good because it gives you more to aim at. As long as their target is low, that's fine, because that's where my sights are."

Koplove said that pitchers feel the ideal catcher has certain qualities: "Other than their arm and throwing runners out, their hands—the way that they catch the ball so that they frame it."

Framing the ball improperly or properly, he said, "will cost you or help you get a couple of strikes here and there throughout a game. Younger guys don't know how to catch the ball properly, and you lose those pitches—I think at least two an inning when I come out of the bullpen, all the time. A lot of times borderline pitches come down to the way the catcher presents the ball to the umpire."

The art of framing also includes the knowledge of when to try to steal a strike from umpires. "Obviously they have to know if it's way off the plate, they're not going to get it, but if it's an inch or two, they can just sort of move their hand slightly. And hopefully they'll get the call for you."

Koplove also spoke of the toughest pitches to frame: "In and out are a little bit easier, but the low pitch, kind of lifting it up, and the high pitch, pulling it down, seem to be the hardest pitches."

The best catchers in the game, such as the 5-foot-11, 225-pound Yadier Molina, gave his pitchers everything they'd want, year in and year out. Among other attributes, he was agile and mobile, and he defied opponents to run on him. Lifetime, he threw out 40 percent of all the runners who dared attempt steals, with glistening season highs of 64.1 percent and 54 percent.

CATCHERS WORKING WITH PITCHERS

Eddie Perez was Greg Maddux's personal catcher, handling the first man to win four straight Cy Young Awards more times—by far—than any other catcher. Perez was able to help Maddux, he said, by stressing one simple key: "Being prepared. If you're prepared to block pitches, if you're prepared to throw guys out at second, and if you're prepared to catch the ball, you don't need anything else."

Maddux could throw sharp breaking stuff in or near the dirt with little worries with Perez as his catcher. Likewise, Maddux was never strong at holding runners on first base, but Perez was prepared to try to prevent a conga line of base stealers from hurting Maddux.

Kyle Davies was in the majors for eight years, but he always remembered his first days on the hill. He said younger pitchers do tend to trust their catchers when they're starting out. Some allow the catchers to call every pitch, never shaking off a sign.

"Coming out of the bullpen it's easier to do that," he said, "but when you're starting, you kind of have to play your game plan—whatever's working that day is what you want to go back to. And you've got to make adjustments [when the plan falters]. Your catcher will help you out there—they know the hitters and what's going on.

"But when you're a reliever, you kind of go right after them, and the catcher who's been in the game for seven or eight innings has a better idea of what's working and how to get these guys out, better than you do."

After a few starts, Davies began to shake his catcher off a few times. At inning's end, back in the dugout, his catcher—either Johnny Estrada or Brian McCann—would explain their pitch calls. "They'd say, 'This is what I was thinking,' and we'd go back and forth. They'd want to know what I was thinking, just so we'd be on the same page."

Davies called such moments good learning experiences and appreciated his catchers' "different perspective, too. Maybe I wasn't even thinking [like them]. Maybe they called for a totally different location, totally different pitch. My catcher obviously is a lot closer to the batter, so he can see stuff that I can't."

As for pitchers becoming much less dependent upon their receivers and basically calling their own game, Davies said that simply "comes with experience; I don't know when that's going to be."

In short, said Ausmus, "The best catchers take pride in their defense, take pride in working with their pitcher, and they do all they can to help their pitching staff through the course of the season."

Down-under pitcher Kent Tekulve said that when he pitched, his catchers occasionally prevented his low pitches from becoming wild pitches. One of his catchers, Manny Sanguillen, had the uncanny ability to hunker lower to the ground than a limbo dancer, yet that prowess, although an attribute, wasn't crucial to Teke's game.

"Not really," he said. "I mean, I don't think it was as important for us [submariners] as it was for the power pitchers because our idea was we wanted the guy to hit the ball. We didn't want him to swing and miss. The catcher was more back there for a target, something to aim at, to throw at, but you wanted the guy to hit it. So actually, the successful pitches were the ones that never got to the catcher anyway—those were the ground balls in the infield."

CATCHERS' VALUE TO CLUBS

Brad Ausmus was well known for his baseball instincts and deft footwork. No player sticks around for eighteen seasons unless he is a valuable commodity. Not only did he persist that long (1993 through 2010), he earned three Gold Gloves and topped all catchers at least once in every defensive stat commonly quoted—for instance, he once gunned down 49.5 percent of would-be base thieves.

The media has often said an excellent defensive catcher (or shortstop) could hit in the neighborhood of .200 and still be an asset to his club. Ausmus replied with a chuckle, "Well, nobody wants to hit .200, but you can't really put stats on calling a game—it's not the type of thing that you can track. It's easy to track home runs and RBI or average, but it's not as easy to track the effect that a catcher can have through the course of a season just by calling a game and working with the pitching staff."

Ausmus must have wished that there was a definitive way to statistically measure—say, the number of runs he saves during a season by, among other things, smothering wild pitches. "That's something there *is* no stat for: a guy who consistently keeps a ball in the dirt in front of him, doesn't allow runners to move up, doesn't allow a runner from third to score."

Plus, a catcher who can prevent balls from getting by him will instill confidence in his pitchers, especially those who throw the ball low, such as sinkerball or split-finger-type pitchers.

It's not even fair to judge a catcher by his percentage of runners caught stealing. As Ausmus noted, "It depends a lot on the pitching staff"—referring to the fact that if a staff isn't good at holding runners on base, preventing them from getting good jumps, there isn't much a catcher can do to stop a parade of base burglars.

Another way to halt runners, said Ausmus, is simple: "A lot of times your reputation for being able to throw can control the running game as much as anything. Opposing managers will be more conservative in their attempts."

One such catcher managers dreaded to see was Ivan Rodriguez. With him behind the plate, Rangers manager Johnny Oates said he could afford to use outside-of-the-box thinking. Oates said he would play the infield back in situations that normally wouldn't call for that strategy simply because nobody would run against Rodriguez—sometimes even when the first baseman was playing in somewhat, not holding a runner tight to the bag.

Ausmus could relate to that because, as he said, "Pudge is in a whole other league when it comes to throwing guys out. He's got a great arm and he's extremely quick, so there's no question he changes the running game completely." As a bonus, said Matt Diaz, when it comes to preventing wild pitches, of all the catchers around, "it's Pudge—you gotta give Pudge that one."

Not only are runners reluctant to run on Rodriguez, they are often timid when it comes to taking their leads. Oates said that translates to saving runs—for example, "picking guys off second base means they won't get too big of a lead—primary lead or secondary lead." That means they may not be able to score on a clean single if they only had the luxury of being less fearful of Rodriguez on the base paths, but caution against that catcher was necessary. Likewise, a runner glued near first base in fear of Pudge may not be able to scamper first to third on a single that normally would have allowed him to do so.

In one tie game, Oates pulled his infield in when the Oakland A's got a man on third base, a move he made largely based on who his catcher was. Oates wanted to make it more difficult for the A's to score, but he also knew it's easier to get a grounder through a drawn-in infield—and he had to consider thwarting a big rally consisting of a string of hits.

"Ben Grieve was coming up to hit and there was one out. It was a situation where you want to make them earn a run." Oates said he wasn't too concerned about a big inning if Grieve did get a hit to drive in a run. "You don't have to worry about him stealing second," which could lead to another run or two getting tacked on; however, said Oates, "with Pudge catching, I *know* he's not going to steal second, because if he does run, Pudge is going to throw him out." Case closed.

Oates spoke of another subtle advantage Pudge gave managers: "Edgar Martínez was on first and you got [the left-handed hitter] John Olerud hitting. We can play our first baseman behind Edgar any time we want because he can't steal with Olerud hitting, and having the first baseman play off the bag enables him to have better fielding range."

Oates concluded with a sort of no-brag, just-fact observation of Rodriguez: "If you're a below average runner, he can let you start from halfway to second and you still can't make it."

Aggressive catchers such as Rodriguez (and Yadier Molina for another strong example) keep runners on their tippy-toed spikes, knowing a snap throw behind them to pick them off was an ever-present tactic of the great throwing, aggressive catchers. Ausmus summed up, "As a baserunner it changes you. You don't get as big of a secondary lead, you're less aggressive, you don't want to get caught napping."

GLOVES

Terry Francona, the winning manager of the 2004 and 2007 World Series when he was the Red Sox skipper, got an early start in baseball.

When he was seven years old, he was the only kid on the field to own a major league glove. That's because his father, Tito, a veteran of fifteen seasons, handed it down to him.

Francona remembered the glove's perfect pocket and just how it became just right. "The pocket was always like blackish-brown. My dad had spit tobacco into it probably for years, and rubbed it with pine tar. You could run that glove over with a truck, and the pocket was going to stay nice."

Francona spoke of the importance of using the right glove: "It almost needs to be your best friend. If your glove doesn't feel good, then good luck. Everybody's different, but when it's yours and it feels right, it just feels right."

Players have various methods to tailor their gloves, to get them just right. One of Francona's pitchers once placed a softball inside the pocket of his glove, wrapped it up securely, then put it in a washing machine for a good breaking-in process. Once the pocket is suitable to users, players typically don't use the glove for more than a few seasons at most.

Players are usually quite loyal to their glove brands and makers, and they are *very* protective of their gloves. Francona put it this way, "Some guys—middle infielders—you put their glove on, they'd want to fight you."[2] Boston star shortstop Nomar Garciaparra was fussy about his glove, fearing other hands inside it would stretch it out too much.

Players are, of course, the best judges of how they want their gloves to fit. Cleveland coach Mike Sarbaugh said middle infielders know a glove is game ready when, and only when, they have no difficulty closing the glove on backhand plays.

A glove's life actually depends largely on what position the player holds down as well as the player's personal taste. Some, like second baseman Bill Mazeroski, an eight-time Gold Glove winner, hold on to a treasured piece of leather for a very long time. Seventeen-year veteran infielder Juan Castro once used a six-year-old glove.

In 2007, Scott Hatteberg commented, "I was a catcher for a lot of years, and I'd go through a couple mitts a year. First base mitt? I've had one for all last year and parts of this year, so I would say [my mitts last] a year and a half.

"Each glove, even though they might be the same model, isn't built the same. They all feel a little different and are going to, most likely, break in a little different. So if you get one that you like, you have a tendency to kinda just patch it and re-leather it."

Hatteberg said that he knew it was time to give his gloves their last rites "when it gets to a point when they lose their density or their rigidity and they get a little too flimsy and they kinda lose the life to them. It needs to have a little bit of stiffness, and it's a personal preference, too, but you'll know."

Another catcher, Kelly Shoppach, said, "Mine last me about a month, maybe two; depends on how much I play. I don't like a floppy glove; I like my glove to be real firm. I don't like it to be worn out. Somebody told me a story about Pat Borders the other day. He would get new gloves then trade one of the young kids for an old, beat-up glove because he liked his real old. So it's just a personal preference."

Pitchers naturally don't put much wear and tear on their gloves. All-Star Bronson Arroyo said, "I think a lot of guys probably use one a year; some guys will use one their whole career. I've been using the same one for about three years now."

Of course, players are always breaking in a new glove, ready to replace their game glove. Shoppach said, "Yep, I've always got *two* breaking in and I have two that are game ready."

DEFENDING AGAINST OPPONENTS' TENDENCIES

Craig Biggio played in a time when analytics to help defend against opponents' tendencies was important, but far from as scientific as it is now—call it the difference between the days of early, clunky computers such as UNIAC versus today's "Intel inside" era.

He said, "The charts that they have, if a guy hits a ball in the air, they usually know where it's going. If they hit it on the ground, they know where it's going. If he hits it the other way, you just tip your cap."

Infield shifts were used during Biggio's big-league tenure, but not widely. Some left-handed, dead pull hitters such as Jim Thome were victimized by shifts, but not a ton of hitters had the burden of trying to avoid hitting into the teeth of an exaggerated shift.

Back in 2000, Arizona manager Buck Showalter had already witnessed home run orgies such as Mark McGwire's 70 home runs struck in 1998. Showalter may not have personally inked the handwriting on the wall, but he could read it clearly, recognizing a power trend and how it would impact shifts.

The game was changing, which brought to mind the old baseball logic about defending against power hitters, which paraphrased basically translates to: "You can play them deep (or shift them), but you can't play them high enough." The big boppers would repeatedly try to beat the shift by hitting over—*way over*—them.

Showalter observed, "I think with the home run being such a prevalent thing in today's game, more guys are more likely to stay with an approach to hitting regardless of what you do defensively." So instead of beating the shift by, say, bunting down the undefended third base line for a single (or even a double, depending upon how far over into center the left fielder is stationed), sluggers continued to swing from the heels and for the fences—strikeouts be damned.

"They're not going to say, 'Okay, you're playing over there, I'm going to [place the pitch elsewhere].' They're going to say, 'The last time I looked, you can't put outfielders in the stands, so I'm going to try to hit the ball where grass doesn't grow.' You can't defend a home run. It's like trying to defend a foul ball—there's no reason to try to do it."

So, did he feel the shift was worthwhile—be it against power hitters or contact hitters? "I think what you try to do when a guy gets a track record of being able to do something [is react to that]," he said. "It's obvious that a guy who hits .330 every year makes a living out of hitting the ball where people don't play him. So if you play him straight up, they're going to hit .330 against you, too. So you're better off trying to put some people where they don't normally play." In other words, move them around, even to the extent of shifting drastically. "You try to get in their head a little bit."

Of course, the shift issue became moot when it was outlawed prior to the 2023 season.

Biggio did note that the shifts he saw on display by around 2000 or so were more plentiful than when he broke in back in 1988: "It seems like when I started, we had more power pitchers, more strikeout pitchers. You had Nolan Ryan, Mike Scott, guys like that who struck out a lot of guys, so you didn't have to worry so much about a shift." Biggio said that when such strikeout artists retired, "you have to play for the defense, and that's probably one of the main reasons for the shifts."

CHAPTER FOUR

Managers

QUALITIES OF GOOD MANAGERS

Vern Law, who played sixteen years, all with the Pirates, spent more time under World Series–winning manager Danny Murtaugh than under any other manager. Law knew how vital it is for managers to "know what each player is capable of doing, and then they try to get them in a ball game in which they can succeed rather than fail. We had that in Murtaugh. Not all managers have that ability. The effective guys have the ability to communicate; they let you know where you stand, and those kinds of managers are the ones that are successful."

Sparky Anderson played just one big-league season, hitting a mere .218 and slugging (if you can call it that) at a lowly .249 rate. That season, in 1959, he set a record for the player with the fewest hits compiled over a 154-game schedule, just 104, with all but 12 going for singles. However, his people skills placed him on the road to the Hall of Fame as a wonderful manager. He won four pennants and became the first manager to win the world championship in both leagues.

Though he was nicknamed "Captain Hook" for his propensity to pull his starting pitchers and go to his bullpen frequently, he said that one key to his success was patience: "You can't push or rush young people. They shouldn't have pressure on them to do it all yet."

In 2000, when Buck Showalter was managing the Diamondbacks, he, too, knew patience was needed with rookies who have plenty on their plate. "Young players are going to get tested with fastballs, especially soon after their arrival," he said. "And after that, if they show they can handle that, then pitchers are going to throw the kitchen sink at them." He realized that the good ones would make it—it's baseball's version of survival of the fittest in a world where only the strong survive.

One of Jim Leyland's strong points was his ability to evaluate talent and to put together a balanced squad. He managed quite a few sluggers, but knew how important defense was, too. Managing before the days of both leagues using the designated hitter (DH), Leyland said, "I think defense was always a big thing with me because I ended up managing in the National League, a place where you need as many two-way players as you can get. And by that I mean offense as well as defense. In the American League, you can hide a player by way of the DH now and then."

Kent Tekulve once said that everything on a baseball club filters through the manager. Luis Gonzalez expanded on that theme: "I think the managers are the ones that lead the ship. They're the ones in charge—you're in charge of your own actions as a player, but the managers are always the ones that are held accountable if a team's not playing well. When a team's not playing good, you never hear that the manager's doing a good job, it's always when they're playing bad, 'They're not making the right decisions,' and things like that.

"So players have a lot of responsibility, and I'm sure the managers have a lot of trust in their players, hoping that they can go out there and do the job." Gonzalez felt that one of the most demanding parts of a manager's job is "just hoping that your players are smart enough to kind of police themselves in the locker room and keep things in order. I think most teams that do well, the managers don't really have to worry about the players that much—they know that when they go out there to play, they're going to give their best effort and do everything they can.

"You're not going to win every game—this is the big leagues, and certain things happen on particular nights, but all they ask is that you go out there and play hard and try to concentrate and bear down and come up big in clutch situations when they need you."

Even though Gene Mauch has been vilified for blowing a 6½-game lead his 1964 Phillies held with just 12 games to go, he was still recognized as a tremendous manager. Four teams hired him, and he lasted twenty-six seasons. It's been said that no other manager knew the rulebook inside out as well as he did.

Baseball lifer Mike Cubbage, who played for Mauch, called him "the most brilliant man I've ever been around in a baseball uniform, real sharp." As a bonus, he was good with the media, a job that should never be underrated. "He always had fresh quotes for the media," Cubbage said. "He didn't just say the old, standard, hackneyed expressions that you hear from a lot of managers. He had a lot of original material, and he was a real bright guy who was dedicated to the game."

PLAYERS WHO MAKE THE BEST MANAGERS

Many experts believe catchers, who are the only players who can see (and direct) all the other eight men on the field, make the best managers. This theory gained steam around the turn of the century, when former catchers monopolized World Series titles.

From 1996 through 2003, managers who had been pro catchers won a staggering eight straight world championships: Joe Torre did it four times, while Jim Leyland, Bob Brenly, Mike Scioscia, and Jack McKeon each won one World Series ring.

Over the nine seasons from 2009 through 2017, former catchers won it all seven times: Bruce Bochy three times, and Joe Girardi, Ned Yost, A. J. Hinch, and Joe Maddon once each. (Brian Snitker would add his name to the list in 2021.) Not only that, from 1998 through 2022, former catchers won pennants but not the World Series an additional eleven times. Finally, from 1998 through 2014, the managers who met in the World Series were both former catchers on five occasions. Front offices sought out the men who wore what's been mislabeled "the tools of ignorance."

Torre's credentials—six pennants and four world championships—are impeccable. He mentioned that his experience as a player helped him because "I hit .360 once. I also hit .240. So I think I can communicate with a lot of those players in between."

In a 2003 interview, Luis Gonzalez pointed out that former catchers are highly attuned to the game and its nuances "because of the fact that they were the ones that were calling pitches, and they had to be involved with everything—the infield, checking the outfield, the hitters."

That doesn't mean men who play other positions can't become good managers. Gonzalez continued, "There are other guys. I think Mark Grace could be a great manager when he's done playing because he relates to the players and knows a lot about the game. And I think if you've been in the war and been out there and played on an everyday basis, you're pretty much qualified to be a manager up here."

There have been many critics who say that as a rule, pitchers, who aren't on diamonds daily and are mainly wrapped up in one dimension of the game, do not make good managers. From 1989 through 2012, not one former pitcher/manager won a World Series, and only five have ever won it all. All-Star reliever Mike Stanton understood the logic, but didn't totally agree, especially concerning the men who work out of the bullpen.

"Obviously we [relievers] have to pay attention to the game," he said. "With the possibility of being in there every day, you have to really pay attention.

"A lot of times, the starters were starting all their lives. I didn't pitch until I got into college, so I was a position player. Even in college I played a little bit out in the field, so you have a different outlook on the game. And you get to learn the nuances of the game and the little things that go on in the field, whereas if you're just a starting pitcher, you're just a pitcher, and you know you have no chance of getting in the game, so you're not going to pay as much attention. That's just human nature, even as a kid."

During the years when only the AL utilized designated hitters, he said relievers could excel as managers: "Especially an American League manager. Basically, he makes out his lineup and he works his bullpen; that's the job."

Gonzalez said that as a pretty firm rule, the one type of personality that is no longer conducive to effective managing is that of the old-school, my-way-or-the-highway mentality. But couldn't a man with a drill-sergeant leaning conceivably succeed in the twenty-first century? Gonzalez said, "I think it all comes on reputation. Everybody knows Lou Piniella and the way he played. Everybody knows Buddy Bell and the way he played.

"There are certain guys as managers now whose reputations preceded them because of the way they were as players—Art Howe and guys like that, Felipe Alou, and Bob Brenly. You knew what type of attitude they took every time they took to the field. In Lou Piniella's case he was a hard-nosed player who played hard and was demanding of his teammates a lot as a player. You knew he was going to take a stance like that as a manager. It just all depends on what kind of team you have."

A team packed with young players has different needs than a veteran squad. Gonzalez gave the example of Alan Trammell running a young Detroit Tigers team: "He's patient. I think if you had more of a hard-line manager the young kids would be on pins and needles, so I think they've hired the right guy because he's good with kids. He knows how to work with the younger players and develop them."

Trammell was wise enough to hire a contrasting coach to complement his personality in Kirk Gibson. "I think Tram wanted him to come on board just to kind of give a different approach—maybe toughen some of these young kids up.

"And it's not a bad fit. I mean, you have two sides of the coin—you have Trammell, who went about his business very quietly but spoke with a loud stick and glove, and then you have Gibby, who's a very emotional guy and showed his colors when he went out there and played—and wasn't afraid to yell at somebody, or get pissed off, or charge the mound if he had to. When you've got good coaches, it makes your job a lot easier."

Gonzalez also felt the old theory that star players don't make good managers is wrong and that Trammell, for one, dispels that notion. "You look now and most of the managers are [former] catchers," he said, "but at the same time a guy like Trammell knows the game; he played in the middle of the infield, so he had to be on top of the game." Gonzalez felt that a man can be both a great player and teacher/manager: "It just all comes down to patience and attitude."

POWER HITTERS' INFLUENCE

Any manager loves having a slugger batting in the heart of his order. For various reasons, some managers have been known to put some power hitters atop the order. Examples include Bobby Bonds, Kyle Schwarber, Mookie Betts, and George Springer. Willie Mays and Aaron Judge have even batted leadoff on some occasions.

Charlie Manuel guided the Phillies to the 2008 world championship. He spoke beyond the obvious importance of having power hitters in a lineup, factoring in how much the very existence of a powerful hitter in the lineup means to the rest of the lineup: "Ryan Howard's presence puts fear in the opposition, it also gives our team a lift to know we've got a guy in the lineup who, every time he walks up to the plate, is capable of hitting the ball out of the yard." That, he felt, becomes contagious, permeating the lineup. "When he's hitting, it definitely breeds confidence, a chain reaction—they'll get happy and start hitting with him."

Danny Tartabull said power hitters are helped when "you have other power hitters around you in the batting order to protect you"—think Murderer's Row or the 2023 Braves, for example.

HANDLING PLAYERS

Alex Grammas managed Hank Aaron in 1976 when the reigning lifetime home run king was playing out the string of his marvelous twenty-three-year career in the city where he began his pro days, Milwaukee, but this time with the Brewers, having been traded by Atlanta for Dave May.

Grammas said there "was no problem at all with Aaron. He probably knew it was going to be his last year. I wish that I could have done a better job, but as far as Hank was concerned, hell, he was as good as they come. A good-natured guy—he was a lot like Stan Musial, a friendly guy—he was just a good person."

Some aging superstars dictate to their manager what days they want to play. Aaron, said Grammas, "didn't do that. As I recall, we talked—probably said, 'If you don't feel like playing, let me know,' or something like that, because he was getting up in age and, what the hell, when you played as many years as he had, you're going to get tired. The door was wide open for him."

Jeromy Burnitz, who crushed 315 home runs, felt that modern managers face more friction from both the great players and even the average players than managers of long ago. "Yeah, without a doubt," he said. "I mean, the manager is now expendable, and the players are not because we have guaranteed contracts that are worth a lot of money. So the player knows that he's not going anywhere because they're not going to just send you home with your paycheck. I think that, in and of itself, is the reason why the manager is going to take more flak."

They also must put up with, or usually just ignore, the second-guessing some players do while watching games unfold. Burnitz commented, "That's probably something that's never changed. *Absolutely*, players do that. That's just human nature, unfortunately. I mean, that happens in probably every walk of life. It's certainly not just baseball where people second-guess their bosses' decisions. And, yeah, it's usually after the fact that the decision [the manager] made ended up being the wrong one. It's easy to say, 'I wouldn't have done that.' But yes, I believe that happens an awful lot, and it's probably been that way from the get-go."

TEAM MEETINGS

One strategy managers use at times is the closed-door meeting, which serves such purposes as chewing out a team or clearing the air by saying, "Hey, let's stop this skid. What can we as a team do to get back on track?"

Luis Gonzalez said such meetings can be effective "because managers care. At the same time, how you play pretty much reflects on a manager. I think managers all have pride and they want to go out and win, but it just all comes down to the manager can only fill the lineup card out." Much hinges, he said, on the "effort that he gets . . . from his players, and they have to be accountable and responsible for the way they go out there and play."

On the other hand, sometimes the players will initiate a closed-door meeting and their manager is *not* invited—which can signal problems for the manager. Gonzalez felt otherwise: "No, I don't think so. It's just leadership—it leads more to 'Let's get it together, we got to turn the ship around.'

"I think players are more open to that now because they kind of police themselves in [the clubhouse] and sometimes it takes something like that, a little wakeup call, because you play 162 games, and this is your family in here, your second family. Sometimes you're around these guys more than you are your wife and kids because of travel and spring training and things like that. So you got to learn to get along.

"There's going to be times when things get a little tense in the locker rooms with players having arguments, but as quick as you can put that fire out and get everybody back on the same page, that makes a winning club."

He stated further that players-only meetings, "usually called for by veterans," aren't necessarily called for by a team captain or a take-charge leader on the team: "It just all depends—it depends what it's about and who feels like it's necessary to call it. Players are always open to that."

He said such meetings are not as rare as the average fan might believe. "It depends," he said. "If you're playing well, there's no need to have something like that, but when times are tough, sometimes you gotta close those doors and let guys air things out and just let them know how you feel and what's going on in your mind and other players' minds. Usually those things work out pretty well."

MANAGING A BULLPEN

Kent Tekulve was a durable, dependable reliever who, in 1987, at the age of forty, became the oldest pitcher to lead his league in appearances. Twelve times he finished in the top ten for games pitched, with a season high of 94. Upon his retirement, only Hoyt Wilhelm had worked in more games than Tekulve's 1,050.

He was clearly the type of pitcher who wanted the ball in his hands, but he said that for him, the ideal work schedule was this: "I never work three games in a row, and I never sit three days in a row." Under his plan, he would avoid being overworked and would not accumulate rust perched on a bullpen bench. Any wise manager would keep this concept in mind in handling his relievers.

Now, what if a manager's bullpen had, say, three men who were all experienced closers. How do you keep them all happy? The answer is mixed, and sometimes you simply can't.

When Sparky Lyle was with the Yankees in 1977, he was the undisputed king of the world champion's bullpen hill. Never satisfied and always seeking to gobble up more and more talent, Yankees owner George Steinbrenner signed the Cooperstown-bound Goose Gossage for the 1978 season. Gossage then got the bulk of the vital work out of the pen, leading the AL with 27 saves and 55 games finished, while Lyle had just 9 saves and wrapped up 33 contests. It was time for the 1977 Cy Young Award winner to say sayonara—he was sent packing to the Texas Rangers. There wasn't room for these two closers in the New York bullpen.

On the other hand, in 2007, Philadelphia's Charlie Manuel had an overload of men with experience as closers, and he was initially faced with determining a viable workload without stepping on egos. He did so, winning the National League East with former firemen Tom Gordon (who led the AL with 46 saves and 69 games finished in 1998), Antonio Alfonseca (who had saved 45 games to top the NL in 2000), and José Mesa (the 1995 AL leader in saves, with 46, and games finished, with 57).

Early in the season Manuel felt a juggling act of relievers would not "be that big a challenge. Basically, for me, these guys have all been closers, and if you look back, and if you think about it, they know what closing the game is—and actually, closing the game starts in the seventh inning. That's when you do your job, and actually you're stopping the game for where the next guy takes over, [allowing the team] to get to the ninth inning.

"And the guy who finishes the ninth inning gets credit for being the closer, but actually the game really starts, from a closer's standpoint and for me, in the seventh inning. Once your starter leaves the game, that's when you start working to close the game out, and no matter how many pitchers you use, they did the job on that day closing the game.

"I know the guy who finishes the game and is recognized as the big closer might make more money, but if you do a job from the seventh inning and eighth inning on, unofficially you will be a closer."

To be honest, none of the three men wound up as the team's closer (that was Brett Myers, with 21 saves), but Manuel did get 15 total saves and about forty-three innings apiece from the former closers.

UNORTHODOX STRATEGY

If necessity is the mother of invention, then a manager's vexing situation is the father of unorthodoxy. In 1968 Detroit manager Mayo Smith was faced with a perplexing situation, even though he had breezed to a pennant with 103 wins.

His outfield was strong, with Al Kaline in right, Mickey Stanley in center, and Willie Horton in left, but an injury to Kaline resulted in Jim Northrup playing in right field more often than Kaline. Smith had four outfielders but only three spots out there and no DH rule to fall back on.

Stanley finished the regular season having played 130 contests in center field, all errorless games, earning a Gold Glove Award for his play. So when the World Series began, where did Smith use him? At shortstop.

He had actually begun placing Stanley at shortstop late in the season, even though Stanley had never played the position even once as a pro. So Stanley replaced Ray Oyler, who had hit a meager .135 for the season. That risky move meant Northrup could play center and add his 21 homers and 90 ribbies to the World Series lineup, flanked by Horton and Kaline.

Stanley did an adequate job at shortstop in the Series, while Northrup hit 2 homers and led the Tigers with his 8 runs batted in. Detroit overcame the Cardinals' three games to one advantage to charge back and win it all. The *Boston Globe* called Smith's strategic juggling "the gutsiest move in history."[1]

Horton recalled the specifics of the moves, remembering that Kaline had played in only 102 games that season. "That was a smart move," he said. "We wanted to get Al in the game because he was hurt that summer. We wanted him to get in the World Series. We wanted that move, but we didn't know who wanted to move to shortstop, and Mayo made the decision with Stanley, which was the best decision because he was the best athlete on the team."

Thirty-five years after the Tigers' stunning comeback, Horton said, "Mickey was in center field for many years. I don't know if I could have done that, but Mickey's a good athlete. You see him today, you see his body, and you'll say he's a great athlete.

"The move took a lot of guts, but I'll tell you, it was something that we all wanted—we adjusted to it. We had been talking about it for a week or two, 'How are we gonna get Kaline in the lineup?'

"Everybody says, 'Well, how did Ray Oyler feel?' He wanted it, too. He didn't feel bad. People don't realize it takes a whole team to win, and whether you're on the bench or you're part-time, pinch hitter, or whatever, we had that chemistry, a team."

It was clear with superstar Kaline returning that *some* move had to be made to get him back in the outfield. Had Stanley not moved to short, said Horton, "I guess you'd have to reshuffle the outfield. Al kinda said, 'What's going on?' because he was a father to all of us and he's a team guy. He kinda said he appreciated it, but he wanted to let us go, let the guys go that had been winning. It wasn't none of Al Kaline's doing, but it worked out good for all of us."

An old baseball adage states, "The ball will find you." That means that when a manager puts a poor fielder into a game, often trying to "hide" him at a not-too-busy position such as left field, sooner or later (seemingly sooner more than later) the ball will be hit to that man. Shortstop is a key position, so Smith was gambling that the ball wouldn't "find" Stanley and hurt the Tigers. Turns out the first ball put in play, a sharp grounder off the bat of Lou Brock, was hit to Stanley, who threw him out. Later, Stanley did commit two errors, but harmless ones. The experiment worked.

GENERAL STRATEGIES AND MANAGERIAL OPINIONS
Wally Westlake was an All-Star in 1951 for the St. Louis Cardinals. In a 2008 interview, he said how puzzled he was by how much baseball's strategies had changed over the years: "I can't believe the way they play

the game in this day. They don't take pitches like they used to or hit and run, and I don't know how long it's been since I've seen a suicide squeeze."

He knew, of course, that it's not easy to hit and run when so many batters aren't concerned about making contact. That season, for example, Mark Reynolds set a new and dubious record by fanning 204 times, the first time the 200 plateau had ever been attained. The next season, he upped the ante with 223 K's, still the all-time season record.

"Criminy! Two hundred times?" muttered Westlake. He was so flabbergasted because as a teammate of Stan Musial, he had never seen "The Man" fan more than 46 times in a year over his twenty-two-year career. Inconceivably, between 1920 and 1933, Joe Sewell played in 1,903 big-league games with 8,333 plate appearances and struck out just 114 *total times*, with a nadir one season of 3 strikeouts over 576 plate appearances, albeit in a different era.

In 2002, Bob Brenly was coming off his incredible performance as the manager of the world champion Diamondbacks, winning it all in his rookie season as a big-league skipper. He pointed out the difference between two once-popular managerial strategies.

He said that on the run and hit play, a manager wants to have a runner with the skill "to straight steal second base," in case the batter doesn't make contact with the pitch. "You definitely need a guy who can steal the base." By way of contrast, he said that on the more commonly used hit and run play, "you're counting on that batter to protect the runner—he's gotta put the ball in play somewhere, or at least put a swing on it to hold the catcher back. On the run and hit, you're just trying to straight steal the base, and the pressure is more on the hitter to make a judgment on whether to swing at the pitch or not."

Another ploy—taking a strike—seems to be dead, or at least at death's door, nowadays.

First, a strategic distinction: There's a difference between taking a pitch, usually with a count of 3-and-0, and taking a strike. At lower levels of baseball, if your team is losing late in the game and you are desperate to start a rally (especially against a pitcher who might be tiring and/or getting wild), a coach might instruct his batters not to swing at a pitch until the pitcher proves he can throw a strike. In other words, the batter is taking each and every pitch until there's a strike on him. Do—or did—major leaguers do this?

Alan Trammell said, "Certainly there are times to do this. I played for Sparky Anderson for seventeen years, and it was mandatory in the eighth and ninth inning if you were trailing to take a strike.

"There were a few exceptions: a guy like Dennis Eckersley, who, of course, would come in there and get strike one on you all the time. So you didn't want to give him one.

"But most of my career playing for Sparky, we'd take a strike. That's the 'old-school' way. That has changed somewhat depending on who's pitching nowadays, but, yes, you do take a strike."

Mike Bordick, a veteran of fourteen seasons through 2003, agreed about control pitchers: "Late in the game, especially when an established closer is in the game and his role is to get ahead, you don't do it." He cited examples of strike-throwing closers such as John Wetteland and Mariano Rivera.

Bordick said that taking a strike is not as common as it was in the days of Anderson, even against starters who are still in the game in the late innings. "Unless they've shown that they're tiring in the end, they're going to want to get ahead," he said, so they *will* try to throw a first-pitch strike.

Nowadays things have changed even more, as starters are rarely around in the late innings and so many teams insist on swinging for the fences rather than being a bit more discriminating, trying perhaps to draw a walk.

Likewise, the new logic dictates against putting on a suicide squeeze play when a deep drive might either go over the wall or at least produce a run on a sacrifice fly.

When Larry Rothschild managed the Tampa Bay Devil Rays in 1999, he said that for him the squeeze play was not dead: "It depends on your team [and game situation]. I'd squeeze here. If it is going to put you ahead going into the ninth inning, any way you can get ahead you take advantage of it."

He liked the play when it either gave his team the lead *or* brought home a late insurance run. In short, he favored the play "if the situation is where you feel it's your best chance to score that run. Maybe you're not comfortable with the hitter hitting a sac fly, or where the infield is playing, or whatever the elements might be dictating you to say, 'My best way to score right here is to squeeze.' The only thing you worry about is if they're going to pitch out, because *they* know it's your best chance, too."

Though today the squeeze play is pretty much roosting atop a dusty shelf gathering cobwebs, when it was used more often, managers took into consideration the all-important count on their bunters. In 1998, Mike Hargrove said if a player like Omar Vizquel was at the plate, "I think with a 2–0 count I'd give him one swing—see if he couldn't get a base hit or drive the ball in the outfield. If you got to 2–1, yeah, you'd think about a squeeze." Other favorable counts include 1–0, 3–0 at times, and even on occasion a full count.

Hargrove said the squeeze was an option some of the time, but "the American League does play for the big inning. You've got high average hitters and run producers, so you're really kind of cutting your nose off to spite your face if you play for one run all the time. It doesn't do you any good to squeeze with a Jim Thome or a David Justice. You've got to have the personnel that fits a squeeze situation."

Hargrove also said that he felt that even with his powerful Indians lineup around the 1995 time period, "there *are* times you'll play for one run. It depends on who's pitching for the other team and what point in the game it is."

On the other hand, he agreed with those who contend the safety squeeze play is pretty much a relic. In that play, the runner from third base doesn't break toward the plate as soon as the pitcher begins his delivery, but waits until after the bunter makes contact with the pitch. Hargrove said that play is discarded because "it's a real chancy play," explaining that it's too easy for the runner to get nailed at the plate. "It's a tough play—you're willing to take gambles, take risks, but to me the safety squeeze is one of those where you better be really desperate if you're going to use it." While it was a play used long ago from time to time, Hargrove said, "it was a different game then than it is now."

In 1999, Orioles manager Ray Miller described a no-win type of situation he and his peers sometimes faced: "Nowadays, your bench really only contains one hitter, one offensive guy, and sometimes you have a two-run lead, bases loaded in the eighth inning, and you've got Harold Baines on the bench. You say, 'Should I hit here? But I'm not going to because the game might get tied up and then Baines wins the game for you.'

"You know what you have, and you're prepared for it. And the thing is, if you hold him back, and later he gets a base hit, it was a good job of managing. If he doesn't, everybody says, 'Why the hell didn't you hit Baines in the eighth?' But you go with your gut feeling"—a gut feeling based on experience and knowledge of one's personnel.

That same season, Kansas City manager Tony Muser discussed going against the book, calling that a matter of "talking about taking risks. I think the longer you're in the game, the more you understand the percentages."

He said that a manager, in the end, has to go with his gut feeling and "be somewhat of a risk taker. You can't play the game the same way every day, because now you become predictable. If you don't try anything different, you never make a mistake. If you're always cautious in your managing, pretty soon your club turns out to be a cautious type club. If we're going to make mistakes, make aggressive mistakes, and take a risk once in a while."

Muser gave an example of a time he went against the book. Johnny Oates, the opposing Texas Rangers manager, had bunted a man over to second with one out and Rusty Greer at the plate. Muser intentionally walked Greer because "we needed a double play. They had Juan González coming up and he's leading the world in RBI. The only way out of the jam was a ground ball double play. We got our ground ball, but González hit it in the seam in between third and short and we got beat."

Muser was ripped, but said that with a ground ball pitcher on the mound, "I had confidence that we could get a ground ball. So I *will* pitch to the meat of the order [at times]. I think once in a while you have to do that. You can't pitch around people all the time. You're cutting your own throat in the American League if you do because [with the league's constant potential for high-scoring innings] the league is going to gouge teams' eyes out."

Oates scoffed at "the book," saying there was none as far as he was concerned. "I never read the book, so I don't know if something's against the book or not. You just do what your heart tells you, and sometimes what the numbers tell you."

One of his moves from the heart was "based on the feel of the dugout. We were down, 5–2, and the first two guys got on, and I had my Opening Day pitcher on the mound. And I just felt that if they scored another run there, the dugout was going to die. So I made a pitching change with the feel of the dugout being part of the decision making."

The ultimate, to-the-point comment about defying common strategy came from Jesse Orosco, who said, "If you do go 'off' the book, you better make sure it works."

MOVING RUNNERS UP

Playing for big innings and striving to jack the ball out of the park nowadays (and not having pitchers come to bat) means the sacrifice bunt is pretty much an archaic weapon, a slingshot in a nuclear world.

Compared to Carl Warwick's era in the 1960s, another move-the-runner strategy is less popular, too. He commented, "Back in those days, if you had a man on second base and no outs and you didn't try to hit a ball to right field to get him to third base up to two strikes, you got frowned on when you got in the dugout. You at least had to take a shot to right field or the right side of the infield. When you went up to bat, you didn't have to have a sign; you tried your best to get him to third base. We played the fundamentals. That is one of the things I see different now that they don't do any more." Forgive him if he comes off like an old-timer carping about today's game—his point about changing/evolving strategies remains true.

Clearly, the days when managers widely bought into the "get 'em on, get 'em over, get 'em in" approach are over.

Other Changes in Managerial Methods

Joe Cunningham was a two-time All-Star who played mainly for the St. Louis Cardinals. In a 2008 interview, he stated that in his era (1954–1966), "they didn't take starters out of the lineup to give you a rest. There was no such thing, and if you're a regular, you're playing every day and that was it. Now, sometimes managers are giving ballplayers rest in April."

There can be no doubt that front offices dictate that their multi-million-dollar investments be protected. Old-timers might whine that modern players are coddled, but what rational manager would risk ruining, say, their ace pitcher by overworking him? That's also true because pitchers are often fragile creatures.

In 1963, Warren Spahn, at age forty-two, and Juan Marichal locked up in a sixteen-inning game, with both men going the distance and a combined 428 pitches expended. (Willie Mays won it for Marichal, 1–0, on a home run.) Nolan Ryan is said to have thrown 259 pitches in a twelve-inning game once, but some sources say the record for total deliveries, although just an estimate, is 360. That came when Leon Cadore pitched a twenty-six-inning complete game in 1920—that game, the longest in big-league history, ended in a 1–1 tie, with the opposing pitcher, Joe Oeschger, also working all twenty-six innings. (By the way, despite the number of innings, the contest still came in under four hours—by ten minutes.)

Such numbers are now unthinkable. Adherence to strict pitch count limits and restrictions on total innings pitched is as big a part of today's game as playing for the big inning. In 2012, when Johan Santana, after missing all of the previous season due to injury, fired the first no-hitter in New York Mets history, he had to burn 134 pitches to get the job done. That total far exceeded what was the norm. He would never again pitch in the big leagues after that season, causing many to speculate that grueling outing caused the demise of his career.

Santana's June 1 no-hit performance lowered his ERA to 2.38. Subsequent outings resulted in him giving up 6 earned runs four times, 7 earned runs once, and a disastrous 1 1/3 innings start in which he was battered for 8 earned runs. That fiasco left him with a bloated season ERA of 4.85. His manager, Terry Collins, said of his decision to stick with Santana during the no-hit bid, "I respected him so much, I thought he deserved the chance to finish. I had guys warming up in the seventh. If there was a hit, he was out."[2]

While Collins agonized over his decision—and while he did give some consideration to relieving Santana—in earlier years, pulling a pitcher working on a no-hitter was just about unfathomable. Manager Preston Gomez made headlines when he defied that standard way of managing by yanking a starter from a gem in progress twice—both times for a pinch-hitter after eight no-hit innings—once when he was the San Diego Padres manager and another time when he was with the Houston Astros. In both cases, the bullpen lost the no-hitter.

In 2013, Jacob deGrom of the Texas Rangers made his fourth start of the season by throwing no-hit ball through four innings. The prospect of a complete-game no-hitter early in a season nowadays is highly unlikely, so when deGrom complained of soreness in his wrist on his pitching arm, the early hook came out.

When the highly touted Stephen Strasburg was in his first full season in 2012, his Nationals decided to keep the number of his innings pitched low, to a maximum of 160, in order to protect his arm. He averaged 93 pitches per game and threw as many as seven innings only five times—and never that many after July 25. In fact, despite making the playoffs, the team chose to shut his season down after a September 7 start with the Nats leading their division by 6 1/2 games.

Strasburg, a fifteen-game winner, wound up throwing 159 1/2 innings, making some wonder why Washington hadn't limited his innings down the stretch, perhaps by allowing him to miss an occasional start. Such a move may have enabled him to work in the postseason. They certainly could have used him there—they lost in the Division Series, ending their World Series dreams.

Washington manager Davey Johnson said that Strasburg had reached his limit: "I just told Stephen that his year is over. . . . My job is to do what's best for the player. And this is what's best."[3]

Meanwhile, a disgruntled Strasburg said of his plug being pulled, "I don't know if I'm ever going to accept it, to be honest. . . . You don't grow up dreaming about playing in the big leagues to get shut down when the games start to matter."[4]

For the record, it would be seven more years before Washington finally won a World Series. That year Strasburg went 18–6, throwing 209 innings pitched to lead the NL.

When Vern Law worked eighteen innings (ten strikeouts, one earned run), he did so "on two days' rest. My regular turn came on four days, not five like today. The 100-pitch [limit] pitcher is something I don't approve of. If a pitcher is in shape, 100 pitches is a breeze."

Cunningham had a final thought on the topic, one that agreed with Strasburg and all proud pitchers who want the ball: "There must be a reason for it and there must be a reason for starters only pitching five innings now, but I don't get it. How about the Cleveland teams when they had so many twenty-game winners [three Hall of Famers, Bob Feller, Bob Lemon, and Early Wynn, who won twenty-plus games a combined seventeen times], and the Dodgers had all those twenty-game winners, and the Yankees. Do you think those guys would want to pitch five innings and get out of there? Heck, no. Once they took that ball, they wanted the ball game. Now we use four or five pitchers a game"— and more.

GAMBLING STYLE

Chris Chambliss, who has seen a lot of managers come and go over his fabulous career, said, "As far as somebody who's not afraid to try things, Zim [Don Zimmer] is really the best man to talk to. He's a gambling kind of guy."

Mark Grace played under Zimmer in Chicago and agreed that he would sometimes try very unusual, daring strategies. Grace said, "He was just a gambler by nature—on the field, off the field. That's his passion, and that's the way he managed.

"The good thing about it was you were always on your toes, you were always in the game, because he was doing something all the time. He'd put hit and runs on with two strikes, and he'd put them on with two outs. He'd squeeze with two strikes—he'd do all kinds of stuff. He'd get hunches and he'd play them. If it didn't work, it looked bad, but that was the way he did things and it worked for him."

His risk taking was not, however, based on whims, but was instead calculated. Buck Rodgers, who managed in the majors for thirteen seasons, said Zimmer factored in many things before making unconventional moves such as his unique hit and run plays: "He'd have a batter at the plate who usually makes good contact, a pitcher who has good control and is usually around the plate with his pitches, and who isn't a big strikeout pitcher." Making contact was the key, so Zimmer naturally also considered the count, often putting his runners in motion with a count that required a pitcher to throw a strike—say, a 3–1 count.

Cy Young Award winner Dwight Gooden was taken aback by one particular Zimmer move. "One year when Zimmer was with the Cubs," he said, "with less than two outs, he sent everybody. It was the hit and run with the bases loaded. Lloyd McClendon was the hitter. I'd never seen that. It worked."

"The first time I did it was with Bob Montgomery in Boston," said Zimmer. "I mean, you've got to have everything right to even think of doing it." A strike blown by the batter or a line drive to a fielder meant doom.

"I happened to have a sinkerball pitcher pitching against us, and Montgomery was a slow runner, but a pretty good bat handler, and I didn't think he could strike Montgomery out. And I didn't want Montgomery to hit a ground ball because he's slow, and any ground ball that he hit that a fielder could catch is a double play. So it just struck me: play hit and run. I did this maybe four or five times in the major leagues.

"If you think about it and when I explain it, it doesn't become that big of a deal. You got men on first and second and one out or no outs, and the count goes three and two on the hitter, nine out of ten times the runners are running." So, he figured, by an extension of that logic, why not let three men run with the bases loaded?

Joe Torre mulled over such a play: "With a contact hitter at the plate, why just sit back and wait for the double play?" So, would Torre become a Zimmer copycat? No. "Some of those strategies of his I just don't have the courage to do."

Bobby Cox, like Torre, a Hall of Fame manager, concurs, "There's nothing wrong with that strategy. Why not try something? I like that type of stuff. There's no book." Plus, he said, smiling, "It's a lot more fun."

Grace disagreed a bit about Zimmer's well-thought-out explanation: "I think Zim was a hunch guy. I'm sure being around baseball as long as he obviously has been, [such logical factors are] in the back of his mind, but I think he sometimes just gets a gut feeling and goes with it."

Yet another Hall of Fame manager, Sparky Anderson, was unafraid of playing the riverboat gambler role at times. Baseball lifer Johnny Goryl said of Anderson, "He'd put on a hit and run with a runner on third only so the runner could score on a ground ball. The disadvantage is if the hitter misses the ball, you're 'out to lunch,' or you could hit into a line drive double play. The situation has to be with a contact hitter at the plate who'll put the ball in play on the ground. Of course, the count must also be favorable to the hitter, a count where the pitcher is going to throw a strike."

As former player and coach Frank Howard said, "Rather than wait for contact, he's getting his runner in motion, and if contact is made, it's a walk home."

Former Twins and Orioles manager Ray Miller added another fearless manager to the list: "I saw Warren Spahn when he used to manage in the minor leagues. He used to hit and run with a man on third all the time. It's not a real envious position for the base runner coming down the line and a guy's swinging, but it was different."

TRICK PLAYS

When Cy Young Award winner Mike Flanagan was with the Orioles during manager Earl Weaver's days, Baltimore was a sneaky squad. Flanagan said, "We worked a lot of different trick pickoff plays. We'd put the first baseman behind the runner and have a timing play [with the fielder sneaking over to the bag].

"Plays at second base we'd use a combination pickoff with the second baseman and shortstop. The second baseman would go to the bag [taking a pickoff throw from the pitcher]. Then as soon as that play ended, the second baseman would leave. Then the shortstop would come in behind the runner—that was a little bit different." The runner would see the second baseman return the ball to the pitcher and resume his position. At that moment the runner would relax a bit "and take his lead. Then the shortstop would come in [for the kill]."

Another former Oriole, Roberto Alomar, delved back into his minor league days to mention a bizarre trick play: "It was around 1986 when somebody was at first base and the pitcher threw the ball over. Then a guy who was on the bench rolled a ball toward the outfield. The guy who was diving back to first base looked up and saw the ball rolling away. The first baseman started going after that ball.

"When he did that, the runner started going to second [thinking the pickoff throw had been errantly fired into the outfield]." Once the runner bolted, he was picked off with the ball that the first baseman had all along. Although the play hardly seems legal, Alomar says that the defense, "got away with it—he got the guy out at second."

When Pat Corrales was an Atlanta coach, he said the successful team didn't need to rely upon trick plays. "We stick with basics," he said, then joked, "The trick is not to let the guy get on first base."

However, he did recall a play Oakland used: "Billy Martin had that bunt play when he had a left-handed hitter up. Rickey Henderson would take off stealing, and the guy would bunt the ball to third base. Henderson wouldn't even think about stopping at second. He'd continue to third. It was a good play. Basically a bunt and run, but instead of getting one base, they'd get two."

Bobby Cox may not have needed tricks, but he did comment, "Why not use them? I think Gene Mauch and Sparky Anderson invented all that type of stuff. Roger Craig and those types of guys would surprise you with stuff. You had to be on your toes. They gave a lot of thought to strategies. I learned a lot from just watching those guys do little things.

"None of us goes by the book unless you're catering to the fans or the sportswriters and making the obvious moves when you really think something else would work."

When Roger Craig managed the Giants, he used a clever scheme against the Reds. Former Tampa Bay skipper Larry Rothschild described the play: "They had a bunt play where the third baseman charged with men on first and second. The shortstop went to second base, and they'd throw there to try to get a double play. You have to have a slow runner to do that. Cincinnati had Joe Oliver [a slow-footed catcher on base]. The play actually happened twice in the series, and it worked both times."

Cox went on to say that even on what might be called routine trick plays, there are nuances to be aware of. He gave the example of stealing home: "The batter [almost always a righty] should get as deep in the box as he can to force the catcher even further back in order to make a later tag. I'm sure Mauch is the one who thought of that—him or Sparky."

Furthermore, Cox did not find the hidden ball trick to be bush league. "Why not try it?" he said. "Gene Michael was the master at that—he was the best, and Spike Owen was real good at it, too."

Managers' Tirades

What do players think when their managers go nuts, arguing with umpires? Jamie Moyer, winner of 269 games, grinned, saying, "I've always enjoyed Lou Piniella's tirades on the field. I mean, I love playing for Lou, he has a lot of passion for the game, and I have a lot of respect for Lou and how he goes about his business and what he expects of his players. He's taught me a lot in this game. I really enjoyed the opportunity to play for Lou, he's just a very good guy." However, when he went off on umps, his act was something to behold.

There's a famous clip of Piniella going wild followed by a quick camera cut to the Mariners dugout where his players, most notably Ken Griffey Jr., were erupting with laughter (although many were hiding their faces behind their caps so as not to show their reaction openly).

"Nothing was scripted," recalled Moyer, "and when he went out there you never knew if he was going to take a base out of the ground, kick dirt on home plate, throw his hat, or kick his hat. Actually, that night I think he was kicking his hat all over the place. So there's nothing you can do but laugh."

Interestingly, said Moyer, when Piniella came into the clubhouse after the game, he didn't get angry with his team for their amused reactions. "No, I just think it was the heat, the passion."

Several minor league managers made headlines with their unbridled passion. Phillip Wellman of the Class AA Mississippi Braves put on one of the most demonstrative shows ever. He buried home plate under a heap of dirt, à la Earl Weaver, and unearthed and tossed a base, doing his best Piniella imitation.

Then, as if striving for creativity points, he invented a few moves of his own, crawling commando style to the mound, seizing the resin bag, which he pretended to bite as if he was pulling out a grenade pin, then heaving it toward the umpire at home plate. He concluded his histrionics by blowing a kiss to the crowd as he finally exited the game. His players' reaction had to have been a blend of utter astonishment, with mouths agape and stifled laughter.

Buddy Hunter managed the Carolina League Salem Red Sox in 1980, and he, too, put on an unforgettable show. He blew up after home plate umpire Bob Serino made what Hunter felt was a horrible call. Bolting out of the dugout, Hunter went toe-to-toe with Serino, spewing expletives like so much spittle.

Then, referring to a call Serino had made the previous night, Hunter, acting as if he were Serino, pantomimed a flipping-a-coin gesture. Glancing at the imaginary coin, he signaled "home run," then flipped it again, this time giving the "out" indication.

Just getting warmed up, Hunter then raced over to, and slid into, first base, where he again gave two calls, safe and out. Next, Hunter took off his shoes, bit one of them as if yanking the pin from his imaginary hand grenade, which he then used to blow up Serino—apparently explosives are as big with minor league managers as they are with Warner Brothers' cartoonists. Using his other shoe as a reserve grenade, he ran near second base umpire Bob Duncan and blew him to smithereens.

Finally, taking an exaggerated bow, he left the field to a chant of, "HUN-ter. HUN-ter." As for his team's reaction, well, sportswriter Mike Blake suggested Hunter may have lit a fuse for them, as they had gone 4–18 over their previous twenty-two contests, then went 27–14 after his meltdown.

CHAPTER FIVE

Covering All the Bases

RESPECT FROM PEERS

Every generation has at least a handful of players who earn the deep respect of their contemporaries. Stan Musial's teammate Marty Marion succinctly said, "If you didn't like Stan, you didn't like anybody."[1]

When Frank Howard was with the Washington Senators, from 1965 to 1971, his size and power earned him the nicknames "The Washington Monument" and "The Capital Punisher." He saluted Hank Aaron: "Probably one of the two most amazing things you'll ever see are Henry Aaron swinging a bat and the quality type pitches he would hit for distance. Maybe not so much for home runs, but for singles and doubles [624 lifetime]. From a hitting standpoint, Aaron is probably the most amazing hitter I've ever seen."

Batting champ Harry Walker said of Aaron, "He's one of the best and most complete ballplayers I ever saw. He'd steal twenty, twenty-two bases out of twenty-four attempts. He'd steal them when you'd need them, not when you're ten runs ahead or behind, like so many others. There was nothing he didn't do that wasn't good. You'd love to have nine Hank Aarons on your team."

Howard then lavished praise on Willie Mays and his defense: "You go back to some of the plays that Mays made in center field. I've seen film of the ones he made in the 1954 World Series—going into the gaps and cutting off balls that looked like sure doubles, throwing the ball on the run with a one-hop accurate throw to nail base runners trying to go for two. We're talking about two of the greatest ever to play."

Former Pirates manager Harry Walker said, "Roberto Clemente was the most colorful player I had. He was a dedicated individual and the most exciting player I ever managed."

Gene Clines was a Clemente teammate who praised him—but could never figure out one thing: "Whenever he came in the clubhouse and said he felt good, he'd have a bad game. When he complained, 'My neck hurts,' or 'The kids kept me up all night,' he'd have a great game." He must have had a whole lot of aches, pains, and insomnia, as he wound up with 3,000 hits and the admiration of millions.

Clemente's Pittsburgh teammate Willie Stargell awed peers by powering 475 home runs. Milt May was with the Pirates long enough to admire Stargell's bombs. "In LA, he hit one *over* the bullpen, and out of the stadium," he said. "He's got a few spots marked around the league, a few seats with marks on them [to commemorate noteworthy homers]. He hit the ball as far as anybody and with as much power as anybody."

Jeff Bagwell came along in 1991, in time to list a few peers whom he admired: "The Mo Vaughns of the world, and Matt Williams is a perfect example of a guy that gets a lot of respect because of the way he plays the game. He does everything the right way. He's a great leader *and* a great person. Those are the kinds of guys who are respected."

So was Bagwell. Houston teammate Roger Cedeno singled out "Bags and Craig Biggio. Everybody loves their personalities. Robin Ventura, too, when I was with the Mets—John Franco and Joe Oliver, too."

Another Bagwell teammate, Doug Henry, said, "Jeff is a class act. He goes about his business. He plays the game hard. He's somebody who just goes out and plays the game like it should be played." Billy Wagner had the final say: "This guy's always been there, he plays every day, he never makes an excuse, he's a field general out there."

WHAT RECORDS IMPRESS PLAYERS?

David Justice was one of many players who was virtually spellbound by Hank Aaron and his résumé. In a 1997 interview, he said, "Aaron's home run record is unbreakable because you have to play *forever* to break it. If you played twenty years and averaged 35 home runs a year, you're still short of his 755."

Such logic would *normally* hold true, but Justice didn't count on the onslaught of cheating in baseball. Barry Bonds was a star early on, but his career high for homers from his rookie season in 1986 through 1999 was 46. Then, when the laws of nature tell us that athletes inevitably slow down, for the next five seasons—from the age of thirty-five through the year he turned forty—he surpassed or came within one of his former high-water mark each season, with an ungodly high of 73 the year he turned thirty-seven, a gravity-defying leap of 24 (or *49 percent*) from the previous year.

So the (moot?) question was, did Bonds cheat to break the record, greatly enhancing his physical prowess? Well, he broke into the majors with a rather willowy build (6-foot-1 and 185 pounds) and wore a size 7 1/8 cap in 1993. Around 2000, he reportedly required a size 7 1/2 hat, an increase of roughly one inch in the circumference of his head. Critics, reporters, and some scientists contend that taking human growth hormones was the reason for his larger head—and inflated stats. They also accused the self-centered star of literally and figuratively having a big head. His weight remained constant until 1991, when it went up five pounds, but it ballooned more than 10 percent, to 206 in 1997. He had morphed from having a thin appearance into a veritable Incredible Hulk.

As great as Hank Aaron was, he managed "only" 47 home runs when he was thirty-seven. At that same age, Babe Ruth hit 41; Ken Griffey Jr., 30; Ted Williams, 24; Willie Mays and Albert Pujols, 23; Jimmie Foxx, 7; and Mickey Mantle, who retired at the age of thirty-six, had 0.

In 1997, Chipper Jones said that he also found the most laudable record of all time to be Aaron's 755 homers. In the minds of many purists, Aaron's untainted record still stands.

As for single-game feats, Jones stated that perfect games impressed him the most, "especially in today's game, just because of the amount of hitting that there is in the game of baseball. I think for somebody to go out there for twenty-seven outs and not allow another team a base runner is probably one of the most remarkable feats."

One pitching gem he'll never forget was a Kevin Brown near-perfecto. Jones praised Brown's showing, saying, "He should have thrown a perfect game. He hit a guy with two outs in the eighth inning, and I know he's got pinpoint control. It was just a shame because he had that kind of stuff. He could have done something [rare]." Through 2023, there have been twenty-two perfect games dating back to 1880.

Tom Glavine, the next-to-last man to win 300 games, said, "I don't know, honestly, if we'll ever see somebody win four straight Cy Young Awards again, either." He was alluding to his Atlanta teammate Greg Maddux, who won four of those honors in a row from 1992 to 1995. Had he foreseen Randy Johnson (the very last 300-game winner) in his prophecy, he would have been 100 percent correct. The Big Unit won five Cy Young trophies, including four straight running from 1999 to 2002.

Glavine was also in awe of the post-1900 record for wins in a season: 41 by Jack Chesbro in 1904. The pre-1900 high is 60 by Old Hoss Radbourn, but his era was vastly different from the so-called modern era. As for the 40-win plateau, Glavine said, "You don't get forty starts in a year now, so that will never be broken."

He continued, "I'm sure there's a lot of obscure ones that a lot of people don't know about, but the major ones, like the couple that I mentioned, I don't think those are ever going to be broken."

All-Star Jeff Blauser said the 12 hits over 12 consecutive at-bats by Johnny Kling, Pinky Higgins, and Walt Dropo "is going to be a tough one to beat because there are so many variables. You know, you can hit a ball good, a line drive right at somebody, and they make the play on you and you're out. That's a record that's obscure, but I think it will stand for a while." Dustin Pedroia in 2016 and Bernie Williams in 2002 came close with 11 straight hits—close, but not quite there. In 2024, another player, Jose Miranda of the Twins, matched this record.

Glavine spoke of factors that keep old records, such as Hack Wilson's 191 RBI in a season, unassailable. For example, at the All-Star break in 1997, when Andres Galarraga was on a pace to drive in a very lofty total of runs batted in, it was suggested to Glavine that as impressive as his pace was, it was one that was seemingly impossible to maintain, especially down the draining dog days of the season.

Galarraga wound up with 140 RBI in 1997, actually a decline from the 150 runs he had driven in the year before—Coors Field helped, as a stunning 103 of his 150 ribbies came there. Glavine said, "I think that's the big thing. Over the course of 162 games, heat, injuries, fatigue, pennant races down the stretch where teams will start pitching around him—all of those things make it hard to keep up that pace."

The following season, Juan González was outshining Galarraga, with 101 RBI by July 5, at the All-Star break. Only Hank Greenberg (103 in 1935) had more by that point in a season. Of course, it must be remembered that the date of the break varies and is not the true halfway point in a season. Gonzalez ended with a league-leading 157 RBI. So yes, the 191 ribbies record seems to be quite safe.

Glavine also liked Mark Whiten's 4 homers and 12 RBI in a single game, along with "Roger Clemens punching out twenty guys, *twice*"—in games some ten years apart. Hall of Fame third baseman Scott Rolen chimed in on Whiten's home run and RBI jackpot: "That's incredible; I don't know if it's by chance or what it might be, but, I mean, that doesn't happen. It just doesn't happen! And 12 RBIs, that's a month right there in one game!"

It should be noted that other men have swatted four homers in a game, but only one other man ever drove home a dozen runs in a game— Jim Bottomley in 1924.

Glavine's former batterymate, Javy López, said his pick for the most inviolate records are "Nolan Ryan's strikeouts and Pete Rose's hits." As good as Randy Johnson was when it came to absolutely blowing away batters, Ryan's career K total of 5,714 stands 839 higher than that of Johnson. Likewise, as proficient as Ty Cobb was—he owned 481 more hits than the next man on the all-time hit list (Aaron)—Rose compiled more, 4,256 hits, to shoot by Cobb's total of 4,189.

In the meantime, Rolen cited Cy Young's record 511 lifetime wins: "Unbelievable the amount of wins that he had. I mean, that's the most amazing to me." Simple math reveals that a pitcher who begins at as early of an age as, say, nineteen could win 25 games every single season of his career through the age of thirty-nine, and he'd still be shy of Young's total. Not only that, with today's five-man pitching rotations, winning

25 is nearly impossible for any given *single* season, let alone for twenty years running. The last time a pitcher registered 25-plus wins was way back in 1990, when Oakland's Bob Welch went 27–6.

Hal McRae, a Silver Slugger winner and lifetime .290 hitter, commented on Joe DiMaggio's record 56-game hitting streak. "That's the most remarkable," he said. "It's going to be difficult for anyone to get a base hit in that many consecutive ball games because of the sophistication of the defenses now and the scouting."

He knew it had to be tough enough in DiMaggio's time to accomplish his record, and he reiterated that nowadays it's even more difficult. His evidence included the fact that today's pitchers don't usually last very deep into games, so a hitter goes up against the fresher arms of specialists in the art of late-inning relief. Often they have different pitches and different looks than the starter's style and stuff.

Blauser agreed: "Pete Rose went for so long, and he didn't really even come close." Rose's 1978 NL record string was terminated at 44—commendable, but a mile away from a 56-game stretch.

What's also difficult to imagine is that before DiMaggio reached the big leagues, he once strung together a Pacific Coast League record with a 61-game hitting streak. (The all-time minor league record streak is 69 by Joe Wilhoit.) After DiMaggio's 56-game spree was snapped, in part due to several dazzling fielding plays, he proceeded to go gather hits in another 16 straight games. Therefore, he hit safely in an unimaginable 72 of 73 big-league games.

So-called unbreakable records always impress fans and players alike. The only problem is some of those records turn out to be a bit fragile. For decades, everyone was convinced Lou Gehrig's longevity record of playing in 2,130 consecutive games was as untouchable as Eliot Ness and his incorruptible crew of lawmen. Somehow, defying all odds, the strong-willed Cal Ripken Jr., the Iron Man, shattered the Iron Horse's sixty-five-year-old record, stretching the mark by 501 games beyond Gehrig's total.

Rico Brogna, who hit 20-plus homers four times, said, "I would've guessed no one would've had a chance to do what Ripken did. It's just so hard. It's hard to make it through a couple of weeks without missing a game, never mind as many years as he did it—what was it, fourteen full years? [It was just about two-and-a-half months shy of seventeen full seasons in a row.] I'd have to say that record would be the toughest one to break ever. I can't see anybody beating what Ripken did."

Nor should Ripken's other inviolate record within his famous streak tumble, as he played in an unfathomable 8,243 innings in a row. The old record for this was so far behind Ripken's, it was but a flyspeck in his rearview mirror—a mere 5,152 innings set by a nineteenth-century ballplayer. When Ripken's innings played skein came to an end, it was only because his manager, Cal Ripken Sr., felt that in a 17–3 blowout, maybe it was time to give his son a one-inning blow.

Furthermore, the *combined* number of consecutive games played by the men who immediately trail Ripken and Gehrig for durability—Everett Scott and Steve Garvey—is fewer than Ripken's 2,632 total.

Denny Neagle, a two-time All-Star, had the last word on Ripken: "The fact that the guy went out there day in and day out, and I know for a fact there were times when he had twisted ankles, sprained ankles, bad coughs and flus, things like that. A lot of people would take a day off. He just kept going out there."

PLAYERS SHOWING UP OPPONENTS/OTHERS

Players' attitudes on opponents who try to show up their peers with demonstrative antics is a facet of baseball that has drastically changed over the years. Regardless of that, many brushbacks, beanballs, and brawls have broken out after a player who has, for example, stood in the batter's box for too long admiring a home run. That type of behavior, once known as showboating, is, in today's game, no longer a dreaded taboo. Of course, some behavior still crosses the line—but the question always remains: Who draws that line?

Jeff Bagwell is such a class act that the idea of showing up an opponent by any display of brash, ostentatious actions or words would be, as the character Vizzini in the film *The Princess Bride* would say, inconceivable. Bagwell said, "As a hitter, you try not to show a guy up when you hit a home run, and, as a pitcher, you don't want [or should not want] to show a guy up if your strike him out."

So actions such as those of his Houston teammate, the highly emotional José Lima, "would be something I would not condone or try to teach somebody." When asked in a 2000 interview if baseball was seeing too much showing others up, Bagwell responded, "Yeah, the new generation is a part of it a bit, but you know, football is ridiculous now. Every time a guy makes a tackle, he's jumping around. I mean, you watch Larry Bird and Dick Butkus, they never did that kind of stuff.

"But the games change—it's all about marketing yourself, and if you become a so-called character, you get a little more publicity, and sometimes that's what they go after. Dennis Rodman made a career out of that.

"It's not the right way to play the game. It didn't used to happen like that, but that's just the way things are nowadays."

Bagwell said that in days gone by, veteran players would take care of showoffs by, for instance, drilling them with a well-placed fastball to the ribs or other painful targets. The players were governing their own game. "That's the way the game had always been played. Nowadays you can't play it that way as much because the umpires have taken it out of your hands. As soon as you hit somebody, they put up a warning. In the old days, well, if you hit Griffey [Junior], and I'm coming up later that inning, I know I'm getting hit," he said, laughing. "Now the pitcher gets thrown out of the game and that's tough."

There certainly was a time when showing up an opponent was virtually unheard of. Stan Musial can serve as a symbol of the model player who would never put on a theatric display that would humiliate anyone. Vern Law said, "Everybody really respected Stan. He wasn't a griper, he didn't give umpires a bad time, he was even-tempered. If he got a hit, he'd just drop the bat and go down to first base. He was kind of a man's man, and just an outstanding personality."

Nowadays, not only do major leaguers show others up, kids do, too. Luis Gonzalez, the father of triplets, is well aware that kids like what they see on, say, ESPN highlights, and they feel they should copycat the major leaguers. He commented, "I think all you've got to do is just look at the Little League World Series when you see little kids like last year [2002], with the kid pointing to the outfield and things like that. It's good to have fun out there, but there's times when you're like, that's a little bit crossing the barrier there.

"You want kids to go out there and be competitive and have fun, but try not to embarrass the other team because sometimes there are players on the other side that just don't have the kind of talent as some teams do."

Cy Young Award winner CC Sabathia said that when an opponent gets demonstrative after hitting a home run against him, it doesn't faze him "because usually I'm not even looking; I'm looking to see where the ball's going to land." He added that he realized it's difficult to hit a baseball at this level, so "those guys can do whatever they want, it doesn't bother me, but it does bother some people."

He did concede, though, that if an opposing player hit a homer off one of his teammates and his antics disturbed that teammate, "then it would get to me because I'm a teammate and a friend."

Of course, the tendency toward showing other players up has spread to pitchers as well. "Some of these guys, like Ugueth Urbina, they do crazy stuff after even *one strike*, so it's evened out."

Curtis Granderson said, "I think the fact that you see all those [demonstrative moments] highlighted is what gets TV time. That's what gets airtime, that's what people talk about, and 'Hey, I just did something big, let me do something to celebrate.'"

Veteran Jamey Carroll had no problem with celebratory displays, even orchestrated ones like when Prince Fielder celebrated a home run by taking a hop and stomping on home plate as if it was a plunger detonating an explosion. Teammates gathered around the plate reacted as if dynamite had just gone off, tumbling to the ground.

Carroll said, "I can't imagine the Prince Fielder thing not being a planned thing. It's a pretty creative thing to all of a sudden throw out there. I'm sure guys talk about it and say what they're going to do. Heck, you hit a walk-off home run and you win the game. It's not easy to win in this game, so you should have as much fun as you possibly want to. More games are on national TV, so I think it's become more of entertainment than just baseball. It's like guys think . . . of what they can do to entertain even more. It's almost kind of expected—something crazy will happen whenever a walk-off win happens, or what have you."

Bench Jockeying

Long ago, players sitting in the dugout would "ride" the opposition, doing things like shouting out distracting, derogatory comments to the pitcher. Times have changed. In 2009, Andy Van Slyke, a two-time Silver Slugger winner, said he felt that perhaps "one of the things that's missing is a little more fun in the game."

He lamented the demise of bench jockeying: "When I first came up, in 1983, players would rag on the other players, and it wasn't that you were disrespectful, it was just part of the chatter. Again, you weren't really being derogatory, it was just part of the language—and that chatter is basically gone. It's a part of the game that I miss, but the game changes in a lot of ways, and that's one way the game has changed."

It seems players today are more professional about doing their job, but that attitude is a bit more cold or calculating, which eliminates much of the bench jockeying and the color of the game.

Van Slyke said he believes the verbal jousting that men such as his former Cardinals teammate Tom Wallace would dish out to the opponents—"for nine innings he verbally abused the other team"—had its place. "In a lot of ways it creates a closeness with the ball club, you feel connected that we're all on one side trying to beat the other team not only physically but verbally," he said with a smile.

What a difference—baseball has gone from the days of savage bench jockeying, when venom and vulgarities (and even racial epithets) were spouted between dugouts during games, to today's more mannerly ways in which, by contrast, one would almost expect to see a library-like "Silence, please" sign in both dugouts.

Volatile Players

Today's players are much better educated than those from the long-ago era, when many men came to the major leagues from, say, farms rather than institutions of higher learning. Nicknames such as "Rube" were not uncommon.

There are quite a few exceptions to the theory that better-educated players today tend to be more professional and well behaved than some of the wild men from long ago, such as the snarling Ty Cobb. So what does a modern, sophisticated player think of his peers who act outlandishly?

Tom Glavine, a true class act, was specifically asked what he thought about volatile players such as Tony Phillips and Albert Belle, who one writer said was "nuts." Diplomatically, Glavine replied, "I don't know, to say they're out of control? I guess that's open to interpretation. They're probably both just intense, emotional players, and a lot of times as an athlete, your emotions get the best of you.

"We've all played around guys who are emotional. I've seen some guys in here [the Atlanta locker] that are great players who will rearrange clubhouses and that kind of stuff, but because people don't see it out on the field, you don't know about it.

"I think anybody who plays this game, at some time or another their emotions get the best of them and they do something a little off the wall. Just some guys do it more often and in front of more people." Of course, Glavine made those comments in 1997, perhaps assuming Belle's seemingly endless antics were over.

After all, the Cleveland slugger was six years removed from the time a fan heckled him and Belle responded by drilling the fan in his chest with a well-aimed baseball. And he was pushing *two whole years* (sarcasm intended) away from his literal run-in with some teenagers who egged his house on Halloween after Belle tacitly indicated he preferred being the recipient of a trick over giving them a treat. Belle's fuse lit, he chased them down in his vehicle. One boy claimed Belle actually ran into him, but police found no supporting evidence. Belle did, however, tell police that if he found one of the kids he would "kill them."

When asked about some of the wild events from long ago, such as Ty Cobb going into the stands to fight a fan, Glavine replied, "I think the days of those things happening are pretty much over. There's just too much for a guy to lose by doing something like that."

Glavine was a bit overly optimistic, but to be fair, he *did* qualify his answer by saying wild antics are "*pretty much* over." There may always be a few hot-tempered athletes around, such as Milton Bradley and, even more glaringly in the NBA, Ron Artest, infamous for his 2004 "Malice at the Palace," when he charged into the stands in Detroit's home arena to attack a spectator. Artest wound up serving an eighty-six-game suspension, longest in NBA history for a game-related incident, and lost nearly $5 million in salary.

As for Bradley, the onetime Dodgers outfielder's most notorious confrontation with fans also created a combustible situation. Late in the 2004 season he was fined and suspended for the final few games of the season after a meltdown in a home contest. His explosion began after a fan threw a plastic bottle at him. He retrieved it, stormed over to the fan, and slammed the bottle into the front row of seats.

This marked his fourth suspension of the season, including the time he was ejected from a game, returned to his dugout, then went ballistic, tossing a bag of roughly seventy-two baseballs onto the field. Some of the balls became souvenirs when Bradley then hurled them into the stands.

In 2007, three years after he went through anger management counseling, he went off on an umpire's call, then tore his ACL when his Padres manager, Bud Black, wrestled him to the turf to prevent Bradley from going after the ump. It's little wonder that Bradley played for eight different clubs over his twelve-year career, never lasting as long as three full seasons with one team.

Bad boy behavior isn't, of course, limited to the major leagues. In 2006, the Durham Bulls' Delmon Young was rung up on strikes. As he walked back to his dugout, he heaved his bat toward home plate. When the bat struck the umpire, it marked the first time in baseball's annals that a player struck an ump with a bat. It cost Young a fifty-game suspension, longest in the 123-year history of the International League.

Bottom line: crazy behavior is generally frowned upon today, but players snapping isn't nonexistent—intense competitors abound, and frenzied outbursts do happen.

BASEBALL ESPIONAGE

Jeff Francoeur believed that, unlike many of the inviolable unwritten rules, stealing signals is an iffy subject. "If people are going the extra mile to try to steal your signs, and really, really looking at the catchers and giving pitch locations, that's kind of bad," he said. "But if a team's doing a bad job of hiding a sign, I've got no problem of taking advantage of that.

"Now, if you're a runner at second and you're getting all these signs and you're giving the location with your hand signals, then that's bush and you're putting your team in danger. I know for us, the Braves, if we saw a team cheating against us, we're probably going to take care of business [retaliate]."

So, he says, not only should the defense protect their signals, but those who have stolen signs and want to relay them to their teammates must also be circumspect and very inconspicuous.

Robin Yount felt that might be true, but he also insisted, "If you're not trying to steal signs, you're not doing your job."

Francoeur said that the simplest way to combat a team that has stolen a signal is to "make in-game adjustments and say, 'Hey, they know what's coming. We need to change something up.'"

Frankly, said Francoeur, when the Braves have had occasion for a runner off second to pass on intelligence to the batter, "We never really give signs so much as it is location sometimes—trying to help a guy with location. You know, if a right-hander's throwing to me and he's going inside for the most part, unless he's got a good front door slider, you know a fastball's coming in."

Another way to steal a catcher's signals is to play an adult version of peek-a-boo. CC Sabathia, winner of 251 games, doesn't go for that: "No, you don't do that. I mean, I'm really adamant about that, you shouldn't do that at all—that's cheating to me."

That, he said, is different from a runner off second trying to peer in to the catcher to help his teammate at the plate. "You gotta give credit to the guy at second base stealing signs. You change your signs up. You can control that, but you can't control a guy turning around and actually looking."

He added that if someone did that while he was on the mound, he would not escalate things to a brushback or knockdown pitch, at least not initially: "I'd probably say something first. If I have something to say, I'll say it."

But if a player continued his sign stealing, justifying it by saying he was seeking any edge he could get, then Sabathia said he would take a stronger approach, making a sort of veiled threat. "Like I said, we'll have a conversation first, and after that, we'll handle it whatever way."

Cat-and-Mouse Games

Baseball is a game with many subtleties, some not even observable by fans. Take the cat-and-mouse games played—is there a lot of that going on? Mark Grace scoffed as he dismissed such tactics as ploys used by some players, but ineffectively—like catchers pounding on their glove so batters will hear the location of the pitcher's target. The catchers are trying to dupe the hitters into thinking they are situating their mitts for, say, an inside target, then having their pitchers throw to the outside part of the plate.

Grace spoke of better tricks, "Definitely a lot between pitchers and hitters. Sometimes a pitcher will 'fan' his glove, or nod—or the 'shake-off' is another thing that they try to do to mess with you. They'll do this rub, make you think more [about what pitch he's telling his catcher he really wants to throw] than you normally will. It's to try to throw you off."

He elaborated on the 'fan' move by pitchers: "Some pitchers, when they get their signs, will fan their gloves out like they're really moving the ball around [to get a certain grip to throw a certain pitch]. When they get a sign, this [a gesture to the chest area] either means, 'Yeah, I like that pitch, but I want a different location' or 'No, it's the next sign I want.'

"If you see a guy shift around—some guys tip their pitches and give them away. Then, of course, a pitcher could do that to their advantage where it may look like I'm throwing this, but I'm doing something else. There are just a lot of nuances going on."

Hitters prepare for pitchers' tricks by analyzing them through video and other methods, including just thinking things over. Jermaine Dye, the MVP of the 2005 World Series, shared his thoughts: "I basically try and look at what he did to me before and use that to my advantage. Pitchers try to pitch to you different every time, so you basically got to go with what he's doing to the other hitters. I try to watch certain guys that are similar to me and how they're pitching him, and try to use that while I go up to the plate. I try to look for pitches that way."

What about when a catcher sets up on, say, the outside part of the plate hoping the batter will take a peek and think an outside pitch is coming, then he crosses the hitter up. It's been said some catchers know that certain batters have a reputation for sneaking a peak, and they will definitely try this strategy on them.

Scott Pose said batters knowing the catcher's location might not work "unless there's somebody on second base and the catcher's setting up early enough where he could relay it [the information] to the hitter, which happens quite a bit."

COMPETITIVE NATURE

Rickey Henderson said that he was misunderstood throughout his career: "They said I was arrogant, cocky. I was competitive. There's nothing I haven't done in this game that I wanted to do. I never wanted to sit—always wanted to play."

During a 2002 interview, when he was forty-three and in his next-to-last season, his fiery nature continued to burn, though more like an ember than the bonfire of his youth. "If I get to play [full time] I'd get 75 to 100 stolen bases today," he insisted. And though his chiseled body still looked capable of rushing for four touchdowns, as he once did in high school—what schoolboy could catch, let alone tackle this sleek, muscular greyhound—he would steal just 8 bases that season.

Merv Rettenmund was a teammate of Frank Robinson's in Baltimore. "On the Orioles he was the best hitter," he said, "and it was very simple why—he had a tremendous competitive spirit. He was flat violent—a violent, violent baseball player—and he believed in himself. And he never would take a lot of batting practice; he just walked out there and played the game, and played it very, very hard."

So, was he violent as in intense, or almost maliciously fierce? "Oh, I think both ways." It brought to mind the time Robinson slid hard into Eddie Mathews at third base and a heavyweight bout under a glamorous Robinson-Mathews "card" ensued. Rettenmund recalled the melee and the fact that "the next game he hit two home runs after getting the crap beat out of him, and he won the game. I mean, he's just a violent guy."

He concluded, "Frank knew himself, and most of the guys that I've been associated with all through baseball, their success is in the fact that they have a belief in themselves."

When Rettenmund left the Orioles and joined the Cincinnati Reds, one of his next marquee star teammates was Pete Rose. "He was special in as much as the intensity he brought per at-bat," Rettenmund said. "We're talking about believing in yourself—thousands of players that came up the road had more ability than Pete Rose. But he had more than 4,000 hits and he never gave an at-bat away. I think you just can't say enough about a guy that goes up there for five or six at-bats a game and battles for 162 games in a row—he could do it."

HUSTLE

If hustle alone was enough to make a player an All-Star, Ryan Freel would've been a perennial figure at the Midsummer Classic. As it was, his versatility—he played five different positions—and his 75 percent success rate on steals made him valuable enough to last nine big-league seasons. Managers also had to admire his all-out style of play as the scrappy Freel played with linebacker abandon, including leaping head-first into the stands in pursuit of foul pop-ups.

Asked why more players didn't go all-out all the time, Freel replied, "I wonder the same question. I have no idea why they don't. I just think it [total hustle] is part of the game. This is where you play. I guess it's what's inside you—you know, your desire, the will.

"This game's all about inches. I scratched and clawed to get up here, and I'm going to scratch and claw to stay up here. It's part of my game, but I don't know why other guys don't do it."

Naturally, considering the way Freel threw his body around, he paid a price: "I get out of bed every day and I just about have to crawl to the bathroom like [NFL star running back] Jerome Bettis."

Jesse Orosco admired Kirby Puckett for his hustle: "As soon as he would make contact, even if he hit the ball 400 feet, he was already at second base by the time the ball landed because he hustled all the time."

Another former Reds gung-ho player was Pete Rose, who earned the nickname "Charlie Hustle." His trademarks were his headfirst slides and his running swiftly down the first baseline after drawing walks. He didn't draw walks; he coaxed 90-foot sprints.

Rose traced his motivation to go all-out to the letters his father sent him, beginning when he first left home to play in the minors. "I remember, my dad used to write me a letter every week," he said. "At the end of the letter, he would always put 'keep hustling.' That was his signature—keep hustling. That's why I run to first on a walk. That's why I slide headfirst."[2]

Luis Gonzalez felt that he was blessed geographically as he grew up, coming from Tampa, a city teeming with baseball tradition. He said, "I had a unique opportunity, growing up in Florida, being around spring training my whole life." He said that after taking in an exhibition contest he would go home, play stickball with friends, and pretend to be players he had just observed, heroes such as Rose. Throughout his career, he said, he tried to mirror the Rose mentality and to "have the same hustle style as him."

However, even Rose's zeal wasn't enough to influence enough major leaguers. One future Hall of Famer once justified his refusal to run out routine grounders because (a) he just *knew* such balls were going to turn into easy outs, and (b) it's a long season—conserving energy was more important and practical than futile hustle.

On the other hand, an incredulous Eddie Mathews would hear no such justifications, saying in effect, "Look, if you can't bust it down the line, running hard for a lousy 90 feet four times a day, you don't belong in the big leagues."

Breaking up the Double Play

It takes hustle, but also guts and determination to bust up potential double plays. Early in the twenty-first century, Bill Virdon, then the Pirates' bench coach, said that when he played the game, Jim Davenport of the Giants was one of the toughest when it came to sliding hard into second to wipe out a potential double play: "He was probably the best at that."

Later, Hal McRae built a reputation for also going into second with a bang. Among more modern players, Virdon said, "you don't see it as much today as you used to, but on our club, I'd say Brian Giles is probably as good as anybody."

In the meantime, Jeff Bagwell felt there were others nowadays who still have the Davenport/McRae mentality. "Guys like Ken Caminiti are very good at it," he said. Logically, the men who go in rough-and-tumble are the hard-nosed players who go all-out in all phases of the game. Bagwell noted, "That's what you're supposed to do. If you can get [to the bag], that's what you're supposed to do—take 'em out. The question is, can you get there?"

TEAM CAPTAINS

Are team captains really necessary now, in the twenty-first century? Few teams appoint captains anymore. Going back to the years early in this century, there were a few, such as Barry Larkin with the Reds and Derek Jeter of the Yankees. As recently as a couple of months before the 2023 season opened, the Yankees kept a long tradition of captains going when they gave that title to Aaron Judge. That season began with just one other team having a captain: Salvador Pérez of Kansas City.

Veteran catcher/first baseman Scott Hatteberg said during a 2007 interview, "I've never been on a team that had a captain. There have always been maybe certain guys that are the leaders of the team. I think a lot of it is nobody sticks around teams too long anymore; they're gone." Free agency has meant that fewer and fewer players, even big stars, stick around with a club long enough to earn the title of captain.

As for his 2007 Reds, there were players who were, so to speak, unofficial captains: solid leaders, "some veteran guys. Jeff Conine is certainly one of them, and David Weathers. They're not outspoken guys, but they're very well respected."

Mike Stanton, who stands second on the all-time list for games pitched, saw no need for team captains because "on good teams there are usually several 'captains.' That's something that kind of falls on the shoulders of the veteran players."

When Judge was given his captaincy, ESPN ran a story about what leadership responsibilities a modern team leader has, including "thinking about, guiding, and motivating teammates, setting a proper tone, and even representing the community."

In that story, Yankees captain Ron Guidry said he once had the task of confronting team owner George Steinbrenner "about the sorry state of the team's in-flight meals." Guidry said there was nobody else for his teammates to turn to. "You're a spokesperson."[3]

So he made his way into Steinbrenner's office, where the intimidating owner barked at Guidry, "What's your problem now?" Guidry shot back, "*I* don't have a problem with you. *Your* team does."[4] After listening to the captain's issue, a placated Steinbrenner said he would take care of the problem. The next road trip featured a new airline carrier and a lavish meal of chateaubriand and lobster tail.

One thing is certain: Being appointed a team captain is an honor, so teams should choose wisely. An egregious example of a mistake was the Yankees' selection of Babe Ruth as captain in 1922. He lasted a measly five days, hardly fitting in with their other fifteen captains over the years such as Lou Gehrig, Thurman Munson, Don Mattingly, Graig Nettles, Willie Randolph, and Derek Jeter, who was the longest-tenured Yankees captain, from 2003 to 2014.

The Yankees brass had placated the Babe by anointing him with the position, but their real feelings about him as a man who could handle his peers was evident when Ruth told team owner Jacob Rupert that he wanted to manage the team. After presenting his case about how he could help both pitchers and hitters, he cringed when he heard the response: "How can you manage the Yankees when you can't manage yourself." Looking back eighty years later, Ruth's daughter Julia Ruth Stevens correctly concluded, "His wild ways haunted him."

Stanton emphasized his feelings about team captains when asked if Derek Jeter had never been given that role, wouldn't he still have taken on the same leadership duties anyway? Stanton, a former teammate of Jeter's, nodded, saying, "Oh, absolutely. Him getting the captain title is something that George Steinbrenner gave him, but he leads more by example than by being a stand-up, rah-rah guy. If he needs to talk to a young guy or something like that, he'll pull him to the side, he's not going to do it out in front of everyone."

PLAYERS' PICKS: LEAST PRETTY PARKS

Players, just like fans, react to the aesthetics of ballparks, and some of their workplaces leave them cold.

Paul Byrd commented that he is not "a fan of the cookie-cutter park, the stadiums they built in the '70s—they really weren't designed for baseball."

Tom Grieve's "ugly" vote is split between Tropicana Field, home of the Tampa Bay Rays, and Minnesota's Metrodome, which closed in 2013. When Montreal's old Olympic Stadium was mentioned, Grieve added, "Oh, yeah, I forgot about that place; I haven't been there enough for it to stick out, but that's probably the worst."

Phil Nevin also listed Tropicana as one of the least attractive parks and recalled the days of Olympic Stadium in Montreal. "I haven't been to RFK, but I hear that's not too good. Also Shea, and we'll leave it at that."

Jamey Carroll's first major league team was the Montreal Expos. He began by noting that his home park was Olympic Stadium, a place that sometimes seemingly drew more flies than fans: "I was just getting into the big leagues, so it was probably helpful for me to be in that situation where it didn't make me as nervous. I was in a little bit better situation as far as the transition into the majors, so I may have used that to my advantage.

"At that point in time it was our gig, it was our home and we had to deal with it. There was nothing we could really do about [the empty seats in an unattractive setting]. You kind of just look past that. I don't know if more guys came in from the road and dreaded coming in. I would assume. Especially if maybe you come in from a place where there were [crowds of] forty-five to fifty thousand, and now there's five thousand. It's a tough thing, but we tried to use it to our advantage. We knew what we were getting into."

WHEN FOES BECOME TEAMMATES

What takes place when there is bad blood between two opposing players and then one of them gets traded, making the two enemies teammates? Will the situation fester and become worse due to their proximity?

"Not really," said Mike Stanton. "Even if you don't like somebody on a personal basis, you still respect them because of either what they've done or the ability they have—or whatever. To say that you get along with absolutely everyone on the team, that wouldn't be true, but you respect everyone, and you realize that everyone has a job to do and that you all have the same goal. Knowing that, you're able to put things aside and get your job done."

Cleveland outfielder Kevin Rhomberg said that the awkwardness of having an enemy become a teammate evaporates quickly: "Just think of Pete Rose. He was kind of hated among everybody else, but if he's your teammate you love him. There's really nobody that comes to mind to me who was involved in any trade, at any level [who didn't gain acceptance].

"Like a Brett Butler—I played against him a ton in the minor leagues when he was in the Braves organization. Then, in my first or second big-league camp, he got traded to us and we were both center fielders at the time. We were fine. You got your job to do; I got mine to do. You got traded to us, so be it. It was thought of as being awkward, but you still have to have your own tunnel vision, but he's a good guy, too."

Therefore, when two teammates do clash, it becomes noteworthy. Take the case of Barry Bonds and Jeff Kent, who became San Francisco teammates when Kent joined the Giants in time for the 1997 season. Their personalities clearly didn't mesh, and things soon came to an ugly head that season when the two fought, their fisticuffs captured on television. If it had been a Las Vegas title fight, it could have been billed as the Bout of MVPs.

When the two were separated, Kent shouted that he no longer wanted to be a part of the Giants, but the men would remain reluctant teammates through 2002.

Stanton said that it's only natural that feuding teammates become news, "especially when [a confrontation] happens in the dugout during the game or something like that, but, you know, a lot of that has to do with each player's approach or where they are in their careers and how they look at themselves as far as how the dynamics of the team goes, stuff like that. Those are the unfortunate situations that don't really happen very often, even behind closed doors."

He went so far as to say that as time goes by after an incident, even one as blatant as the "Slugout in the Dugout" between Kent and Bonds, it is forgotten (though perhaps never forgiven): "I can guarantee they both put it behind them now and it's just something that happened in the past."

PLAYERS' HAPPIEST MOMENTS

What on-the-field moments stick out as the happiest ones for players? Ben Grieve joked, "Every time I hit a home run, I'm pretty happy." More seriously, he added, "Probably a game in Texas, because my first game there I had a really good game, and my first game in Oakland I had a good game [in his home park], but I'd probably take the one in Texas.

"I was playing that first game there, against the team I grew up watching. It was pretty special." Born in Arlington, Texas, when his father, Tom, was with the Rangers, Ben's first homer in Texas came with his father as the Rangers color commentator.

Jason Bay looked back to when "I was eleven years old. I was fortunate enough to go to the Little League World Series for Team Canada. So winning that, the Canadian championship, and going to the Series in Williamsport were probably the highlights of my life."

Todd Hollandsworth said, "You have games that stand out. There's an awful lot of different games, special days. I think probably one of the bigger days I was proud of was when I had a three-homer game on Easter Sunday of 2001.

"I had a big pinch-hit against the Cubs in the 2003 NLCS. I remember standing on second base watching seventy thousand flash bulbs going off. It was just one of those moments that you capture and you keep for a long time. I drove in the tying run in the eighth inning in Game Three. We lost the game, but at the time it was a huge hit for us, and at that moment in time, just standing on second base getting caught up in all that was pretty awesome." It was, he felt, the kind of moment one dreams about as a kid, and it doesn't come much better than that.

In Brad Wilkerson's case, his memorable moment wasn't, like so many players, his very first day in the big leagues, since he was "more nervous than happy" that day, which came shortly after he got the official call-up to Montreal at the All-Star break of 2001.

"That next year," he said, "being able to start Opening Day in the big leagues, to be involved and in the starting lineup, was a dream come true for me—to know that I finally made it, it was amazing."

Players as Fans

Bill Hasselman said most big-leaguers are, at heart, fans. He said he loved the game even before he played it at a serious, elevated level. Further, he said that he believes all his fellow major leaguers are, in fact, baseball fans: "Now that we play it, we're probably more wrapped up in our team winning rather than being a fan of anybody. But I think before and after you play the game is when you're really going to be a fan, or maybe in the postseason just watching some team if you're not in it."

Players, when impressed enough by dramatic, unbelievable, and/or exciting events, react like fans. Asked what left them with lasting impressions, players came up with a variety of responses.

Rico Brogna said, "I think one of the most amazing things that I've seen was what Kirk Gibson did in the 1988 World Series [for the Dodgers in Game One] against Oakland. He could barely walk, and he pinch-hits the two-run, game-winning home run off Dennis Eckersley." Gibson was so badly hobbled with injuries to both legs, he wasn't expected to play at all. He barely did—his home run represented his only appearance in that entire World Series.

Gibson was undergoing physical therapy in the clubhouse as the ninth inning rolled around. He heard broadcaster Vin Scully say that he was "nowhere to be found" in the dugout, Gibson notified his manager that he could pinch-hit. After taking some cuts in a batting cage, he entered the game to face an elite reliever in Eckersley.

With an 0–2 count, Gibson took a terribly awkward swing that resulted in a foul ball dribbler. The odds of him hitting with power seemed to be nil, but several pitches later he slashed his dramatic home run.

Less dramatic but truly newsworthy is something Greg Maddux once did with the Braves. Teammate Denny Neagle recalled,

"[Pitching coach] Leo Mazzone keeps a stat on first-pitch strikes, and there was a game down in Florida when Greg pitched against the Marlins and he threw first-pitch strikes to the first twenty-one batters, and went through a total of thirteen balls the whole game, something like that—I don't remember the final numbers, but that, to me, was amazing."

As the game unfolded, the drama of the situation increased, at least for those in the know, if not for the average fan: "We knew because we're so conscious of it, and we take pride in who has the most first-pitch strikes.

"John Smoltz came up to me in about the fifth, he goes, 'You know what? There's something happening here tonight that's unbelievable! I'm not going to tell you, because I don't want to jinx him, but you just think about it.' The more I thought about it, I checked the chart, and there it was: strike one, strike one, strike one. He didn't miss a spot that whole night. That's incredible. That night he was *on*."

Paul Byrd said, "Maddux, execution-wise, could throw a ball on the corner any time he wanted, and a lot of people know that up and in or down and away gets guys out, but not everybody can throw the ball there. He doesn't overthrow, just nice and easy. People get labeled as being really super smart, but the reality is you have to be able to execute the pitch. I think he's a *great* executioner.

"You can know everything in the world about a hitter, but if you can't execute the pitch, it really doesn't matter. You watch the guy throw his bullpen, and he misses maybe five times out of forty pitches; not a lot of guys can do that."

As for Maddux himself, he picked an isolated moment for his lasting impression: "Andre Dawson when he got [a pitch] right at his head against Nolan Ryan—and then, next pitch, almost the same place, and he hit it in the upper deck in the Astrodome."

Ryan said he'll never forget another one of Dawson's shots: "The one he hit in the Astrodome off Frank LaCorte. That's the longest one I ever saw there." It was one of just a few blows ever hit into the dome's fifth level. The ball flew so high and far that Dawson said, "I actually lost the ball straight down the left field line in the lights. Only when I came back to the bench did someone tell me that it went into the upper deck in the yellow seats."

Joe Carter said he hated to see Dawson come to the plate: "He's intimidating. He's got that wiry body, but he's a strong as ever, and he's got tremendous bat speed."

Sparky Anderson called a September 14, 1991, Cecil Fielder home run in Milwaukee unforgettable. "I've never seen one hit better than that," he said. Rick Dempsey was the Brewers' catcher that night, providing him with a perfect "seat" to view the homer and appreciate it as if he were a fan. "It was the longest ball I ever saw," Dempsey said. "He hit it out of the entire stadium. Dan Plesac threw a fastball and it just disappeared into the night. I looked up to see the fans and see who was going to catch it, but they were all just looking up.

"One kid ran up the stairs and got to the top row, looking as if he was going to catch it, but it went over the eight-foot fence up there. The ball went 30 feet above *that*, and that's a conservative estimate. It went halfway up the light tower in left field. It was estimated that the ball traveled 520 feet, landing in a dumpster by the parking lot." It is the only ball ever launched out of Milwaukee County Stadium.

Aside from being slack-jawed at the feats of their peers, players who see themselves as fans of the game do have gripes about baseball, just as all fans do. Hall of Famer Craig Biggio pointed out an odd rule that states that a batter who hits a ground ball is awarded a hit if the ball strikes a teammate on the base paths. The runner is ruled out, but the batter lives at first base.

Biggio joked, "That's a great team rule because if a guy's struggling and you're going to be out anyway [on a force play at second], you might as well kick the ball for the guy so he can get a hit." Naturally, he knew that such occurrences are almost always unintentional.

He tossed in another peculiar rule: "Why is it that the [45-foot restraining path] line running down the side of the first base line is in foul territory when the base is in fair? So you gotta run in foul territory and step in fair. That's pretty stupid."

Curtis Granderson said that employing safety bags like those used in youth baseball would solve that situation. As a fan/player, he also had a different mild complaint: "If you foul tip with two strikes and it's caught by the catcher, you're out, but if you foul tip with zero or one strike, you still get to bat. That one doesn't make any sense to me."

SELF-SACRIFICING

Some players love the game—and winning—so much, they'll "take one for the team"; in other words, they'll willingly get hit by a pitch to reach base. All-Star Ron Hunt made that practice into an art form, leaning into pitches and utilizing tricks such as wearing a baggy jersey so that tight pitches might nick him. For quite some time he was the all-time leader in reaching base by way of getting hit by pitches. He led his league in that department seven seasons running, including a sky-high total of 50 in 1971, for an average of being plunked once in every three games.

He once said of opposing pitchers, "If they throw too hard [to hit against], I'll take one for the team." In other words, he added, "If you can't him them, let them hit you." Borrowing an old line from Dizzy Dean, Hunt went on, "I got hit in the head a couple of times. They X-rayed my brain, but the X-rays showed nothing."

Toby Harrah, an All-Star with a palindromic surname, respected Hunt's dedication. "There aren't too many Ron Hunts around any more," he said in 1990. "I don't think so, even with the protective gear worn now. Guys don't like to get hit. There aren't too many players left today who will hang out over the plate trying to get hit on purpose."

Occasionally, a starting pitcher who is getting roughed up very early in a ball game willingly becomes a sort of baseball martyr. This occurs when the shellacking he's absorbing comes at a time when his bullpen has been badly overworked. Rather than tax the fatigued relief corps, he sucks it up and lets his manager know he'll go deeper into the game, his ego and his rapidly inflating ERA be damned.

Former Arizona manager Bob Brenly once commented that players who are willing to put the team ahead of their stats are invaluable to a manager. Those players, he added, are also "in a minority, a small minority."

How Tough Is It to Win a World Series Now?

It's never been easy to win the World Series, but it is now more difficult than ever before, especially earlier than 1969, when division play began. Prior to that revolutionary change, the team that had proven over the long haul that they were the best in their league won the pennant (a term not used now nearly as much as it had been from 1903 to 1968). After that, it was usually a case of winning four more games to be crowned the champions.

Nowadays, a team could be the most competitive, talented team in the world but not become world champs. In theory, a team could win all 162 games of their season and get eliminated in their first round of playoff action. Instead of the top two teams being in the running to win it all, there are now twelve teams involved in postseason play. In 1968, for example, two of the twenty clubs in the majors went to the postseason, or 10 percent. In 2023, twelve of the thirty teams—or 40 percent—go. In 2017, the Twins made the playoffs with a winning percentage of .525. In 2005, the Padres made it to the postseason at only two games above .500 (82–80) thanks to division play—six other teams had better NL records.

Tom Grieve commented, "There's a big element of luck now. Over the course of 162 games, there's no such thing as luck because you play every day for six months, and the teams that win deserve to win, and they were the best team, and there's no doubt about it.

"What happens in postseason play includes an element of luck because *anything* can happen in a short series. The Canadian team beat the US [in the 2006 World Baseball Classic]. If they played 162 times, the US would probably go, you know, 130 and 32, something like that. But on any given night in baseball anything can happen. And in postseason play anything can happen."

When the Atlanta Braves were mathematically eliminated from the 2006 division title race on September 12, it marked the first time they had failed to win their division since 1990. That covers a span in which they won fourteen division titles and five pennants. It was the longest such winning streak in sports history, with the next-best such streaks at the time being nine seasons (by the Colorado Avalanche, the Boston Celtics and the Los Angeles Lakers). Despite such a dynasty, even the Braves managed to win just one World Series.

CHAPTER SIX

Life in the Big Leagues

UNWRITTEN RULES OF BASEBALL

Baseball has its clearly drawn-up, etched-in-cement rulebook covering everything from balks to strike zone boundaries. However, baseball also has much hazier, far from carved-in-stone unwritten rules.

Many players spoke of how irate and belligerent they get when an opponent breaks such rules, and because these rules sometimes change from one era to another and seemingly from player to player, major misunderstandings and even fights result.

Curtis Granderson believed most of the unwritten rules of baseball "really don't make any sense. It's kind of one of those things where, 'You can beat me, but you can't beat me too bad.' And it's okay for me to hit a home run to break up a no-hitter, but I can't bunt."

A team—even one with a speed demon who could outrun a beam of sunlight, such as Rickey Henderson—will not attempt to steal a base with, say, a ten-run lead, nor would a team with such a lead squeeze home a run or bunt a runner over, but, Granderson said, "squeezing to score a run? Whether you're up five or six, every run counts."

He thought it foolish that a base-stealing artist is expected to refrain from swiping a bag with his team holding a big lead, even though there is a chance that the opponent may eventually rally and engineer a shocking win. "Everybody's going to be talking about you [blowing] the game when you had the opportunity to add to your lead," he said. "I see it in other sports. For example, in basketball the other team doesn't stop shooting with a big lead, and in football they don't just stop running plays anymore. If the other team can't stop you, why [ease up]?

"And I never understood if I'm not supposed to run here, then why are you holding me on? If you're not holding me on, that's one thing, but if you're holding me on, then that gives me the option to run. I see no wrong with going—if I'm the manager of a team, I'd let my guys go."

Fear of retribution keeps some unwritten rules alive—nobody enjoys getting plunked by a pitch. Granderson said, "I've never understood if you're batting second and I'm batting third, and you just hit three home runs, why do you hit me [for retaliation]? I didn't do it! I've never heard of a pitcher striking out ten guys in a row and then a batter throwing his bat at him. You never see it, it's not okay, but it is okay for the pitcher to say, 'Oh, they're too comfortable on me,' and throw at him."

Yet another aspect of the game, this one from the days when the NL wasn't using the designated hitter, puzzled Granderson. Pitchers often avenged a star player who had been a target of a fastball by hitting the other team's star. "Why not hit the pitcher? He's the one that hit you?" The typical reply Granderson received was, "Well, that's just one of those no-no things. You definitely can't do that." However, Granderson's thinking was, "Well, when guys are constantly hitting guys, maybe pitchers will stop when they start getting hit. Hit the pitcher."

Because there are gray areas, there will always be disputes. Just when does a manager with a big lead call off his dogs and instruct his team to, for instance, quit stealing bases or stretching singles into doubles?

In recent years, with numerous teams splurging on offense, an aggressive manager might reason, "Well, okay, if the other team promises not to try to hit home runs, then I'll promise to have my runners be passive and play station-to-station baseball." Perhaps a manager feels the opponent's offense is so powerful, a six-run lead in the seventh inning isn't necessarily safe, so he unleashes his speed burners. The other team might interpret the strategy as bush and retaliate.

Jeff Francoeur explored the issue of taking an extra base. "If you hit a clear-cut double, go to second base, do what you got to do, but [if] you're up more than six, seven runs in the eighth, ninth inning, you got to stop there," he said. "For the most part the game's over with. If it's any time before the seventh inning, I don't care if it's 12–1, I think that's fine. Later innings, you tone it down a little bit. The game's gotta be really out of hand for you not to want to [ease up]."

So what about a scenario in which a team with a lead of, say, nine runs cruises, then the other team rallies and upsets them? Wouldn't the team regret not playing hard, even with their big lead? Francoeur laughed, saying, "If you blow that much of a lead, you don't deserve to win."

Similarly, there's the matter of not stealing with a big lead. On April 22, 2011, the Dodgers were playing the Cubs. With Los Angeles up, 8–1, in the fifth inning, they were enjoying a Good Friday. However, things turned a bit ugly when their catcher, A. J. Ellis, with pitcher Chad Billingsley at the plate, attempted the first stolen base of his career, irritating Chicago manager Mike Quade in the process.

Ellis was gunned down by his counterpart, catcher Geovany Soto, but Quade was still fuming after his 12–2 defeat at Wrigley Field. Dodger manager Don Mattingly later explained that a missed sign is what caused Ellis to be running, but he defended the strategy in that situation, nevertheless.

Francoeur said, "That's more of a big deal than the going for an extra base, because if you go for an extra base, you know, you hit it, you deserved it [the next base]; but to steal is a no-no, especially if a guy is playing off [the bag, not holding the runner tight]. That's bush league."

One rule everyone seems to agree on is on what count not to take a vicious cut at the ball. Silver Slugger winner Aubrey Huff said, "I've seen some guys swing at a 3–0 pitch, up 10–0, something like that, late in the game, and that's a bad one. That always looks bad."

An ancient rule, though one not to be found in any edition of Major League Baseball's Official Baseball Rules, is never to bunt to break up a no-hitter. In 2001, San Diego catcher Ben Davis was at the plate with one out in the eighth inning against Arizona's overpowering Curt Schilling. With his team down, 2–0, Davis said, in effect, "He's too much for me today. I just can't hit him, so I gotta try anything to get something started. If I reach base, that brings the potential tying run to the plate." He laid down and beat out a bunt to break up Schilling's gem.

The Diamondbacks were livid. Manager Bob Brenly bristled, and Luis Gonzalez, normally a very mild-mannered man, had quite a bit to say on the subject. Indignant, he felt baseball had seemingly reached the point where it had become acceptable to flaunt the traditional unwritten rules of the game. "You ask the old-school guys, and it's not so much accepted," he said. "We had a situation here with Schilling throwing a no-hitter, and the unwritten rule is you don't bunt to break up a no-hitter because of the respect for the pitcher out there—you try to earn it. And they bunted.

"We didn't see it as a good play in baseball, and shoot, man, we got barbecued for it. Actually, the media and the fans got on us because of some of the comments we made after the game because it broke up a no-hitter. We felt like if you're going to [break up a no-hitter], especially that late in the game, do it the right way—get a clean hit instead of bunting. It didn't set well with us."

Gonzalez seemed quite surprised when fans reacted as if what the light-hitting Davis did was fine. He pointed out that they felt like, "What's the big deal? But the big deal to us is we're old-school and, just like the old days, when a guy got hit on one team, somebody would have to get hit on the other. Once in a blue moon there were guys charging the mound, but it was, 'You get one of ours, we'll get one of yours,' and that was it. Now, times have changed"—and not, in his view, for the better. Some rules, he believed, are *not* meant to be broken.

However, there is another side to the story, and it can be argued that under certain circumstances, maybe some rules need to be edited a bit. As Francoeur said, "I got no problem with that bunt—you're right in the ball game, you got a chance—it's part of the game.

"That's like saying it's 2–1 in the ninth inning and the pitcher has a no-hitter—maybe he walked in a run or something, and some guy tries to drop a bunt to get something started. Come on, it's 2–1. Now if it's eight to nothing and he drops a bunt, I *totally* disagree with that, but in the 2–0 [Schilling game], you're a bunt and a home run away from a tie ball game. Not a big deal. Why not bunt?" Why not, he felt, use every weapon at one's disposal?

CC Sabathia agreed that due to the score, the bunt was not a bush-league move. "He was trying to get on base," he said. "If somebody hits a home run, it's a tie game. I could see [being angry] if it was 5–0 or 4–0. I don't think it was that bad." After all, it was Davis's job to get on base, and, as Granderson fully understood, it is the job of the defense to guard against bunts. "He's trying to win the game," Sabathia noted. Still, like beauty, a bush-league play or a violation of an unwritten rule is often in the eye of the beholder.

UNWRITTEN CODE FOR ROOKIES

Veterans' expectations and treatment of rookies has changed over the years, but Wade Boggs said that when he broke into the majors, he knew he was to keep a low profile. The old line "Speak only when spoken to" applied. In 1998 he said, "Rookies are to be seen and not heard. You keep your mouth shut, you learn your business, go about it, and put your time in. I think that's a lost art of paying your dues and keeping your mouth shut."

Joe Charboneau, 1980 AL Rookie of the Year, said, "You know what, pretty much everybody treated me real well as a rookie. You don't talk a lot, you kind of wait until you're spoken to, and you kind of know your place."

Gene Clines said rookies even take flak from people in the club-house, as happened when he broke into the majors in 1970: "Some veteran clubhouse men let the young kids know, 'I run the show in here.' As a rookie, you take what's there when it comes to equipment."

Kevin Rhomberg, who played only forty-one big-league games, added an insight on how umpires treated him in his 1982 rookie season: "They'd all treat you very differently—some were very outgoing and welcoming, 'Congratulations. You made it.' Another umpire said, 'Hey, don't say a word to me. You're a rookie; just play the game.' He wanted to get that established right away."

The treatment a rookie gets can depend upon his status, though. For example, Dwight Gooden was already a big name by the time he made it to the majors with the Mets in 1984. He said, "I was lucky, actually, they were pretty good with me."

However, he said that when Ryan Thompson made his debut with the Mets, "We made him wear a dress in Philadelphia because he's from that area. His family was there, and we hid his clothes so he had to wear a dress and high heel shoes on the bus."

The 1995 Indians went a slightly different route with rookie Herbert Perry. Shortly after the last game of his first Indians road trip to Toronto, he was about to get dressed when he noticed that "all of my clothes were missing from my locker. I had to wear these hobo clothes [thoughtfully provided by veterans] all the way back through the airport. I swear I thought there was no way the American customs officials were going to let me back into the country."

Rafael Palmeiro said during a 1998 interview, "Earlier this year we played the Marlins, and they have a bunch of rookies. They have to come onto the field through a tunnel where we come out of our clubhouse doors. It was the funniest thing—there were twelve babies with nothing on but big diapers, half their team with these diapers."

Infielder Shane Halter recalled a few favorite dress-the-rookie-up gags: "The funniest thing I ever saw was probably Mendy López. He had a wrestler's uniform on with combat boots and they [Kansas City veterans] made him wear hairpieces and everything else. Another one that we saw was Andy Stewart; they had him in leotards and that was quite a sight to see. Those are always funny because they always have to be done in front of fans, and they had to sign autographs."

Carl Erskine spoke of one mild prank he experienced during an early road trip. At his Dodgers hotel in Pittsburgh, he asked a veteran how to get to Forbes Field. "He told me to take a taxi." He did. The trip lasted seconds to the park just around the corner from the hotel.

In 1964, when veteran catcher Pat Corrales broke in, there was very little levity. He echoed the words of Boggs, "You kinda had to keep your mouth shut and do what you were told."

When Brad Wilkerson first walked into a big-league clubhouse as an Expos rookie, he was intimidated. He explained the etiquette of being the new guy: "A lot of veterans are knowledgeable about the game and they understand it's a team game, and they usually initiate the contact with younger players.

"Younger players are kind of nervous walking in, and they don't know what to do. You kind of creep around. Some rookies are more boisterous than others, but a lot of veterans do a great job of being leaders and coming up to them and taking them under their wings, then go on from there.

"When I first came to Montreal, they had veterans like Lee Stevens, and Graeme Lloyd and Mike Mordecai. Just being around those guys for even a half season [Wilkerson was called up at the All-Star break in 2001], I learned so much."

Kenny Lofton, the sixth man on the University of Arizona's 1988 Final Four team, was thrilled to reach the majors, mainly because "I'm playing against a lot of guys I've seen on TV."

Rookies aren't mistreated now, and they aren't awestruck as they once were. "I think the game's different now," said Chris Chambliss. "The money that they make now is so much different. So some of those traditions have started to fade away."

Chambliss, who played from 1971 to 1988, can remember the era when rookies were made to serve the veterans when a group of players went out to eat. Of course, even eating out with a bunch of players, he says, has pretty much disappeared. Players aren't together as much as they used to be, so, as he put it, "some of those pranks don't really exist anymore."

Wade Boggs gave his opinion on when rookies' reactions to being treated like peons began to change: "It's probably less tolerated by rookies now; they get a little bit more offensive more often now. I don't know when the transition period [to intolerance to being mistreated] happened, probably in 1991 and 1992.

"Rookies get to the big leagues and sort of have an attitude that they've been here ten years. I'm sure their money [from huge contracts] has changed their attitude. When I came up [in 1982, at the age of twenty-four] with Carl Yastrzemski, Mike Torrez, Dennis Eckersley, Jerry Remy, and those types of individuals [established veterans], it was *a lot* different."

Chambliss also pointed out that in the old days "the older guys even got more swings in the batting cage than the rookies, but everybody gets the same amount of swings because batting practice is so structured now."

David Bell, a rookie in 1995, has baseball roots that date back to the 1950s. His grandfather, Gus, was a major-leaguer, as was his father, Buddy. That made the Bell family the second of just three three-generation baseball families. Bell theorized on why rookies were treated a lot more roughly in the old days: "Maybe guys stayed with a team longer and they developed more of a close-knit thing where you had to break into their circle." Bell, who once wore an "initiation" skirt, much to the delight of Cardinals veterans, concurs that "guys *are* easier on rookies now."

Luis Gonzalez explained one reason for that. When he was with the Diamondbacks in 2003, he said he and the other veterans had been around the game long enough to appreciate the fact that times have changed and even rookies can be vital to team success. "We've learned you treat the young guys the same way as you do the veterans because they could be just as important," he said. "So the quicker you make these young kids feel welcome around the veteran guys, the more comfortable they're going to feel, and the more they're going to feel like, 'Hey, I belong up here; let me relax and just go out there and do what I know I'm capable of doing.'"

Ryan Zimmerman is something of a modern rarity in that he spent his entire sixteen-year big-league career with one club. When the All-Star infielder got called up to the big club, the Washington Nationals, in 2005, he was highly heralded. Like Gooden, he didn't face hazing at all, but he did have to learn.

When asked what went through the mind of a big-league newcomer, he replied, "Well, you just got to go about your business the same way, the way that got you here. You're here for a reason. You can't come up here and try to do too much or be out of character; you have to stay with your game and take advantage of the guys around you—they've been here for a long time and you can learn a lot from them. That's one of the bigger things: just to learn as much as you can while you're up here."

ROOKIES' LEARNING EXPERIENCES

In Michael Young's rookie year, he was just one year younger than his Texas Rangers double play partner, Alex Rodriguez—but A-Rod was already a six-year vet, having broken into the bigs in 1994 at the age of eighteen.

Young commented, "As a rookie, you don't need people to take you by the hand, you just see people doing what they do and maybe you take something that you should from them. At the time, I didn't need people to pat me on the back all the time, I just needed to see people do their job and go out and play hard and play to win—that's all I cared about." Seeing A-Rod play every day and display a strong work ethic reinforced what Young, too, was all about.

In 1992 and again in 1993, Cleveland's Carlos Baerga became the first second baseman since Rogers Hornsby (in 1921 and 1922) to put up consecutive seasons with 20 or more doubles and homers, 100-plus runs driven in, and 200 or more hits while topping the .300 level. In 1993 he also became the first switch-hitter to hit home runs from both sides of the plate in the same inning.

Baerga said he had the pleasure of playing with Dave Winfield, Paul Molitor, Roberto Alomar, and Tony Gwynn. When you play alongside men who handle the bat with such prowess as those, you learn about "the way they prepare themselves for the game and how they react to pitches—what they look for. That's what you learn from them."

Similarly, All-Star Phil Nevin noted his biggest influence: "Once I got to the big leagues, I would say Tony Gwynn." Nevin learned from him by both studying his dedication and "watching how he goes about his business."

Meanwhile, 1998 Rookie of the Year Ben Grieve said he soon learned the importance of "getting a good pitch to hit, just not going up there swinging at everything—being patient."

Jason Bay said that the best lesson he learned was "to try and stay inside the ball. The more you try to fly open and pull the ball, that's the first thing a pitcher sees, your weakness, and you're so exposed to breaking balls and stuff away. In BP that's what we're trying to stress the whole time—just staying inside the ball. And you can't work the other way. You can work away and react to it; that's the best way to go."

People often learn from making mistakes, and that's certainly true of minor leaguers learning to ply their trade. But what happens when a young player makes a glaring mistake during a game at the big-league level—will someone approach him with advice? Do they *teach* at such a high level, or is a matter of sink or swim?

Jeff Francoeur said that someone will definitely instruct the youngster, but "not during the game. Maybe quietly—one of the guys, a veteran, or our hitting coach will say, 'Hey, listen, in this kind of situation maybe next time you might want to . . . .' And that's good, everybody needs to hear it. Sometimes guys eight, ten years in the big leagues need to hear it, too."

Ryan Zimmerman, who blistered the ball to a .397 tune over his fifty-eight at-bats as a rookie, felt that the biggest surprise for baseball debutantes is the precision of big-league pitchers. They don't tend to miss their locations or make costly mistakes nearly as often as minor leaguers. "They still make a few mistakes," he said, "and you gotta get them when they make a mistake, but they're good up here—they're here for a reason, too."

In just his first few days, Zimmerman faced some tough pitchers, including Dontrelle Willis, who was on his way to recording a 22-win season, and Todd Jones, a crafty veteran who was closing out a 40-save season. Zimmerman summed up another learning experience: "Whatever it says on the scouting report is what they got. The pitchers aren't that much better than down in Double-A, it's just that they spot it up a lot better and they know when to throw [their best pitches]. They're a lot smarter up here, pretty much everyone."

He also quickly learned several other non-baseball matters that every rookie from Babe Ruth to today's upcoming stars has discovered. "The travel is easier than it was at Double-A," he said. "We fly everywhere, there are no busses and you're treated real well up here, so that's also nice. It's more than I had expected. Everyone's dream is to get here, and you don't realize how nice it is until you actually get here."

Playing with the Senators in Harrisburg, he had been getting "pretty much $20 a day" per diem. In one of his earliest big-league interviews,

Zimmerman said he wasn't sure how much the meal money allowance was because he had yet to make a road trip, but he knew it was "a lot more." He was correct, and it kept getting better. Shortly after he retired in 2021, a new basic agreement called for players to get $117.50 per day for food, tips, and other basic expenses while on the road. Not a bad perk for players whose average yearly salary in 2023 had soared to $4.9 million. Even a player making the major league minimum earned $720,000, so it's safe to say he could afford to pay for his own food.

By way of contrast, Class D players circa 1948 were given $3 a day for meals, while big-leaguers back then received around $6. By 1972, in Class A ball the allotment was $3.50, compared to $18 per day in the majors. In the 1990s major league meal money hit $59,and by 2005 it was $80.50. It's now $117.50 during the season on days when the team is on the road and the club doesn't provide players a meal.

ROOKIES AND SELF-DOUBT

Even men who are destined for stardom can experience self-doubt as they advance through the minors and reach big-league rookie status. Thoughts of "Can I make it? Do I belong here?" infiltrate young players' minds.

Derek Jeter said that when he broke into the minors in 1992, "I cried all the time. . . . I had no roommate because I signed late. Third baseman spoke no English. Second baseman spoke no English. I struggled for the first time. I cried almost every day. That was tough." He hit a paltry .210 and whiffed fifty-two times in fifty-eight games, giving no indication that he would someday be headed to Cooperstown.

Jeter and Mariano Rivera got the call-up to the Yankees—briefly—just days apart in May 1995. When Rivera served up a home run to Edgar Martínez in a game that saw his ERA blow up to 10.20, the Yankees certainly did not feel as if he belonged. Jeter said, "He gave up a home run and they sent me down, [too]. We were miserable."[1]

Naive rookies, new to the world of the majors, are susceptible to being duped. Back in 1975, Cleveland pitcher Fritz Peterson kept things loose in the spring training locker room. A teammate of his, Duane Kuiper, recalled a favorite trick. "Cy Buynak [the clubhouse attendant] would leave the weekly bill for clubhouse dues, say, for $30, on players' chairs," said Kuiper. "Fritz put a '1' in front of the '30' on the rookies' bills. They'd see it [a bill for what was then the astronomical amount of $130] and almost die! They didn't know anything, and they'd believe everything."

PREFERENTIAL TREATMENT FOR VETERANS

To paraphrase a line from George Orwell's book *Animal Farm*, "All ballplayers are equal, but veteran players are more equal than others."

Travis Hafner and Don Mattingly share a record: six grand slams in one year. Hafner spoke about a baseball fact of life—stars and established veterans get preferential treatment over others—by saying, "You have to respect veteran ballplayers and what they've done in this game, because everybody knows how hard it is. With our [Cleveland] clubhouse it's things like veterans getting the best parking spots. You just try to take care of the veterans—if you're ahead of them in line, you'll let them go ahead, just things like that. Doing what they've accomplished, they deserve some, I wouldn't say special rights, but some privileges."

Carl Erskine said that when he played with the Brooklyn Dodgers, "there was a pecking order in the clubhouse. Nobody talked about it, but it existed. A rookie would get a locker in the back of the clubhouse. It would be smaller than the others, or he might have to share a locker. At first they give you a uniform that didn't fit to see how you'd handle it. You had to prove you belonged. As you got more established, you'd find you had a better locker. Our captain, Pee Wee Reese, had the choice, bigger locker and a captain's chair—the rest of us had stools."

Joe Charboneau added, "When you first come up, umpires will call more strikes on you. If you're facing a veteran of ten years in the big leagues and you're a rookie, he's going to get more strikes called. It's not that they're not fair, it's just you have to kind of learn your place, that you're a rookie and you gotta pay your dues."

Baseball's first player to appear at the plate as a designated hitter was Yankee Ron Blomberg. He said, "If you are a Hall of Famer or a star, they're going to give you more leeway, and we understood that. Rookies better not say anything to the home plate umpires when they get up to bat, and they better not make them look bad. You have to respect them."

This disparity in getting calls was vividly on display in a 1998 game when rookie Rolando Arrojo started on the hill for Tampa Bay versus Atlanta's Greg Maddux, who was in his thirteenth season and already owned four (consecutive) Cy Young Awards. Even though Arrojo would soon head to the All-Star Game, and even though his record going into the July 2 game was 10–4, the home plate umpire squeezed the strike zone on him. That was far from the case when Maddux pitched.

Tampa teammate Kevin Stocker said it wasn't a mano a mano duel: "It was Maddux *and* the umpire against Arrojo. Maddux gets another four inches off the plate. It was tough to see Rolando not get calls. You have to realize, this is Maddux; Rolando is a rookie." Clearly, a double standard was on display.

PREFERENTIAL TREATMENT FOR STARS

Stars naturally are treated better than other players on many, if not all, clubs. There is a fine line, though, between a grateful, appreciative manager giving a star some perks and privileges others might not get versus bending over so far as to cause dissension on a team.

When Barry Bonds was bombing balls all over the Bay Area with the Giants, he demanded special treatment. One of the most salient examples of how he was different from his teammates was the seating arrangements in the clubhouse—he sat isolated in a plush Sharper Image massage recliner with a $3,000 price tag, tucked away from the rest of his teammates, watching a large for-his-eyes-only TV. He had not one or two lockers to himself, but four wood paneled stalls, including the largest one in the room. Teammates such as Jeff Kent resented Bonds, and clubhouse strife followed. "Off the field," Kent said, "I don't care about Barry and Barry doesn't care about me. Or anybody else."[2]

In 2004, at the age of forty-one, twenty-year veteran Roger Clemens insisted on a clause in his contract with the Astros stating that he did not have to make any road trip in which he wasn't slated to pitch. There's no way of knowing if any teammates begrudged that stipulation, but anyone who subscribes to the age-old concept that teammates belong together and that they stick together no matter what would have been upset at Clemens's absence.

It should be noted that the Astros organization was wise enough to consult venerated vets Jeff Bagwell and Craig Biggio before consummating the free agent deal with Clemens. Asked what their reaction would be to such favoritism, they said they had no problem with the treatment, they were just delighted at the prospect of having the 300-plus game winner aboard.

David Wells said that not traveling with teammates on any trip was an act of disrespect to the Astros and every teammate, and an act that would cause them to lose respect for Clemens. Greg Maddux agreed, saying he could not even imagine doing what the Rocket was doing and continued to do when he signed on for his second stint with the Yankees for the 2007 season. "That's not the Yankee way," said Wells. "The Yankees have changed."[3]

One rather noncommittal player said, "He's a special case, I guess," and let it go at that. Another, pitcher Mike Stanton, took a stronger and more supportive stance. He said, "Me personally, no, there's no resentment. I mean, if you can get that contract or you can get an organization to agree to that, there's not anyone here [in the Cincinnati locker room] who wouldn't take that. Obviously some of our jobs [the everyday players] wouldn't really allow that, but as much as managers and general managers would say there's not a double standard, there absolutely is a double standard.

"People who are having problems with that, it's really just a personal problem, because you're not going to change it. It's something you have no control over, it's got nothing to do with you, so that's just the way the world is—the world's not fair."

Stanton pointed out that there certainly are teammates who inevitably think that they should also be given those special perks, too. It's easy to imagine aggrieved and/or jealous players mulling over the inequity: "If he can leave the team, I should be able to do it, too." Imagine, too, the chaos that would then unravel.

Scott Hatteberg opined, "It's pitchers that are able to do it. It's hard for me to relate, because I'm not a pitcher. I'm sure there's jealousy. The season's really long and you want everybody to be involved in the toil of the whole season. I mean, it's a grind, and being an older guy [such as Clemens], you're kind of thrust into the leadership role, but you're not there for it."

Stanton concluded, "There is definitely some of that [envy], and a lot of those guys probably think very highly of themselves."

Another example of a Hall of Fame pitcher wandering away from teammates is Jack Morris, who finished his eighteen-year career with a twenty-three-game stay in Cleveland in 1994 with 244 wins under his belt. Then thirty-nine years old, he began as the number-two starter, but his pitching and his personal life (his fiancée called off their engagement) began to deteriorate. His farm in Montana was plagued by a drought, and between starts Morris began flying there quite a bit instead of staying with the club.

He refused to change his nomadic ways, so the front office, pointing mainly to his performance without getting into his frequent departures from the team, made their move. Fed up with Morris, who had ten wins to his credit but an inflated ERA, the Indians released him in early August. General manager John Hart explained, "From a baseball perspective, the [coaching] staff didn't want the guy."[4]

So poor pitching and too much baggage led to Morris's final days in baseball, even though Cleveland was in a pennant race, one game out of first place. Of course, it should be noted that the 1994 season ended due to a players' strike just three days after his release, wiping out a dramatic race and all postseason play.

On Race and Racism

Larry Doby, the first Black player in the American League, was once asked if it was difficult for him to reconcile the fact that from the day Jackie Robinson broke baseball's color line in 1947 to become the first Black player in the majors in the modern era, Doby was left in Robinson's shadow. "No," he replied. "I never thought of it. I'm not wrapped up in publicity, I don't have an ego. Most of the time you get publicity when you die. Maybe that'll happen to me." On that, he was quite prophetic: He was awarded the Congressional Gold Medal on his hundredth birthday, but not until 2023, almost twenty years after his death.

He chuckled, then continued, "Somebody had to be second." However, he felt it was important to note that "I went through the same things he did—just eleven weeks later than he did." Robinson's debut with the Brooklyn Dodgers came on April 15, 1947, and Doby followed with his first big-league game on July 5 with the Indians. "Nobody cleared all those problems in eleven weeks. It made me a stronger person, though. Nothing comes easy."

Indians owner Bill Veeck tried to make things easier for Doby. Shortly after bringing Doby to the majors, Veeck received more than twenty thousand letters, mostly protesting the integration of the team. Veeck responded by stating, "I am sure you would agree that any man should be judged on his personal merit and be allowed to exploit his talents to the fullest whether he happened to be black or blue with pink dots."[5]

That helped, said Doby, as did the fact that "I grew up in a mixed neighborhood, so I had no trouble adjusting to others. *They* had the problem—facing me for the first time." He said that he eventually made many fans realize "that I was a human being like them. I could play baseball. I could talk."

Still, things often grew very tough, and finding solace was difficult. "My most enjoyable hours were on the ball field," he said. "The worst were off the field. I was only twenty-one years old when I broke in, and there was a lot of loneliness for me, especially on the road. You kinda wished you could go have a beer or dinner with your teammates, but you couldn't.

"In 1952, things started to change, and at times I did have guys like Satchel Paige, Luke Easter, and Al Smith with me, but the first five years were often lonely." That didn't stop him from excelling, though. Over his eight full seasons with the Indians, he made the All-Star squad seven times and he helped lead the team to the world championship in 1948, his first full season with Cleveland.

The genial Doby focused on the positive, especially when speaking of his days with the Indians: "After ten years with them, you gotta have fond memories. The best one would be winning the '48 World Series. Cleveland hadn't had a winner for a long period of time [since their 1920 championship], and to be on a world champion ball club in just my second year was a good feeling." Cleveland fans liked and appreciated Doby. "We had good fans, they treated me real fine. They never gave me any problem. When the fans feel good, you feel good—the town feels good."

He knew it was unfortunate, though, that many people judge others prematurely and do so based on superficial matters. During a late 1980s interview he stressed, "I don't dwell on what happened forty years ago. We have to learn to live on this earth together—and athletics is a great way to do this. There has been a lot of change and improvement in many areas of baseball, but there's always room for more improvement."

He added another comment that has remained timely over the years: "It's a tense time and we should work together. That's the important thing we should strive for. I respect people. Thank God I don't have a problem with color. I just look at people as people."

Doby could certainly relate to Robinson, but he pointed out how different the two trailblazers were. "My 'thing' was being the low emotional type," he said. "Jackie was more political, more aggressive. If I had a problem, I'd take it to our team owner Bill [Veeck]. Jackie would take it to the media. I didn't get involved in that. You have to be yourself. I only ran into Jackie a few times at banquets. I can't say we socialized, but we were friends. We had respect for each other."

Meanwhile, Sam "The Jet" Jethroe initially thought he had a chance to break into the world of white baseball before Robinson. Jethroe had the tools: he was a speedy, rifle-armed outfielder who played on the Cleveland Buckeyes of the Negro Leagues from their initial season, 1942, through 1948.

Coming off a .353 season in 1944, he was proud to read what was called a "special bulletin to the *Cleveland Call and Post*," a weekly African American newspaper of the day that would later be owned by boxing promoter Don King. The April 15, 1945, news release stated that Jethroe "has been notified to report to the Boston Red Sox . . . for a tryout." It was all a sham, though, a pretense of sincerity by the Red Sox under their owner, the known bigot Tom Yawkey.

Jethroe recalled, "Jackie Robinson, Marvin Williams, and myself tried out for their manager, Joe Cronin. He got some of his coaches to go out on the field and we went through the fundamentals. After the workout, they said we had talent, but it was not the right time." It was a verdict that had the same sting as the comment made in the movie *On the Waterfront*, when a prize fighter played by Marlon Brando was told his chances of making the big time were doomed. "This ain't your night," he was told. Like Brando's character, Jethroe absolutely believed he could succeed at any level—it *was* his time.

And so Jethroe and his talented companions were rejected by the Red Sox, who would become the last team in Major League Baseball to integrate, fourteen years and three months later. Even then, they showed a lack of shrewd judgment, signing a marginal ballplayer named Pumpsie Green.

Jethroe believed the tryout he was given was "forced upon the Red Sox by an alderman. If they didn't get Blacks up there, they'd take Sunday baseball away from the Red Sox."

Dick Schofield, a veteran of nineteen seasons, several spent in Boston, said, "The Red Sox didn't have a Black player forever. I'm sure somebody in the front office or owners of some teams didn't want to have Black players in the beginning. That's obvious. That was the culture then."

Jethroe also said that another factor outside of his control prevented him from perhaps being the first Black player in the majors: "Bill Veeck was interested in me first, but the owner of the Buckeyes, Ernie Wright, wanted too much money, $40,000, to let me go. Then the Newark Bears owner let Veeck have Doby for $25,000 with a promise of $25,000 more if Doby did good."

Jethroe said that earlier, when he learned of Robinson's signing with the Dodgers, "I thought nothing about it. I never dreamed his signing would lead to me going to the majors." Afterward, though, it didn't take long for Brooklyn Dodgers general manager Branch Rickey to get the rights to Jethroe. That took place in 1948, when Jethroe was purchased— as if he was a piece of property—for $7,500.

Jethroe later learned for sure that his big-league debut could have come earlier than it did: "*Look* magazine wrote that I didn't know how close I was to being among the very first Blacks in the majors—maybe even going to Brooklyn as Jackie's roommate."

In addition to the influence of Rickey and Robinson, there were others, said Jethroe, who helped open the big-league doors. "I give Bob Feller a lot of credit for helping us get to the majors. He'd organize All-Star games between Black and white players. That was a big step for integration."

Jethroe said that having played in such All-Star games also showed him that he "wouldn't have to worry about any difficulties in the majors. They had good pitchers like Feller and Early Wynn, but we hit them."

On the other hand, he experienced inequities in many places, even south of the border. Owners of Mexican League teams tried to pirate big-leaguers to play for them, attempting to lure such men as Stan Musial with lucrative contracts. In some cases, such as Sal Maglie, they succeeded. However, when Jethroe was offered a three-year contract worth a total of $15,000, he was indignant. "I told him, 'You're giving white boys that much just for signing.'" His refusal wound up being a wise move, as those players who did jump to the Mexican League were subsequently suspended from Major League Baseball.

While he was delighted to break into the majors, Jethroe was taken aback by another fact of frugality in the bigs: he had received more money, $700 a month in the Negro Leagues, than he did with the Dodgers' top farm club in Montreal, $400 per month.

Still, he said he knew he could run on anybody: "My second year in Montreal, I stole 89 bases." That set a new modern International League record. "I could have stolen 150, but I had played all year [in various other leagues, such as winter ball]. By July, I was tired. I wouldn't run.

"Everywhere I played, I led the league in stolen bases. A guy once told me that in one year I led three *countries* in steals: the USA, Cuba, and Canada!" He would end up leading the NL in steals, with 35 in both his first and second seasons in the majors. He also took home Rookie of the Year honors in 1950.

Despite all of that, he was never immune to discrimination—just like Robinson and Doby and others before him. After the 1950 season with the Boston Braves, Jethroe was the only Black player on a barnstorming All-Star team of big-leaguers. When his team tried to play a game in New Orleans, the police told his manager, Alvin Dark, that there would be no game there that day—not with Jethroe on the diamond.

"I couldn't stay in the same hotel in Chicago with the Braves," he said. "The next time through Chicago, our traveling secretary roomed with me there." Jethroe also remembered, "In 1950, when I first went to Florida for spring training, I stayed at a private home. I didn't stay at the team hotel. We'd charter buses for our trips. They'd stop to eat and pile out to go in the restaurant. They'd say, 'Come on, Sam. They'll serve you here. If they don't, we won't eat.'

"I'd say, 'I don't want to start a commotion.' A waiter would come out to the bus and take my order. You knew that's how things are in the South."

Some say that many Black players of that long-gone era weren't as demonstrative as those that followed, those who were unafraid to protest indignities and injustices vehemently. When asked his opinion of more outspoken Black athletes such as a Charles Barkley, Jethroe answered, "He's too outrageous. I see a lot of that when a guy gets to be a big star—they act too crazy." Players of Jethroe's era tended to agree with him, as when he commented, "Barkley's going about it the wrong way. You don't bite the hands that feed you. You never see Michael Jordan do such [outrageous] stuff."

As for his Boston teammates, "Most of them were pretty nice to me, Warren Spahn and Johnny Sain, for example. One day I was in the batting cage and I took too many swings, more than I was [allotted]. Earl Torgeson [a white player] said, 'Can't you count?' Somehow, that broke the ice. After that I melted right in."

Not everything was fine with the team, though. Early on, the team's public relations man said he had been checking up on Jethroe. "I see you don't like to be called Sambo," he said. Jethroe sternly shot back that he was correct, but some of his teammates began to tease him about his "nickname." Jethroe then warned them to stop "before I get me a bat and run everybody out of here."

While his insensitive teammates did change their tune, Jethroe wasn't so lucky a bit later with Braves manager Charlie Grimm. Jethroe said, "He didn't like me. During games in 1952, he called me Sambo from the coach's box. I know I could've stayed with the Braves when they moved to Milwaukee the next year, but Grimm sent me to the minors, to Toledo."

There, he enjoyed an outstanding season, leading the league in steals while hitting .326 with 28 home runs. But with Grimm still in charge, the Braves sent Jethroe to Pittsburgh. "The Pirates never gave me much of a chance [two games and just one plate appearance]," he said. "Black players didn't have much opportunity to sit on the bench. If you were Black, you had to be good enough to start or they'd get a white guy."

Elroy Face, a standout relief pitcher of the 1950s and 1960s, said when he was with the Pirates, he and his teammates saw Roberto Clemente being denied the opportunity to eat meals with the team. Face said the attitude on the club was that they were helpless. "That was the law. What could you do about it? I think when we came north we all stayed in the same hotel."

Many liberal white players in the majors from around 1955 to 1964 or so were either naive about the race issue or simply so unbiased themselves that they were blind to some of the prejudice around them.

Johnny O'Brien, who was with the Pirates from 1955 through part of 1958, may have minimized the problem a little, but he did share a sobering tale. He said, "I saw some racism in spring training in the South, but I didn't see it in the big leagues. I spiked Jackie Robinson on the thigh one time when he blocked the bag, and he dropped the ball and got charged with an error. He jumped right up and immediately said, 'Obie, not a problem. I blocked the bag. My fault,' and that was the end of it.

"About a week later, I got a box of cigars in the mail with a very racist statement about what I should have done to Robinson. The guy who sent them to me was, of course, anonymous. He used a racial term—it wasn't kind, let's put it that way." In effect, the letter writer was saying thanks for spiking Robinson.

"That was the only time I ever saw anything like that, and it bothered me that that would exist in our day because Jackie came up in '47 and this was in '53. That bothered me that someone would be that nasty."

O'Brien said that he felt that by 1960, "the time had passed of the original reaction to Black players in Major League Baseball. It persisted in the South somewhat, but I didn't see it in Pittsburgh. If it was underground, it wasn't apparent to me. I never heard a Black player being booed because he was Black. That may have happened in '47, but it was passé by the time I was there."

All-Star Ralph Terry, who was the MVP of the 1962 World Series with his New York Yankees, seemed to agree with O'Brien: "In Florida there were some restrictions. Black players didn't stay in the same hotel, but as far as I know, on the ball field, there wasn't anything like that. Jackie Robinson put up with most of the problems."

Hal Smith, a catcher with the 1960 world champion Pirates, was a realist. "I would say things were difficult for Black players on our team because they were very segregated," he said. "They had a place in Pittsburgh called the Hill District where many Blacks lived." The handful of minority players on the Pirates "kind of had their own group they ran with." Where Black players lived and where they congregated was often dictated by societal factors.

It's true that the Pirates organization was, in fact, more progressive than many clubs. On September 1, 1971, they made history when they fielded a starting lineup with Black players at every position. Pittsburgh's manager that day, Danny Murtaugh, said he simply put his best nine players for that day on the field, claiming it was no earth-shattering move on his part.

Pirate All-Star Bob Skinner spoke highly of the Pirates atmosphere: "I thought the Pirates were excellent. We were the team with the most minority players earlier than other teams. Branch Rickey [once the Pirates general manager] was very busy in signing minority players, and he got Clemente from the Dodgers, and you know the rest of the story."

His point was that teams that were progressive prospered, while teams such as the Red Sox didn't: Over a period of twenty seasons beginning the year Robinson broke into the majors, the Red Sox's average finish in the standings was fifth place—back when there were just eight teams in each league.

In fact, from around 1947 to 1960 or so, the Senior Circuit overall was much more progressive in signing minorities than the AL, and that head start carried over for a very long time. For example, from 1970 through 1982, the NL won nineteen of twenty All-Star Games, including eleven in a row. From 1970 through 1982, they outscored the AL, 74–41, and out-homered them, 23–10.

From 1947 to 1973, the average season for white ballplayers produced 140 hits and 13 homers. Black players averaged 150 hits and 18 home runs. Also, until the year 2004, the last time a white player led the majors in stolen bases was way back in 1952, when Brooklyn's Pee Wee Reese led with 30 steals.

Ernie "Cokey" Nimmons was an outfielder in the Negro Leagues who played for the Indianapolis Clowns, the Kansas City Monarchs, and the Philadelphia Stars. He said that he believed himself to have been the first roommate of a seventeen-year-old Hank Aaron when the two men were teammates on the Clowns in 1952, the year they won the Negro Leagues championship.

Nimmons once witnessed a horrible scene when he and his team were traveling in the South. In 1952, the Clowns were on the road in Missouri. "Our bus pulled into town," he said, "and they told us that our game was delayed because of something that was going on there." Assuming the town was hosting some sort of festivity, they took the news in stride.

"Then we saw [evidence] of what recently had happened there, a lynching. The man they had killed was being dragged down the street by a rope [attached to a] truck." It was, he said, enough to frighten and sicken him, making him ponder what the world had come to. The ugliness of the lynching was horrifying, he said, but it also made him philosophize about the mindless hatred of racism.

Another Negro Leagues veteran, Norman Lumpkin, remembered, "We'd play a team in a small town we're visiting and I'd hear fans saying, 'Our colored boys are beating the hell out of those [n-word].'" The irony of it was that when Lumpkin played at home, *his* fans would call Lumpkin colored, and the visitors the n-word.

Latino players also experienced varying degrees of prejudice. One example touched on earlier was Clemente. Pirates teammate Elroy Face spoke of how Clemente and other Latino players had to deal with a language barrier, which also resulted in ridicule. Many members of the media offended Clemente by quoting him in print, spelling words he had spoken phonetically. For example, if Clemente said, "I hit the ball good," reporters wrote, "I *heet* the ball good." Clemente grew to distrust many writers, saying they portrayed a bad image of him and that they were prejudiced against him as a Black, Puerto Rican player.

Another Pittsburgh teammate, Bill Virdon, felt that all in all, Clemente managed "to get along all right. I thought he handled it very well." Early on, though, said Virdon, he wasn't always included in the ribbing players do to one another.

The proud Clemente firmly felt that calling him Bobby rather than Roberto, as some members of the media did, was also disrespectful, akin to the treatment immigrants got at places like Ellis Island when officials took the liberty of Americanizing some families' surnames. Several of his baseball cards list him as Bob Clemente.

Many people in baseball circles made no effort to learn the ways and culture of Latino ballplayers, and many indulged in stereotyping both Black and Latino athletes. *Sport* magazine quoted manager Alvin Dark saying of his Giants (circa 1964) that his team had trouble because they had so many Black and Spanish-speaking players. Those men, he contended, were simply unable to play as well as white players in terms of their mental capabilities.

The fact that such thinking existed, and for so long a period of time in baseball, is a shame, and many people contend that to believe racism has vanished in baseball is also shameful.

While Veeck paid the owner of Doby's Negro Leagues team for the right to take him from that club, Branch Rickey did not reimburse

Robinson's team, and before Jackie even concluded his rookie season, Rickey stripped sixteen more players from the Negro Leagues. He even justified his action by saying that the Negro Leagues was something of a racket, alluding to the fact that many team owners in that league made much of their money from running numbers. One owner shot back that Rickey had some nerve and that his robbing the league of players was, in fact, quite a racket.

Robinson may have broken into the majors in 1947, but it wasn't until 1955 that Black players on the Dodgers could eat in the team's hotel dining room. One year earlier, Don Newcombe complained to Robinson that he had just spent two years in the army serving his country, yet he couldn't stay in the same hotel as his white teammates.

Later in 1955, the Dodgers honored Pee Wee Reese on his thirtieth birthday. Among other tributes to the Louisville native, who was sometimes called "The Little Colonel," was the flying of several Confederate flags. Sometimes, as in this display, racism is subtle, maybe even unintended, but Robinson was livid. He ripped those responsible for the flags, yet no action was taken.

ENCOURAGING AND SUPPORTING PLAYERS

At the pro level, one might think that players really are self-motivated and have no real need for encouragement from fans, managers, teammates, and even their teams' broadcasters, but they do.

Sure, at that level players no longer chatter on the field, like kids often do to support their pitchers: "C'mon, kid, fire it in there. You can do it!" But the pros do appreciate praise, and they universally agree that they do hear and react to an emotional and favorable home crowd, which can often psych them up and spur them on to greater showings.

Visits to the mound to calm down a pitcher in peril are sometimes nothing more than a pep talk, an adult version of chatter. Still, those treks are honest attempts to help out a floundering pitcher.

Vern Law recalled the reverse side of that coin regarding Cardinals broadcaster Harry Caray's propensity for getting on players, with a favorite target being St. Louis star Ken Boyer: "He'd say, 'Here's Boyer. There's a fly ball. Oh-for-four.' And he didn't give some of the guys the credit that they deserved. That always bothered me. He was a little bit negative back then.

"He was a real competitor. He wanted the Cardinals to win every game, and when somebody was in a slump, he'd get down on him, [perhaps] rightly so, I guess. But that kind of bothered me. You give your guys credit, you encourage them.

"As a coach I've always felt that you get exactly what you expect out of a player. Criticize them all the time and that rubs off on them. And instead of building somebody up and patting them on the back and saying, 'Hang in there,' you hurt them."

Judging from the constant reinforcing congratulations that take place in dugouts for anything from a sacrifice bunt or sac fly to a grand slam, most teammates are very supportive. However, strong encouragement isn't a given on every team.

"I really think that's the reason the Cubs for many years, even though they had great players at times, never won anything," continued Law. "I know that when my son Vance was with them, I really noticed it a lot because he could hit three line drives right at somebody and he'd go back to the dugout and nobody would say a word or pat him on the back and say, 'You hit the ball well. You'll get 'em next time,' or anything like that. And that's a turnoff as far as I'm concerned."

PLAYERS' PRIDE

Gaylord Perry said there's an obvious reason being voted into the Hall of Fame is special: "It's a great honor because it's recognition by peers. Players I knew like Willie Mays and Willie McCovey were enshrined, so when you get in, it's a great honor."

Looking back on the three biggest highlights of his career, Perry cited his no-hitter, "being a part of all the good teams I played on—we didn't win it all, but we came in second a lot, and the Hall of Fame [induction] is number one."

The 314-game winner spent more time with the San Francisco Giants than with any other club, and they finished in first place during his 1962 rookie season and in 1971, his final season as a Giant. He was correct about his second-place finishes, as San Francisco came in second five seasons in a row from 1965 through 1969.

Perry was a member of eight teams over his twenty-two-year career, and even in retirement, he felt loyalty to those clubs. Perry showed up at Old-Timers' Games wearing a uniform adorned with the logos of each of the teams he had played for. "I follow all eight of those teams," he said. "Of course, when you play for enough teams, some do well and others, not so well."

Fellow all-time great Bob Gibson, like many good-hitting pitchers, was proud of his prowess with the bat. He said, "Pitchers didn't treat me like I was a pitcher at bat. They treated me like a hitter." In seventeen seasons, he hit 24 homers (#7 all-time among hurlers), and he reached a season high of 5 twice. He also owns a career batting average of .206, extremely good for a pitcher.

He had to be equally proud of his fielding ability, having won nine Gold Gloves. Only Greg Maddux, with eighteen, and Jim Kaat, with sixteen, won that award more often. Gibson's all-around athleticism was never in question. He excelled in basketball at Creighton University, and he even spent time playing for the Harlem Globetrotters.

Hank Aaron had tons of reasons to be proud. He touched upon the record he and Eddie Mathews established when they surpassed Babe Ruth and Lou Gehrig for the most combined homers struck by team-mates, 863, four more than the Yankee greats. Aaron noted, "It *always* meant something to us. I don't think that it gets enough attention, but it's always meant to me that we were [productive] teammates for a long time, which is not going to happen now because players have a way of playing out their option and going somewhere else. That's not going to ever happen again where two teammates can set that kind of record."

PLAYERS' EATING HABITS
Maybe Babe Ruth could get away with stuffing himself with a cornuco-pia of hot dogs (and wash them down with endless beers), but modern players tend to be careful about what they eat.

In the 1990s, Matt Williams once topped the National League in home runs, with 43, and in ribbies, with 122 (20 fewer than his best season). He candidly pointed out that "most players have kids, and if you have kids, you can't stay away from fast food completely—that's a given. But I think that in the biggest respect, guys are probably concerned about being in shape, and being in shape all year round because, of course, the longer you play, the more money you're going to make.

"And you got to keep ahead of the Joneses, too. You've got young guys who want your spot, and you have to make sure you keep up with that, too," said Williams, who was thirty-six at the time of his interview.

He said that some players, though, are very particular: "I find that guys aren't necessarily eating as much in the clubhouse. There are guys that have chefs and things like that, but that's few and far between.

"I don't know if it's so much the eating that's the main concern, it's the making sure you're in shape physically and prepared all the time," he concluded.

Autograph Seekers

Players' thoughts on autograph seekers and collectors cover quite a range. Let's begin with Tim Raines, a Hall of Famer who led his league in stolen bases four times. "It seems like there's always a hundred people out there," he said. "It's not that you don't want to sign for them, it's you don't have the time.

"Then there are the rude ones—they'll insult you if you don't sign. It puts a bad taste in your mouth." He said that players may be athletes with their faces splattered all over the place like Hollywood stars, but they are nevertheless human beings with feelings. He said, "You don't like hearing them call you a bum when I run out of time and don't sign. Still, all in all, I enjoy signing autographs."

Frank Thomas said, "I get a pile of letters a day. I'll grab letters and read them, but usually it's not a letter, it's just, 'Sign this.' It's not like it used to be [in the early 1990s] with true fan mail."

Carlton Fisk groused about books that revealed players' home addresses: "I'm totally offended that everybody in the world has my address. Some of my friends don't know where I live!" It's an intrusion, he said. "At home, I'm a dad and a husband, not a ballplayer. I'll sign at the park what I can in the time I have, but fans don't realize it's four, five times a day. They'll shout, 'Just one,' but when you play every day, your attitude is strained. Some days you don't care if it's your mom, you're not going to sign.

"Many fans don't ask; they demand." One time, after signing quite a few autographs, he told the crowd he was through. An obnoxious fans pestered him on and on, demanding "one more." Fisk said, "Fine. I'll sign one more, but not for you," and he signed for a young fan.

Another time, a rude fan reached across Fisk's table at dinner, stretching right by Fisk's wife. "He clotheslined her and just ignored her." And one time the team pulled into their hotel at 3:30 a.m. "We were dragging. There were people waiting for autographs. Your fuse point [is short]." It's difficult to be understanding at times.

Players certainly do have legitimate complaints about those who obtain autographs not to cherish as souvenirs, like true fans, but as items to hawk. One player recognized a young boy after he showed up at the park daily, begging for an autograph. The player soon discovered the boy's father was a collector taking advantage of the kindness players often show to young fans.

Five-time strikeout king Sam McDowell said he wouldn't sign for adults if he suspected they may be a card shop owner or a collector who was asking for his signature simply for profit.

"If there was a way of proving the autograph was for a kid, all players would sign," said McDowell. "No problem. I'm guessing 90 percent of the people now are selling the autographs. This leads to cynicism by the players.

"A kid came up to a player in Toronto and let the cat out of the bag, thanking the player for 'paying for' his vacation. The player had signed seven or eight autographs for the kid over the years, and the father sold them."

Meanwhile, in 2001, Jeff Bagwell said that giving autographs is "part of the territory, but it's getting to the point now where there are so many people not collecting just to collect. They're collecting to sell, and that's what ruins it for everybody else. I think guys get a little bitter at that. You see the same guys there, four days in a city, the same ones out in front of the clubhouse and in front of the hotel every single day."

Bagwell said that type of exploitation still goes on "big time, no question about it. It's a big business; they get a lot of money for stuff, so that is a little annoying."

Nine-year major league veteran Herbert Perry said if he was unable to sign autographs for everyone who was asking him for one, they'd call him selfish. He said players' first concern had to be getting ready to play. He gave an analogy: "I don't know too many people who would want their doctor to be signing autographs and talking to fans before he goes in and does open heart surgery. I know this isn't life and death up here, but it's pretty close. If you don't think so, watch these fans."

He said that fans often get the feeling that buying a ticket means something is owed to them *beyond* watching a big-league contest. He likened it to movie fans who demanded extensive coverage of a Hollywood wedding. Perry said, "That's *their* day; that's *their* time. No, you don't deserve more. You watch what they do for entertainment; you don't watch what they do so that you *own* part of them.

"For the most part, I love signing autographs because you get to meet people, and I like people, but the weird thing about this game is the more you play it, and the more you meet the bad fans, the more it kind of taints your attitude toward the good fans, and that's unfair to them."

Steve Sax was very accommodating, hiring a firm to help handle his mail and taking mail home over the winter. "I go through and sign as much as I can," he said. "If someone wants my autograph, that's flattering."

Jay Buhner said, "I feel you have to give a little something back to those who pay your salary, to make a concerted effort to the fans."

Tim Raines collected Tim Raines cards: "I ran an ad in a collectors' magazine telling people if they send me two cards, I'll sign one and keep one."

Ken Griffey Jr. said that fans should try "to understand and learn that we are humans and we have lives, too. Just because sometimes we can't sign for them, you can't get an attitude and call us names, because that just makes it worse for you and other people. If you're nice and polite, then usually we sign, but if you're not, well, you know."

And Frank Thomas said there are even some players who ask him for his autograph. "Of course you sign for them as a courtesy."

FAME

Lord Byron once said, "Fame is the thirst of youth," but it's debatable as to whether a young Ken Griffey Jr. sought a liquid diet of fame or not. Sure, players crave attention for their outstanding accomplishments, but there is a ceiling for such desire.

Junior became so good so quickly that fame was thrust upon him before he was old enough to crack open and down a cold one. A rookie at age nineteen, he was an All-Star the next year—and for the ten seasons following.

Disadvantages to fame also followed. On Mariners road trips during his early years in the majors, he said he could kill some time out and about depending upon "where I'm at. I go to malls, but I haven't gone to a mall in Seattle—I don't go anywhere when I'm at home." He said that he was too recognizable, so privacy was impossible in his home city.

However, he added, "You get used to it." At the time of his 1993 interview, he said his then-fiancée "does all my shopping for me, but I don't have to twist her arm," he concluded with a grin.

His fame also kept his mailman busy, as he estimated he was receiving "three hundred letters or more a day." He said he had to have a secretary screen his mountain of mail to deal with fan mail and bills.

BOOING AND HECKLING

Within certain logical boundaries, players recognize the fact that fans pay their way into parks and therefore have the right to show their displeasure by booing. After the Astros' 2017 sign-stealing scandal came to light and, as the old saying goes, hit the fan, while also hitting the fans in the face with its harsh reality, players such as José Altuve and Carlos Correa knew they would be greeted by heckling and mocking chants of "Cheater" for a long, long time.

Craig Counsell, a veteran of sixteen seasons who went on to become a manager, said it's not just players who feel bad about being the target of boo birds: "I think what's tough for anybody is if someone you love is getting booed, it's tough to feel good about that—and they know it's part of [the game], but if we switched spots and your wife was playing a professional sport and she was getting booed, it's gonna be kind of tough to handle."

After all, as Matt Mantei said, "we really do care about what people think about us. We do care what the fans say about us. I think a lot of people don't realize that. Fans think we're just out there and the booing goes in one ear and out the other, but it really doesn't. Guys take some things to heart, some guys more than others."

Some cities have reputations for being very rough on their own players—Philadelphia stands out in that regard. However, their biggest star, Bryce Harper disagrees. "Philly gets a bad rap for a lot of stuff people think they are," he began. "They're not. They're just a fan base that really cares. They spent their hard-earned dollars to come and watch you play, and they want the best out of you each night. If you're 0-for-4 and you punch out with a guy on third base to lose a ballgame, they're going to let you know. And trust me, I'm walking back to the dugout doing the same thing to myself."[6]

Fans often boo superstars from other teams simply because they know those players can hurt their team. Tom Grieve has been around the game for more than fifty years as a player, general manager, and broadcaster. He has heard stars such as Alex Rodriguez getting booed, and he commented on the rare type of player who is widely respected: "Probably the only one who achieved that kind of [universal] fame is Cal Ripken, who was never booed anywhere.

"Let's face it, Ted Williams used to get booed in Boston, Mickey Mantle got booed everywhere he went, Mike Schmidt got booed in Philadelphia. The only place they don't boo people is in St. Louis."

Another exception dealt with one special individual: Stan Musial, who destroyed Brooklyn Dodgers pitching yet was admired by fans of Dem Bums. It was in Brooklyn where fans struck up a chant when Musial batted: "Here come the man." Writers picked up on "The Man," and the name stuck.

Sportswriter Stan Isaacs reminisced, "Dodger fans and Giants fans were in awe of him, and they tended to be critical, they liked to find a weakness in opposing players, but Musial transcended that. There was awe about him."

Closely related to booing is heckling. Ben Grieve said, "I think everyone gets heckled, especially in the outfield, because they're drinking all the beer out there. I've had a few things thrown at me—money and stuff like that."

Of course, it can get worse. Pirate outfielder Dave Parker was the target of a fan who threw a battery at him. Still worse, Chris Chambliss said, "When I was with the Yankees, we were in Boston around 1975. I hit a ball that bounced into the stands, but it looked like a fan might've touched it. There was an argument about whether it had been touched or not because I was on third. So was it a triple or a ground rule double?

"I'm standing there with third base coach Dick Howser, waiting for the manager to argue, and I felt something funny go in my right arm. It turned out to be a steel dart thrown from the stands. I looked on the ground and there were about six of them there. That was during the middle of the Yankee-Boston rivalry. It was unbelievable!"

Hecklers, much tamer than those who throw objects, are usually tolerated if they don't cross a line. Plus, Grieve said, most hecklers are pretty unimaginative: "They try to be smart and get the media guide and read your background, but you know where they got their information [and insults] from usually. Usually they're pretty stupid things that come from their mouths."

Jason Bay agreed. "Usually you hear the same stuff over and over again. If someone does have a [creative] joke or yell something funny, I'll be the first to turn around and kinda smile and give them a thumb's up or something, but usually it's the same old, 'You suck,' and that just gets redundant after a while."

In an early 2000s interview, Herbert Perry said, "The fans are tough. I mean, they expect you to be above it all, and they expect you not to be human. Last night there was a guy that called me every name in the book the entire game, and told me how I stunk when I played here [in Cleveland], and how I stink now. And he wasn't using those [tame] words. He's standing up the whole time. Finally, I turned around and gestured like I couldn't hear him, and I get booed by fifty or sixty people sitting over there because I reacted to this guy.

"It's hard sometimes. It's unfair sometimes. They talk about how much money we make, but they don't understand that only one in a thousand that was drafted ever make [big] money.

"I can't understand [the heckling], and I don't think any athlete alive has ever heckled another athlete who's out there trying to do his job. I love the cheering. I love the people to get up and get behind people, but for somebody to sit in the stands when you're on deck and call you every name in the book, and talk about your family, there's no place for that in the game.

"He's calling himself a superfan, but really he's making a jerk out of himself. It's like you're really some big, tough guy if you can sit up in the stands and talk to a guy who's probably twice as big as you are. Actually, size doesn't matter—it's like spitting in somebody's face when he's got his hands tied behind his back. They can't do anything about it, and if you even turn around and acknowledge that you hear that person, then there'll be three or four more people there who are going to have some 'fun' with you."

CONDITIONS TODAY VERSUS YESTERYEAR

Nowadays, even the teams that aren't as wealthy as, say, the Yankees and the Dodgers, go first class all the way. That wasn't the case as recently as the 1950s (and even later for some chintzy owners).

Four-time All-Star Bob Friend said that in the early years of air travel, not all clubs treated their players in major league fashion. Many clubs frequently scrimped. "I remember we [the Pirates] had a game in St. Louis that went into extra innings, and we got on the plane about 2:00 a.m. and flew to San Francisco," he said. "And I'm pitching that day game, and they didn't even fly starting pitchers ahead. So I'm there trying to pitch to the Giants—Willie Mays and company—on three hours' rest after traveling all night."

Today's clubhouses are plush. Friend said that was far from the case in his era: "They were nothing like they are today—it's really something, what they have today. Nobody complained about them when I played. Hey, they looked pretty good when you win; they looked pretty bad when you lose."

If the lifestyle of players in the majors wasn't even close to being luxurious then, how much worse was it in the minors? Aside from the obvious, such as enduring arduous, interminable bus rides and having to subsist on peanut butter and jelly sandwiches, there were other drawbacks.

Bobby Dues paid his dues in the Cardinals farm system from 1960 to 1968 and worked in the Braves organization in many coaching and managing positions for more than thirty years. He recalled that even the lighting in ballparks was substandard. "The lights were low," he said, "so we had a lot of trouble with pop-ups early in the evening. They'd get up over the lights and get lost by infielders. And the fields were kind of rough. In Winnipeg, they used to have a rodeo on Saturday night and then we would play Sunday afternoon games—that was rough fielding." Playing defense came with a unique obstacle course as the field had a "residue" from the rodeo animals, "and the aroma was still there, too. Of course, after the game our manager said, 'Well, I'll match the smell with our defensive play.'"

Perhaps beginning around the time of free agency, the relationship between players from opposing clubs became vastly different from, for example, the days of the bellicose Ty Cobb. For a long time there was even a rule prohibiting opponents from fraternizing on the field.

Today's players frequently rub elbows behind the batting cage as freely and easily as teenagers once mingled at a malt shop. For many years, the don't-get-chummy rule was enforced. During pregame activities, an umpire was stationed in the stands to spy on possible fraternization. If he saw an infraction, he would write up a report and the violators would be slapped with a fine—$25 for breaking the rule the first time, and double that for the second violation.

One imagines a modern player getting such a fine, pulling out a wad of money the size of George Costanza's wallet, peeling off a thousand-dollar bill, and sneering, "Here. When that runs out, come see me again."

While Friend never knew of a player getting fined, he understood the reason for the rule. When players from rival teams socialized with each other, it didn't look good to the fans, who wanted their team to be hungry and to despise the enemy, not pal around with them.

Former umpire Dave Phillips told *Sporting News* writer Stan McNeal that he didn't care for the rule because it meant an ump had to be confrontational with players even before games began. McNeal wrote that the rule simply phased itself out to the point that around the mid-1980s, baseball ceased enforcing it.

Given the mobility players have now under free agency, former friends and teammates are spread throughout the majors. Mark Teixeira propelled 409 home runs from 2003 through 2016 for the Yankees, Rangers, Braves, and Angels. He observed, "It's a friendlier game now. Guys are traded so much nowadays that you could be on four or five different teams within five years. It's definitely changed. It's always nice to see former teammates. Playing against guys kind of makes the big leagues one big happy family. When you're playing against them, you want to beat them, but at the same time you get to enjoy watching some of their accomplishments."

There's even a strong contrast between the uniforms of yesteryear versus today. From the dawn of the game and well into the twentieth century, players' uniforms were made of wool. "That's all we knew, so it was fine," said Elrod Hendricks, a man who spent parts of or all of thirty-nine seasons with the Orioles as a catcher who was a part of the world champs O's of 1970 and as a coach (working though eleven managerial changes). Still, he recalled losing more than just a few ounces during, say, a scorching doubleheader in August.

The 6-foot-1 Hendricks, who had a playing weight listed at 175, grinned, saying, "I remember playing in RFK Stadium in Washington, DC, and God, on a summer night, man, you'd lose twelve pounds easily catching, and I didn't have twelve pounds to lose to begin with.

"I've thought about it, and I asked [fellow Orioles coach] Tom Trebelhorn the other day, 'How did we ever play 162 games with the wool—took infield, batting practice and all that stuff, and never really complained about being tired. And these guys today have the comfort of nice-feeling uniforms and whatnot, and they complain about being tired and they don't take infield. How did we do it?' Tom said, 'We *had* to.'"

Nowadays, after taking batting practice, players switch into their clean, comfortable game outfits. Long ago, said Hendricks, "we didn't have another shirt; that was it. You put it on at 4:00 or whenever you came out, and you wore it for the game—and the undershirts were 100 percent wool, too."

DRAWBACKS TO BIG-LEAGUE LIFE

Life in the big leagues is glamorous and rewarding in many, many ways, but there are some drawbacks. Doug Henry was a solid reliever who lasted eleven seasons (1991–2001) but bounced around with five teams. Being traded, often uprooted in the middle of a season, is no fun. Plus, he added during a 2000 interview, "I love traveling, but people don't realize what a toll it takes on a body and mind.

"It's a physical grind every day. I mean, you go in and out of a city. It's every three days and you're in a different city, and you're living out of a suitcase. You get to the park early—if you don't, you just sit around the hotel and get bored to death.

"[The travel] sounds exciting for the first two months, and it was when I first came up. It was awesome, but you look back: I've got an eighteen-year-old and a fifteen-year-old, and I missed so much of their lives doing what I'm doing. I love what I'm doing, but there is a downside."

In a 2002 interview, Matt Williams agreed: "I think the biggest part is you have to be away from your family, your wife and your children— that's the hardest part.

"It's also a grind, even though it's something that we all love to do and there are a million people out there that would trade places with us, but it can become a grind. One hundred sixty-two games is a lot of games, and you get tired physically and tired mentally, but it's all worth it to have a chance to be where we were at last year [in 2001, when his Diamondbacks won it all]. That's what we all play for. If you get a chance to go to the World Series, it's all well worth it."

He also pointed out that it's not just football players who have significant aches and pains and experience days where they can hardly get out of bed. Williams said, "I've had plenty of them, but we're paid to do our job, and that's no different than any other working man in the United States. You get paid to do your job and to perform on that given day, and that's the way we look at it."

Herbert Perry added, "I've had eight surgeries in ten years of playing professional baseball—we pay a price. By the time I'm fifty years old, if

I'm able to walk and stand up straight, I'll be lucky." He joked about how, at season's end when he returned to his home, he'd take some guff from family. "My sister's always giving me heck about, 'I wish I had the job you have.' And my wife tells her, 'No you don't. He takes painkillers just about every day.'"

Darin Erstad said the most difficult part of his job as a player was "cranking it up every day. Being at the top of your game. Mentally and physically. Every day." Still, he added, "There's nothing I want to change. I love just how it is. That's part of the fun of having a long season—grinding it out and separating the fit from the unfit."

Jim Thome spoke of how being on the road so much makes it "a hard life on your family. You try to mix it to where you can get your family out as much as possible and spend time with them."

Perry also spoke about the grind while touching on the difficulties of exhaustive travel: "Eight months out of the year, you play every day. I mean, you may get a day off one day a week, maybe, if you're lucky, and that's always, like, to fly from Seattle back to Chicago or from Tampa to Chicago. It wears you out. Physically, by the end of the year, you're beat."

Regardless, like Erstad, Perry commented, "There's nothing better than being on the field. We pay a lot of prices, we put up with a lot of stuff, but when you're out there, it's a great feeling."

Infielder Toby Harrah, in the majors for seventeen seasons, philosophized that he tries not to consider things such as draining travel and missing one's family "as a negative. I just think that's part of the game. You know, you just take the good with the not-so-good, and being away from your family *is* a very hard thing to do, but the upside to it is you get about five months off. So you get out there and you play seven months out of the year to get five months off—those are pretty good 'hours.'

"There are really very few downsides as far as being a big-league baseball player goes. When you're in the big leagues, you're living a dream come true, and all the other things like being on the road and living out of hotels are very, very minor, considering the whole picture."

He added that players, unlike tourists, have few worries when traveling: "The team does everything for you." That includes giving him his allotted meal money, making all travel arrangements, and so on.

Henry elaborated, "I'm not going to lie to you, we're spoiled rotten. Our stuff gets packed for us; we don't even pack our equipment. We pack our personal luggage, but then somebody picks it up and takes it up to our room and back down to the bus afterward."

One last—and very large—drawback is being traded. Players are just like everyone else in that they don't relish the idea of being uprooted and having to move their families, sometimes across the country. Matt Mantei pitched for three clubs over his ten-year career. Concerning moving to a new team, he said, "It's pretty tough. When you play somewhere, you'd like to play there for a long time, and you want to make a home there.

"But when you get traded, you basically have to start all over again. You've got to worry about finding somewhere to live, you've got to move your family out, you've got to get everything going again. It makes it tough on you."

Being swapped also has an impact on friends. Thome was saddened when his Cleveland teammate and close friend Richie Sexson was dealt to Milwaukee in 2000. While Thome and his wife made it to Sexson's wedding and managed to keep in touch, Thome's wife, Andrea, pointed out that it's not quite the same. "It's really hard on us," she said.

Son of a Big-Leaguer

There have been more than 250 father-son combinations to make it to the major league level. Obviously, being the son of a big-leaguer gives a player a leg up on others. Cecil and Prince Fielder serve as one example of such success, as they are the only such duo to both enjoy 50-plus home run seasons.

There are, of course, exceptions, such as pitchers Ed Walsh and his son Junior. Of all the father-son combos who were pitchers, the Hall of Fame dad had the best lifetime ERA, at a minuscule 1.82, but his son had one of the worst career ERAs, at 5.57.

Ken Griffey Jr., whose dad hit .296 lifetime and, like his son, made multiple All-Star teams and copped the game's MVP trophy, comes to most fans' minds when they think of offspring of big-leaguers. Junior refuted a story, which had been repeated over and over, about how he spent countless hours hanging around his father's clubhouses, absorbing the ins and outs of the big leagues. "Very seldom was I in the locker room," he said.

Nor, he said, did his father impart baseball wisdom with each passing moment. "No," said Junior, "he just told me to go out and play. My father always told us, 'Don't be anybody else. Just be yourself.'"

Senior said, "He wasn't allowed in the locker room. He wasn't allowed on the field. People always take that for granted, but Kenny was not allowed on the field at any time except for when we played the father and son games, and that was it.

"Other than that, he wasn't in the cages; he wasn't taking batting practice. All that stuff we did, we did at home when I had the opportunity to go outside and throw him batting practice in the backyard or catch with him. Those kind of things happened at home, not at the ballpark."

It worked, and Junior rewarded his father by recording his 500th home run in 2004, doing so on Father's Day. Incidentally, that hit tied him with his father's lifetime base hit total. In addition, in half of his first sixteen seasons, Junior homered on his father's birthday.

Senior said that as his son was growing up, it didn't take long to realize that Junior could exceed his father's accomplishments: "I knew he was that good when he was twelve and thirteen because of his quick hands and how well he handled the glove, and batting. When he got about fourteen, I couldn't strike him out, and I never told him what I was throwing."

Going lefty-on-lefty versus his father was a plus. "That's all he saw," Senior said, "so that's why left-handers really don't give him that many problems. He saw me throwing to him left-handed and I was throwing breaking balls and everything else.

"We took batting practice just like he was in a game. It was always game scenarios that we went through, and I never told him that I was going to throw him a curveball, changeup, slider, whatever. As he got better and better by recognizing pitches, by the age of fourteen I knew that he could handle himself pretty good. He was on the sixteen-and-seventeen-year-old traveling team when he was thirteen and fourteen. That's when he really developed, but mostly when I had him in New York [around 1982 through 1985] during the summers."

Senior listed some of the built-in advantages a son of a big-leaguer can have: "He had somebody there who knew exactly what to look for. When he got to be seventeen, I had eight, nine years in the big leagues, so his experience was what I was teaching—the experiences I learned. So he had shortcuts in understanding exactly what to look for in terms of at the plate—what the pitcher is doing, so he can watch the catcher move in and out, and he has an idea what the pitch is going to be. And defensive prowess—those things you can teach him, and that was the biggest advantage."

When they made their big-league debut as teammates in 1990, the first time Senior came to the plate he heard some words of encouragement that had never before been uttered from an on-deck circle. Junior shouted out, "Come on, Dad!"

Asked if he still sees Junior as his little boy or as a Hall of Famer, Senior said, "He's not my little boy, he's my son, and that's more important than anything. He's my son first, before he's this superstar, this baseball player, and that's the way he feels. He was always, 'That's my dad.'"

SUPERSTITION

Given the fact that players today are better educated than ever before, are there fewer superstitious players around now? Not according to ten-year veteran Lee Stevens. "It's part of the game," he said. "Every guy in here [the clubhouse] is superstitious, and they're lying if they say they're not, because that's part of your routine, and that's part of how you get mentally prepared to play this game. It's a crazy game, a real mental game, and everybody in here has a certain routine, whether it's with your batting gloves, your clothes, what you eat for lunch, whatever. There are things on and off the field."

Stevens's argument may be a matter of semantics. For example, if a player always takes a shower at a certain time as part of his pregame routine, is that a superstitious move or is it merely his style, his way of doing things before a game?

"Your routine *is* a superstition," Stevens continued. "When you break that routine, you kinda get out of whack. Every player does that and tries to find [a routine] that he likes."

One of the most notable cases of a fastidious player, one totally dedicated to his routine/superstitions, was Wade Boggs. Jim Lefebvre said, "He definitely has routines. He eats chicken at a certain time on game days; takes batting practice at an exact, specific time; warms up and takes ground balls at a certain time. Boggs is probably one of the most prepared [people] in the game. That's why he's successful. It's not a superstition, it's just a form of preparation, I think."

If a player deviates from his routine and perhaps goes into a slump, he can explain or rationalize his problems by attributing them to bad luck. It's a sort of self-fulfilling prophecy. "You think that [the variation of a routine] is why you didn't get any hits," continued Stevens. "So you're superstitious and you don't even realize it sometimes. Whatever makes you feel better when you go out there to take the field [is fine]."

Gene Clines agreed: "Everybody has their own little superstition, like wearing the same T-shirt, especially when you're hot."

LOVE OF MONEY, LOVE OF THE GAME

With today's top players negotiating contracts that pay them more than $40 million a year ($70 million if you're Shohei Ohtani), some fans grumble that they're more concerned about money than the love of the game. Some time ago, when salaries began to climb to what were formerly considered to be outrageous heights, All-Star pitcher Herb Score said money wasn't everything to modern players.

He felt that many former players make the mistake of thinking their eras were more innocent than the modern times. "Now, younger players are exposed to the media more, so they might act tough," said Score. They learn to act a bit jaded, as if they are detached, but Score insists that "inside, they're excited. They love to play the game," just as players from his day were delighted to be on a big-league diamond. Score went on, "A competitor is a competitor—forget salary. When a player crosses those foul lines, he's not thinking about money; he wants to do his best."

Of course, not everyone agrees with Score. Hall of Fame manager Dick Williams saw players as being too businesslike. "Players make more money now, but they have less fun than we did when we played."

Regardless, one constant remains: Money is *always* important, but to players who love baseball, arguably the game is just as, if not more, important. Manager Tommy Lasorda once, perhaps half-jokingly, said, "My wife tells me one day, 'I think you love baseball more than me.' I say, 'Well, I guess that's true, but hey, I love you more than football and hockey.'"[7]

Maybe infielder Al Gallagher may have been exaggerating, too—but maybe not—when he said, "There are three things in my life which I really love: God, my family, and baseball. The only problem—once baseball season starts, I change the order around a bit."[8] Like the love of God and family, the love of baseball is also enduring.

Notes

Introduction

1. Jeff Hurt, "Your Senses Are Your Raw Information Learning Portals," Velvet Chainsaw Consulting, May 23, 2012, https://velvetchainsaw.com/2012/05/23/your -senses-your-raw-information-learning-portals/.

Chapter One

1. John Denton, "Gold Standard," *Baseball Digest*, November/December 2022, 31.
2. SI Staff, "1969," *Sports Illustrated*, November 15, 1989, https://vault.si.com /vault/1989/11/15/1969.
3. Larry Stone, "Great Expectations," *Baseball Digest*, January/February 2023, 27.

Chapter Two

1. As an aside, a few other men infamous for their fearlessness in pitching inside and plunking batters are intimidators Don Drysdale, who hit 20 men in 1961, led his league in hit batsmen for five seasons, and was in the top ten a dozen times; and Bob Gibson, who made the top-ten "hit list" for eight seasons. Walter Johnson once hit 20 batters in a season and finished in the top ten for nailing men fourteen times. Ryan's high-water mark for those two statistics were 15 batters in a season, with thirteen top-ten finishes.
2. David Adler, "The Secret Weapon McClanahan and Strider Have in Common," MLB.com, June 3, 2023, https://www.mlb.com/news/spencer-strider -shane-mcclanahan-release-extension.
3. "Before There Were Radar Guns, There Were Pitchers Racing Motorcycles," *San Jose Mercury News*, March 28, 2017, https://www.mercurynews.com/2017/03 /28/before-there-were-radar-guns-there-were-pitchers-racing-motorcycles/#.
4. Tim Kurkjian, "Mastery of Splitter Led to Sutter's Success," ESPN, July 28, 2006, https://www.espn.com/mlb/columns/story?columnist=kurkjian_tim&id =2531648.
5. Todd Rosiak, "Burning Desire," *Baseball Digest*, May/June 2023, 44.

6. Brian McTaggart, "In a League of His Own," *Baseball Digest*, September/October, 2022, 25.

7. John Denton, "Q and A with Adam Wainwright," *Baseball Digest*, July/August 2023, 20.

Chapter Three

1. Tom Verducci, "Somebody's Perfect," *Sports Illustrated*, September 22, 1997, 53.

2. Joe Noga, "It Almost Needs to Be Your Best Friend," *Plain Dealer* (Cleveland, OH), May 14, 2023.

Chapter Four

1. Bob Ryan, "Talk about Being Put in Tough Position," *Boston Globe*, August 10, 2009.

2. Anthony McCarron, "A Heart That Can't Be Measured," *Baseball Digest*, March/April 2023, 60.

3. Maury Brown, "Bizball: The Strasburg Shutdown and How It All Could Have Been Avoided," Baseball Prospectus, September 10, 2012, https://www.baseballprospectus.com/news/article/18288/bizball-the-strasburg-shutdown-and-how-it-all-could-have-been-avoided/.

4. Ibid.

Chapter Five

1. Wayne Stewart, *Stan the Man: The Life and Times of Stan Musial* (Chicago: Triumph, 2010), xi.

2. Mike Thomas, "Pete Rose Lived by 2 Words His Father Always Wrote to Him When He Was Away Playing Baseball," Sportscasting, January 26, 2022, https://www.sportscasting.com/pete-rose-lived-by-2-words-his-father-always-wrote-to-him-when-he-was-away-playing-baseball/.

3. Joon Lee, "Former New York Yankees Captains on What Awaits Aaron Judge," ESPN, January 9, 2023, https://www.espn.com/mlb/story//id/35391647/former-new-york-yankees-captains-awaits-aaron-judge.

4. Ibid.

Chapter Six

1. Tom Verducci, "So Far, So Good," *Sports Illustrated*, May 3, 2010, https://vault.si.com/vault/2010/05/03/so-far-so-good.

2. Mohsin Baldiawala, "A Battle of Egos between Barry Bonds and Jeff Kent Robbed the Giants of a World Series: '. . . Barry Doesn't Care about Me,'" EssentiallySports, September 5, 2022, https://www.essentiallysports.com/mlb

-baseball-news-a-battle-of-egos-between-barry-bonds-and-jeff-kent-robbed-the-sf
-giants-of-a-world-series-barry-doesnt-care-about-me/.

3. "Wells Doesn't Agree with Clemens Not Traveling," ESPN, May 7, 2007, https://www.espn.com/mlb/news/story?id=2863411.

4. Tyler Carey, "Hall of Famer Jack Morris' Brief (and Forgettable) Time with the Cleveland Indians," WKYC, July 28, 2018.

5. Bill Veeck, *Veeck—As in Wreck* (New York: G. P. Putnam's Sons, 1962), 170.

6. Scott Lauber, "Unfinished Business," *Baseball Digest*, July/August 2023, 26.

7. "Baseball Love Quotes," AZquotes, https:/www.azquotes.com/quotes/topics /baseball-love.html.

8. Ibid.

REFERENCES

The following sources were used for general information such as records, stats, dates, and game scores detailed in this book:

Baseball Reference, https://www.baseballreference.com
Bleacher Report, https://bleacherreport.com
The Official Site of Major League Baseball, https://www.mlb.com
Sporting News, https://www.sportingnews.com

INDEX

About the Author

Wayne Stewart was born and raised in Donora, Pennsylvania, a town that has produced several big-league baseball players, including the father-son Griffeys and Stan Musial (whose biography, *Stan the Man: The Life and Times of Stan Musial*, Stewart wrote). Stewart was on the same Donora High School baseball team as Ken Griffey Sr.

Stewart has covered the sports world since 1978. He has interviewed and profiled many stars, including Kareem Abdul-Jabbar, Lenny Wilkens, and Larry Bird. His key football interviews have been with legends such as Joe Montana, Raymond Berry, and Lenny Moore, and he has also interviewed numerous baseball legends, including Nolan Ryan, Bob Gibson, Tony Gwynn, Greg Maddux, Rickey Henderson, and Ken Griffey Jr.

Stewart has written more than twenty-five baseball books, along with others on football and basketball. His works have also appeared in seven baseball anthologies. This is his fortieth book.

Stewart has also written more than five hundred articles for publications such as *Baseball Digest*, *USA Today/Baseball Weekly*, *Boys' Life*, and Beckett Publications, and he has written for the official publications of many Major League Baseball teams, including the Braves, Yankees, White Sox, Orioles, Padres, Twins, Phillies, Red Sox, A's, and Dodgers.

Stewart has also appeared, as a baseball expert/historian, on Cleveland's Fox 8, on an ESPN Classic television show on Bob Feller, and on numerous radio shows. He also hosted his own radio shows, including a call-in sports talk show, a pregame Indians report, and pregame shows for Notre Dame football.

Stewart now lives in Amherst, Ohio, with his wife, Nancy.